TOWARDS UNDERSTANDING THE QUR'ĀN

Towards Understanding the Qur'ān

Vol. XIII

SŪRAHS 66–77

English version of

Tafhīm al-Qur'ān

SAYYID ABUL A'LĀ MAWDŪDĪ

Translated and edited by
Zafar Ishaq Ansari

The Islamic Foundation

Towards Understanding the Qur'ān, Vol. XIII, SŪRAHS 66–77
English version of *Tafhīm al-Qur'ān*

Published by
THE ISLAMIC FOUNDATION,
Markfield Conference Centre,
Ratby Lane, Markfield,
Leicester LE67 9SY, United Kingdom
E-mail: publications@islamic-foundation.com
Website: www.islamic-foundation.com

Quran House, PO Box 30611, Nairobi, Kenya

PMB 3193, Kano, Nigeria

Distributed by
KUBE PUBLISHING LTD.
Tel: +44(0)1530 249230, Fax: +44(0)1530 249656
E-mail: info@kubepublishing.com

Translated and edited by Zafar Ishaq Ansari

British Library Cataloguing in Publication Data is available from the British Library.

ISBN 978-0-86037-664-4 *casebound*
ISBN 978-0-86037-659-0 *paperback*

Typeset by: N.A. Qaddoura
Printed by: MEGA PRINT, Turkey

بسم الله الرحمن الرحيم

Contents

Foreword vii

Transliteration Table x

Sūrah 66: Al-Taḥrīm (Madīnan Period)
Introduction 1
Text and Explanatory Notes 8

Sūrah 67: Al-Mulk (Makkan Period)
Introduction 29
Text and Explanatory Notes 32

Sūrah 68: Al-Qalam (Makkan Period)
Introduction 47
Text and Explanatory Notes 50

Sūrah 69: Al-Ḥāqqah (Makkan Period)
Introduction 63
Text and Explanatory Notes 66

Sūrah 70: Al-Maʿārij (Makkan Period)
Introduction 79
Text and Explanatory Notes 81

Sūrah 71: Nūḥ (Makkan Period)
Introduction 93
Text and Explanatory Notes 95

Sūrah 72: Al-Jinn (Makkan Period)
Introduction 105
Text and Explanatory Notes 111

Sūrah 73: Al-Muzzammil (Makkan Period)
Introduction 123
Text and Explanatory Notes 126

Sūrah 74: Al-Muddaththir (Makkan Period)
Introduction 137
Text and Explanatory Notes 142

Sūrah 75: Al-Qiyāmah (Makkan Period)
Introduction 159
Text and Explanatory Notes 161

Sūrah 76: Al-Dahr (Madīnan Period)
Introduction 179
Text and Explanatory Notes 184

Sūrah 77: Al-Mursalāt (Makkan Period)
Introduction 205
Text and Explanatory Notes 208

Appendices 219
Glossary of Terms 229
Biographical Notes 237
Bibliography 245
Subject Index 251
General Index 267

Foreword

The Qur'ān is a book of guidance for mankind. The real significance and uniqueness of this guidance lies in the fact that it is from our Creator, *Rabb*, Sustainer, Master and Lord — to Whom is our return. He has been kind enough to bless us with guidance and not leave us to grope about in the dark in search of pathways to success and salvation.

Allāh Subḥānahū wa ta'ālā has blessed human beings with whatever they need for their survival and growth in the world; both, to ensure their physical existence and development, as well as, their moral, spiritual and social flowering. Endowed with powers of intellect, intuition, experience, innovation and capacity to develop technology, and equipped with moral and spiritual guidance provided by God, the Creator, human beings have been enabled to relate themselves correctly to the Divine Reality and build their relationship with their Lord on the right foundations, and in the light of this relationship, develop their own personality and promote the entire network of relationships with other human beings — individuals and institutions: the family, community, society, economy, state, humanity, and the universe at large in a manner that leads to the establishment of a truly just and harmonious social order. This is a divine recipe for the promotion of true wellbeing and tranquillity in society in this world, and success in the eternal life after death.

The Qur'ānic guidance has two very pertinent dimensions:

1. It addresses all human beings inviting them to a life of obedience to their Creator and Lord- i.e. Islam, and secondly, it provides all those who accept Islam as their faith with:

   (i) a clear road map to build a relationship with God, their Creator;

   (ii) to develop their own personality and character as true believers;

(iii) and to live with other human beings and institutions in a manner that is just and fair, in accordance with the values and principles spelt out in the Qur'ān.

2. These aspects come into sharp focus as we reflect upon some of the key terms used in the Qur'ān spelling out its nature, role and significance. Guidance (*hidāyah*) being the real objective of the Book, (*al-Kitāb*) which also refers to the destiny of mankind.

The Qur'ān describes itself as *Hudā,* guidance for the heedful (*al-Baqarah* 2: 2), a guide to the way that is the most straight (*Banī Isrā'īl* 17:9), *al-Dhikr* and *al-Shifā',* an Exhortation, a Remembrance and a Healing for the ailments of the heart, and a Guidance and Mercy for those who believe (Yūnus 10: 57) *al-Furqān*, a Criterion and a Warner (*al-Furqān* 25: 1), *al- Nūr* and *Kitābun Mubīn* – a Light and a Clear Book through which Allah shows to all who seek His pleasure the path leading to peace and wellbeing – bringing them out from darkness to the Light and directs them to the Straight Way (*al-Mā'idah* 5: 15-16)

The Qur'ān is the greatest blessing of Allah to mankind. To benefit from this divine bounty, it is important to understand this guidance, to accept it with sincerity and dedication, to strive to follow it and live by it, making it one's true companion in life and finally to share it with all seekers of truth. The *Tafhīm al-Qur'ān* is a major effort to present the meaning and message of the Qur'ān in the language of our own time.

Mawlānā Sayyid Abūl A'lā Mawdūdī (1903-1979) is one of the chief architects of contemporary Islamic resurgence. He has written over 150 books on different aspects of Islamic thought and civilization. He has been one of the most widely read authors of the Muslim world in the 20th century. *Tafhīm al-Qur'ān*, however, is his greatest contribution, rightly described as a window to the meaning and message of the Qur'ān. *Alḥamdulillāh,* its English translation has been sponsored by the Islamic Foundation. My lifelong friend and academic and literary partner, Dr Zafar Ishaq Ansari, has rendered this service with profound rigour and superb competence.

The original Urdu edition of *Tafhīm al-Qur'ān* has been a lifelong effort of Mawlānā Mawdūdī, a work he began in 1942 and completed in mid-1973. This *magnus opus* appeared in six volumes, spread over

4000 pages. The first volume of the English translation appeared in 1988. Originally, the whole work was planned to be published in 12 volumes of roughly equal size. As work progressed, it became clear that it would take 14 volumes to complete the project. However, in between it was decided to publish separately a shorter version of *Tafhīm al-Qur'ān* containing a complete translation of the Qur'ān with short notes, as written by Mawlānā Mawdūdī, and published separately in Urdu. Dr Ansari rendered the translation of this shorter version which appeared in 2005. He was also able to translate and edit the first 10 volumes covering up to *sūrah* 46, and volume 14 containing the last *juz'*, (*sūrahs* 78-114). While he did prepare a first draft of some of the remaining *sūrahs*, unfortunately, he could not complete the work and breathed his last in May 2016. The present volume (volume 13) was mainly prepared by him although he could not finalize it. Two of our senior colleagues at the Islamic Foundation, Dr Muhammad Manazir Ahsan, the Chairman and Dr A.R. Kidwai, a senior research consultant, both of whom had long been involved with the project, now shoulder the responsibility for completing and revising the translation and editing the three remaining volumes. Final responsibility rests with Dr Manazir Ahsan.

Volume 13 of *Towards Understanding the Qur'ān* is currently being published which covers *sūrahs* 66-77 under this new arrangement. It is hoped that the remaining two volumes (volumes 11 and 12) will be published within the next two years, *inshā' Allāh*. May Allah (*Subḥānahū wa ta'ālā*) give the best of the rewards to the author, Mawlāna Mawdūdī, and the translator, Dr Ansari, for their lifelong effort to communicate the Divine Guidance to human beings searching for light, felicity and salvation. May Allah enable Dr Manazir and Dr Kidwai to complete this work and may Allah reward them and all the colleagues at the Islamic Foundation and Kube Publishing who have worked hard to see the translation of this historic work reach the English reading public. Finally, may Allah open the hearts of all seekers of truth to the message and meaning of the Qur'ān and enable them to make it their real guide and companion in life.

Khurshid Ahmad
Leicester
5th April 2018

Transliteration Table

Arabic Consonants

Initial, unexpressed medial and final: ء ʼ

ا	ā	د	d	ض	ḍ	ك	k
ب	b	ذ	dh	ط	ṭ	ل	l
ت	t	ر	r	ظ	ẓ	م	m
ث	th	ز	z	ع	ʻ	ن	n
ج	j	س	s	غ	gh	هـ	h
ح	ḥ	ش	sh	ف	f	و	w
خ	kh	ص	ṣ	ق	q	ي	y

With a *shaddah,* both medial and final consonants are doubled.

Vowels, diphthongs, etc.

Short:	ـَ a	ـِ i	ـُ u
Long:	ـَا ā	ـِي ī	ـُو ū
Diphthongs:		ـَوْ aw	
		ـَيْ ay	

Sūrah 66

Al-Taḥrīm

(Prohibition)

(Madīnan Period)

Title

The expression *limā tuḥarrimu* occurs in the opening verse of this *Sūrah* and hence constitutes its title. Let it be clarified that the title (literally meaning "prohibition") is not reflective of the contents of this *Sūrah*; rather it signifies that it contains, amid other things, the account of the prohibition of a particular item.

Period of Revelation

According to reports in *aḥādīth*, two wives of the Prophet (peace be upon him) – Ṣafīyah and Māriah the Copt are alluded to in the incident of the prohibition referred to in this *Sūrah*. The Prophet (peace be upon him) had married Ṣafīyah after the conquest of Khybar which, according to unanimous reports, occurred in the seventh year of Hijra. As to Māriah, she had been gifted to the Prophet (peace be upon him) by Muqawqis, the ruler of Egypt, in the same year. She gave birth to the Prophet's son, Ibrāhīm in the month of Dhu'l Ḥijjah of 8 AH. In view of these chronological details, it is almost certain that this *Sūrah* must have been revealed some time during 7 or 8 AH.

Subject Matter and Themes

This is a very important *Sūrah* which, while alluding to some events related to the Prophet's respected wives, highlights the following significant points:

First, Allah alone has the absolute power to declare the bounds of the lawful and the unlawful, the permissible and the forbidden. He has not delegated this authority even to His Messenger, let alone any ordinary person. The Prophet (peace be upon him) in his capacity as a Prophet may declare something lawful or unlawful only when Allah directs him to do so, either through the directive of the Qur'ān or some subtle mode of revelation. However, the Prophet (peace be upon him) is in no way authorised to prohibit something which Allah has made lawful. As for the ordinary person, under no circumstance can he declare any such prohibition.

Second, the Prophet (peace be upon him) occupies a very delicate and lofty position in society. A minor incident in an ordinary person's life may not be of any significance, but if the same happens to the Prophet (peace be upon him), it will have its bearings on law. Accordingly, Allah watches every incident in the lives of the Prophets intensly. This is done to ensure that even a slight step may not be discordant with His will. If a Prophet ever swerves, his action is rectified immediately. This helps protect and preserve the Islamic law and its principles to ensure that it reaches mankind in pristine purity, not only through the Qur'ān, but also through the Prophet's illustrious life, which should not include anything that may not be in keeping with the Divine will.

Third, another self-evident truth emerging from this *Sūrah* is that the Prophet Muḥammad (peace be upon him) was reproached for his minor oversight. His momentary lapse was not only rectified but was recorded in the Qur'ān. This forcefully assures us that all actions and directives which appear in the Prophet's illustrious life, including those for which he was censured, represent the truth and are in consonance with God's will. We may thus, with full confidence, derive guidance from the excellent example he has set.

Fourth, the Qur'ān states that Allah asks the believers to accept the honour and dignity of the illustrious Prophet (peace be upon him) as an important part of their faith, even though this *Sūrah* states that the Prophet (peace be upon him) once prohibited for himself something declared lawful by Allah to placate his wives. On the one hand, Allah the Almighty declares the respected wives of the Prophet as the mothers of the believers and asks all Muslims to hold them in great esteem. On the other, it reproves and criticises them severely in this *Sūrah* for some of their lapses. The criticism directed at the Prophet (peace be upon him) and the warning issued to his wives have not been conducted secretly, but are recorded in the Book which is and will be recited by the entire Muslim *ummah* forever. In so doing, Allah did not intend to lower their prestige in the sight of the believers; the study of this *Sūrah* has never caused a Muslim to develop any disrespect for the Prophet (peace be upon him) or his wives. The only reason therefore, for its inclusion in the Qur'ān, is that Allah seeks to instruct the believers in the norms and limits of respect for their elders and the great personalities. A prophet is a prophet; not God, that he may commit no error at all. He is respected not because he is infallible. Rather, he enjoys his exalted position for being the perfect embodiment of Allah's will. Allah did not leave him without correcting even his minor oversights. This reassures the believers that the Prophet's legacy of the role model is faithfully reflective of Divine Will. Likewise, one learns from this *Sūrah* that the Prophet's Companions and his respected wives were after all human beings. They were not angels, superhuman beings. Nor were they exempt from committing any mistake. Allah's guidance and the Prophet's training uplifted them in their ranks and made them excellent examples for mankind. Indeed, whatever respect and esteem they command, it is based on the above considerations and not on any presumption that they were infallible beings. This explains that during the Prophet's sacred life, they were immediately reprimanded whenever the Prophet's Companions and his respected wives committed any human mistake. The Prophet (peace be upon him) corrected some of their errors whenever required, the incidents of which are recorded in several *aḥādīth*. Allah Himself corrected some of the errors by mentioning these in the Qur'ān, so that Muslims may not inculcate such excessive veneration for them which could elevate them to the status of gods and goddesses. When studying the Qur'ān objectively, one comes across several instances of this nature. In its critique on the battle of Uḥud, the Qur'ān tells the Companions:

> *Allah surely fulfilled His promise (of succour) when you were slaying them by His leave until the moment when you flagged and quarrelled among yourselves about the matter, and disobeyed (the Prophet), after He showed you what you intensely desire; for some of you sought this world and some of you sought the Next. Thereupon, to put you to a test He turned you away from your foes. Still, He pardoned you after that, for Allah is Bounteous to those who believe.*
>
> (Āl 'Imrān 3: 152)

Likewise, regarding the slander directed against the mother of the believers 'Ā'ishah, the Prophet's Companions are instructed thus:

> *When you heard of it, why did the believing men and women not think well of their own folk and say: "This is manifest calumny?" Why did not they bring four witnesses in support of their accusation? Now that they have brought no witnesses, it is indeed they who are liars in the sight of Allah. Were it not for Allah's Bounty and His Mercy unto you in the world and in the Hereafter, a grievous chastisement would have seized you on account of what you indulged in (just think how wrong you were) when one tongue received it from another and you uttered with your mouths something you knew nothing about. You deemed it to be a trifle while in the sight of Allah it was a serious matter. And why, no sooner than you had heard it, did you not say: "It becomes us not even to utter such a thing? Holy are You (O Allah)! This is a mighty calumny." Allah admonishes you. If you are true believers, never repeat the like of what you did.*
>
> (al-Nūr 24: 12–17)

While addressing the Prophet's respected wives the Qur'ān directs them:

> *O Prophet, tell your wives: "If you seek the world and its embellishments, then come and I will make some provision for you and release you in an honourable way. But if you seek Allah and His Messenger and the abode of the Hereafter, then surely Allah has prepared a great reward for those of you who do good."*
>
> (al-Aḥzāb 33: 28–29)

About the Prophet's Companions, one comes across this observation in the Qur'ān:

> *Yet no sooner than they saw some trading or amusement, they flocked to it and left you (O Prophet) standing by yourself. Tell them: "That which is with Allah is far better than amusement and trading. Allah is the Best Provider of sustenance."*
>
> (al-Jumu'ah 62 : 11)

In *Sūrah al-Mumtaḥinah* the Prophet's Companion, Ḥāṭib ibn Abī Balta'ah, who participated in the Battle of Badr, is censured for leaking the Prophet's military plan to the disbelieving Quraysh before the attack on Makkah.

All the above instances feature in the Qur'ān itself; the same Qur'ān in which Allah showers praise on the Prophet's Companions and respected wives and points to their exalted rank. They have been blessed with glad tidings that they are pleased with Allah and He is pleased with them. This teaching of moderation and balance in the veneration of elders and great personalities has protected Muslims from descending into the pitfall of human worship which the Jews and Christians fell into at an earlier date. The works on *tafsīr*, *ḥadīth*, and history authored by leading Muslim scholars while recording the excellence of the Prophet's Companions and respected wives did not hesitate to mention their mistakes and weaknesses whenever they occurred. Today, there are people who claim to have greater regard for them than the classical Muslim scholars, but the latter were more well-informed and conscious about the desirable limits of respect for the Companions and respected wives of the Prophet (peace be upon him).

Fifth, this *Sūrah* makes it plain that Islam, being the faith prescribed by Allah, is quite candid and forthright. It allocates to everyone what he deserves in the light of his beliefs and practices. One's association with a great personality will not help him in any way. Likewise, one's relationship with an evildoer will bring him no harm if he himself does not do any wrong. Three examples of the women from the past are presented for the special attention of the Prophet's respected wives. The first one is that of the wives of the Prophets Noah and Lot (peace be upon them). Had they embraced faith and assisted their illustrious husbands in their noble work, they would have earned the same position and respect from the Muslim *Ummah* as the Prophet Muḥammad's respected wives have. However, since they acted on the contrary, their marital ties with Prophets will not avail them. They are destined to be thrown into Hell.

The second example is that of the Pharaoh's wife. Although she was the wife of Pharaoh, the worst enemy of Allah, she stood firm on faith and followed the straight path, steering away from the ways of Pharaoh and his people. Even marital ties to such a staunch disbeliever as the Pharaoh did not cause her any harm. Allah made her worthy of Paradise.

The third example is of Mary, who attained an elevated rank after being put through a severe trial by Allah. She rose to the occasion and passed the test with distinction. No chaste and noble woman other than Mary has ever been given such a severe trial. Though she was a virgin, Allah caused her to miraculously conceive a child. Mary was given her task by Allah which she accepted without any protest. Rather, as a true believer she put up with all that was concomitant with this trial. In recognition of her excellent performance, Allah bestowed upon her the title of the leader of women in Paradise, as is reported in a *ḥadīth* cited in the *Musnad* of Imām Aḥmad (5, 391).

In addition to the above realities, this *Sūrah* highlights another important fact, that the knowledge and guidance the Prophet (peace be upon him) acquired was not limited to the Qur'ān alone, but he was also blessed with receiving divine guidance (*waḥī*) on several issues not included in the Qur'ān. This point comes out sharply from verse 3 of this *Sūrah*:

> *The Prophet confided something to one of his wives and then she disclosed it (to another); so, after Allah revealed to the Prophet (that she had disclosed that secret), he made a part of it known to her and passed over a part of it. And when he told her about this [i.e. that she had disclosed the secret entrusted to her], she asked: "Who informed you of this?" He said: "I was told of it by Him Who is All-Knowing, All-Aware."*
>
> (al-Taḥrīm 66: 3)

This naturally raises the question as to which Qur'ānic verse informs the Prophet (peace be upon him) that the secret entrusted by him to his wife had been disclosed by her to someone else. Since there is no Qur'ānic verse to the above effect, this is clear evidence that the Prophet (peace be upon him) used to receive also divine revelation other than the Qur'ān. This forcefully refutes the standpoint of the deniers of the *ḥadīth* who allege that the Prophet (peace be upon him) never received any divine revelation other than the Qur'ān.

In the name of Allah, the Most Merciful, the Most Compassionate.

بِسْمِ ٱللَّهِ ٱلرَّحْمَٰنِ ٱلرَّحِيمِ

(1) O Prophet, why do you forbid what Allah has made lawful for you?[1] Is it to please your wives?[2] ▶

يَٰٓأَيُّهَا ٱلنَّبِيُّ لِمَ تُحَرِّمُ مَآ أَحَلَّ ٱللَّهُ لَكَ ۖ
تَبْتَغِى مَرْضَاتَ أَزْوَٰجِكَ ۚ

1. Although this sentence is phrased in the form of a question, it is in fact an expression of disapproval. These words are not said to enquire about as to why the Prophet (peace be upon him) acted in the manner described here, but to let him know that God does not approve of his act of making something unlawful for himself which God Himself had proclaimed lawful. This incident gives a clear message that none has the authority to declare something unlawful which Allah has made lawful, not even the Prophet (peace be upon him). Despite the fact that the Prophet, in this incident, did not regard it as unlawful from the point of view of belief or because it is non-compliant to the *Sharīʿah,* rather he only exhibited dislike and prohibited it for himself to consume it. From this Prophetic action, some people may misconstrue that in following his footsteps, there is no harm in placing some lawful thing into the unlawful category. For this apparent reason, God censures the Prophet (peace be upon him) on this account and asks him to refrain from prohibiting for himself something God has made permissible.

2. It is evident from the wording of the verse that the Prophet's act of making lawful things unlawful was not actuated by his desire. Instead, he did so in deference to some of his wives' desires. This raises the question as to why, apart from reprimanding him for this act, Allah mentions in particular the reason behind his action. Had the intention been only to dissuade him from this act of prohibition, this could have been achieved well by the opening part of verse 1. In that case, there was hardly any need for specifying the reason behind his action. It is clear from the specific mention of the reason that the purpose was not only to dissuade the Prophet (peace be upon him) from that act, but also to chide his respected wives over their negligence of their exalted position. They had erred in forcing the Prophet (peace be upon him) to do something

which could lead to the danger of making something unlawful which Allah had deemed lawful.

The Qur'ān does not specify the item which the Prophet (peace be upon him) had forbidden for himself, yet scholars of *tafsīr* and *ḥadīth* identify the following two incidents as relevant to the circumstantial setting of the above verse. One of these is related to Māriah the Copt and the second one to the Prophet's vow that he would refrain from using honey.

The story of Māriah is that, after concluding the Ḥudaybiyah treaty, the Prophet (peace be upon him) had sent letters to the kings and rulers around Arabia, inviting them to accept Islam. One of them was to the Roman patriarch of Alexandria, known to Arabs as Muqawqis. When Ḥāṭib ibn Abī Balta'ah delivered the Prophet's letter to him, he did not embrace Islam. However, he treated the Prophet's emissary well and in his reply, wrote: "I know about the Promised Messenger. In my opinion, however, his advent would be in Syria. I have nonetheless treated your emissary very well. I take this opportunity to present you two slave girls who enjoy a respectable position among the Copts." (Ibn Sa'd, *al-Ṭabaqāt al-Kubrā*, 1, 34) The two were Sīrīn and Māriah. While returning from Egypt, Ḥāṭib introduced the message of Islam to both and they accepted it. When they were presented before the Prophet (peace be upon him) he handed Sīrīn over to Ḥassān ibn Thābit and admitted Māriah to his household. In the month of Dhu'l Ḥijjah 8 AH Māriah bore the Prophet's son, Ibrāhīm (*al-Istī'āb*, 4, 465 and *al-Iṣābah*, 8, 311). She was exceedingly beautiful. In his *al-Iṣābah* (8, 311) Ibn Ḥajar records 'Ā'ishah's observation about her as follows: "I resented much her entry into the Prophet's house. For she was very pretty and the Prophet (peace be upon him) liked her very much."

Varying reports appear about her in some of the collections of *aḥādīth* which could be summarised as follows: One day the Prophet (peace be upon him) visited Ḥafṣah's home while she was not there. Māriah then joined him and spent some time with him in privacy. This was resented by Ḥafṣah who lodged a strong protest with the Prophet (peace be upon him). To assuage her hurt feelings, he vowed that he will not have any marital relations with Māriah. Some reports state that he forbade her for himself. Some add that he took an oath to the above effect. Most of these *mursal* reports are on the authority of the Successors of the Companions. However, some of these are also narrated by such outstanding Companions as 'Umar, Ibn 'Abbās and Abū Hurayrah.

In view of various reports to the above effect, Ibn Ḥajar in his book *Fatḥ al-Bārī* (8, 765) says that there must be some substance in the above incident. However, this incident is not reported in any of the six authentic collections of *ḥadīth*. Nasā'ī relates only this much on the authority of

Anas: "The Prophet (peace be upon him) had a slave girl with whom he had conjugal relations. Since this was disliked by Ḥafṣah and 'Ā'ishah, he forbade her for himself. Against that background the opening verse of *Sūrah al-Taḥrīm* was sent down: 'O Prophet, why do you forbid what Allah has made lawful for you?'"

The second event is reported on the authority of 'Ā'ishah in the *ḥadīth* collections by Bukhārī (*K. al-Tafsīr, Sūrah al-Taḥrīm*), Muslim (*K. al-Ṭalāq, Bāb Wujūb al-Kaffārah)*, Abū Dāwūd (*K. al-Ashribah, Bāb fī Sharāb al-'Asl*), Nasā'ī (*K. 'Ishrat al-Nisā', Bāb al-Ghayrah*) and others. The Prophet (peace be upon him) used to visit his wives at their homes after 'Aṣr Prayer. During a particular period, he started spending more time at Zaynab bint Jaḥash's residence. She had received honey from someone, which she offered to the Prophet (peace be upon him) and he liked it very much. He used to have a honey drink at her apartment every evening during that period. 'Ā'ishah states that this made her jealous. She took Ḥafṣah, Sawdah, and Ṣafīyah into confidence and decided that they would tell the Prophet (peace be upon him) when he visited any of them that his mouth is giving off the scent of *maghāfīr*, a flower with an offensive smell. Honey made from this flower carries its peculiar smell. They knew it well that as a person of refined taste, he would react strongly to any suggestion about the bad smell emanating from his mouth. They had devised this strategy to dissuade him from staying at Zaynab's place. And this worked, for when his several wives told him that his mouth smelt of *maghāfīr*, he vowed never to take that honey. A report cites his words: "Never will I drink it again. I swear by this." The other report, however, quotes him saying only this much: "Never will I take it." It makes no reference to his taking a vow. Ibn 'Abbās's report, as cited by Ibn al-Mundhir, Ibn Abī Ḥātim, Al-Ṭabarānī and Ibn Marduwayh, reads thus: "By Allah, I will not drink it."

Leading scholars regard the latter version more authentic and relevant to the circumstantial setting of this verse. They tend to dismiss the former as unreliable. Imām Nasā'ī opines: "'Ā'ishah's version regarding honey is sound. As to the incident about the Prophet (peace be upon him) forbidding Māriah for himself, it is not recorded in any authentic report." (*al-Fatḥ al-Rabbānī*, 18, 310). Qāḍī 'Iyāḍ holds: "The truth is that first verse of *Sūrah al-Taḥrīm* was sent down with reference to the Prophet's forbidding the drink of honey for himself, not Māriah." (*al-Fatḥ al-Rabbānī*, 18, 310) Likewise, Qāḍī Abū Bakr ibn al-'Arabī links the incident of honey with this verse (*Aḥkām al-Qur'ān*, 4, 294). The same stance is endorsed by Imām Nawawī (*Ṣaḥīḥ Muslim*, 10, 66), and Ḥāfiẓ Badar al-Dīn al-'Aynī (*'Umdah al-Qārī*, 20, 242). In his *Fatḥ al-Qadīr* Ibn Humām says: "The incident of the prohibition of honey is related on 'Ā'ishah's authority by

Allah is Most Forgiving, Most Compassionate.[3] (2) Allah has prescribed for you a way for the absolution of your oaths.[4] ▶	وَٱللَّهُ غَفُورٌ رَّحِيمٌ ۝١ قَدْ فَرَضَ ٱللَّهُ لَكُمْ تَحِلَّةَ أَيْمَـٰنِكُمْ ۚ

Bukhārī and Muslim. Since she was a party to this incident, her version is more reliable." (8, 160) Ibn Kathīr holds the view: "In all reality, this verse was occasioned by the Prophet's prohibition of honey for himself." (*Tafsīr*)

3. The Prophet (peace be upon him) is told that his act of making a lawful thing unlawful for himself to please his wives does not befit the august office of Allah's Messengership. However, in doing so, he did not commit any sin which would incur punishment. Allah therefore only reprimanded him and forgave his lapse.

4. To come out from the self-imposed constraint of turning *ḥalāl* into *ḥarām*, Allah is directing the Prophet (peace be upon him) to break the oath and offer an expiation in the same way as mentioned in verse 89 of *Sūrah al-Mā'idah*. This has given rise to an important juristic question – whether the above command is applicable when one forbids for himself a lawful thing after taking an oath or when one employs such words which are synonymous with an oath. Jurists answer the above question variously.

According to one group of jurists, prohibition alone does not amount to taking an oath. If one forbids for himself something lawful, for example, his wife, without taking an oath, it amounts to doing something foolhardy and it does not entail any expiation. Without offering any expiation, one may resume his relationship with his wife or taking what he had prohibited for himself. This is the stance of Masrūq, Sha'bī, Rabī'ah and Abū Salamah, which is endorsed by Ibn Jarīr and Ẓāhirīs. For them, only when one takes an oath, he must offer expiation. Their argument rests on the point that since the Prophet (peace be upon him) had declared for himself a lawful thing as unlawful, Allah directed him to free himself from the constraint, concomitant upon taking an oath in accordance with the prescribed method.

The other group of jurists is, however, of the view that if one forbids for himself something, without using an expression synonymous to an oath, it does not constitute an oath, except one's utterance of such words about his wife. It is wrong for someone to forbid for himself some item of food or clothing. He may start using it without offering any expiation. However, if one forbids for himself his sexual relations with his wife or slave girls, she will not automatically be forbidden for him. However, he must offer expiation if he wants to approach her sexually. This is the stance of the Shāfi'ī school (*Mughnī al-Muḥtāj*). Almost the same view is held by the Mālikī school (Ibn al-'Arabī, *Aḥkām al- Qur'ān*, 4, 294).

The third group of jurists maintains that one's act of forbidding something for himself constitutes an oath, even though the words of oath have not been used. Among the exponents of this view are Abū Bakr al-Ṣiddīq, 'Ā'ishah, 'Umar, 'Abdullāh ibn Mas'ūd, 'Abdullāh ibn 'Umar, Zayd ibn Thābit and 'Abdullāh ibn 'Abbās. A different view is ascribed to Ibn 'Abbās as well. According to a report cited by Bukhārī, Ibn 'Abbās appears as saying: "If one forbids his wife for himself, it is something pointless." (*K. al-Ṭalāq, Bāb limā tuḥarrim*) For him, it does not represent any form of divorce. It is only an oath and for breaking it one has to offer expiation. Ibn 'Abbās's opinion is also quoted by Bukhārī (*K. al-Tafsīr*), Muslim (*K. al-Ṭalāq, Bāb Wujūb al-Kaffārh*) and Ibn Mājah (*K. al-Ṭalāq, Bāb al-Ḥarām*): Nasā'ī reports that on being asked to give his ruling on this issue Ibn 'Abbās said: "She (your wife) is not forbidden for you. However, you must offer expiation." Ibn Jarīr (23, 86) quotes Ibn Abbās's following ruling: "If people forbid for themselves something which Allah has declared lawful, they are obliged to offer expiation for breaking their oath (*K. al-Ṭalāq*)." This viewpoint is endorsed by Ḥasan al-Baṣrī, 'Aṭā', Ṭāwūs, Sulaymān ibn Yasār, Ibn Jubayr, and Qatādah. Ḥanafīs abide by the same ruling. Imām Abū Bakr al-Jaṣṣāṣ maintains: "The wording of verse 1 of *Sūrah al-Taḥrīm* does not imply that the Prophet (peace be upon him) had also taken an oath while forbidding something for himself. It therefore emerges from the verse that the act of forbidding something does amount to taking an oath. For, after that incident, Allah prescribed the expiation for breaking an oath while forbidding something for oneself. Ḥanafīs equate the act of forbidding with taking an oath when one's intention is not to divorce his wife. If one forbids his wife for himself, it amounts to his taking an oath that he would not approach her sexually. This would be an *īlā'* (an act of temporary separation) for him. If he forbids for himself an item of food and drink, it is akin to his taking an oath that he would not draw upon it. In this verse, Allah censures the Prophet (peace be upon him) for forbidding for himself something which He has declared lawful. This verse suggests also the way out. Allah thus equates his prohibition (*taḥrīm*) with an oath and the word *taḥrīm* in its meaning and sense becomes equivalent to taking an oath." (*Aḥkām al- Qur'ān*, 3, 621 and 623)

In the public interest, the juristic ruling about forbidding one's wife for himself and other items is clarified below:

The Ḥanafīs maintain that if one forbids his wife for himself without any intention to divorce her, or takes an oath that he would not approach her sexually, it is tantamount to committing an act of *īlā'* (temporary separation). He should offer expiation for an oath before he resumes conjugal relations with her. However, if the above act is accompanied with his intention to divorce her, he will be asked first to clarify his intention. If he intended a triple divorce, it will come into force. However, if his intention was to pronounce divorce less than the above in degree, be it single or double, only a single divorce will be counted. If one employs very broad, general words for forbidding for himself all that is lawful, it will not affect his conjugal relationship to forbid his wife for himself. Until one offers expiation for the oath, he cannot resume the thing he had prohibited for himself (*al-Badā'i' al-Ṣanā'i'*; *Hidāyah*; *Fatḥ al-Qadīr* and *al-Jaṣṣāṣ's Aḥkām al- Qur'ān*, 3, 623).

The Shāfi'ī school of thought is of the view that if one forbids for himself his wife, with the intention of divorce or *ẓihār**, it will come into force. This holds true for both revocable and irrevocable forms of divorce as well as *ẓihār*. If one intended both while using the expressions for prohibition, he will be asked to indicate his choice for either of the two as both divorce and *ẓihār* cannot come into force at the same time. In fact, divorce brings an end to the marriage whereas *ẓihār* does not. If somebody takes an oath forbidding his wife for himself without the intention of divorce, she will not be lawful for him, but he must offer expiation (*kaffārah*) for his wrongful oath. If one takes an oath not forbidding his wife but forbidding other things, it will be regarded as a foolish and useless act and will not require any formal expiation (*Mughnī al-Muḥtāj*).

Mālikīs hold the view that, except for one's wife, if someone forbids any other thing upon himself, it will neither make the thing unlawful nor will he be required to expiate before resuming its use. However, if one forbids himself for his wife or her for himself, irrespective of whether his marriage with her has been consummated or not, it amounts to pronouncing a triple divorce unless his intention was for less than this. Aṣbagh points out: If one says: "All that is lawful is forbidden for me" and he does not specifically exclude his wife from this assertion, his wife will be forbidden for him. In *al-Mudawwanah,* a distinction is drawn between the wife with whom one's marriage has been consummated

---

* To say to one's wife (according to a pre-Islamic practice) that her back is as forbidden to one as the back of one's mother.

Allah is your Guardian. He is All-Knowing, Most Wise.[5]

(3) The Prophet confided something to one of his wives and then she disclosed it (to another); ▶

وَٱللَّهُ مَوْلَىٰكُمْ ۖ وَهُوَ ٱلْعَلِيمُ ٱلْحَكِيمُ ۝٢ وَإِذْ أَسَرَّ ٱلنَّبِيُّ إِلَىٰ بَعْضِ أَزْوَٰجِهِۦ حَدِيثًا فَلَمَّا نَبَّأَتْ بِهِۦ

and the wife with whom it has not been. If one forbids for himself the former, it amounts to a triple divorce, regardless of his intention. In the latter case, however, one's intention for the number of divorce will be taken into account. If he did not specify it, it will be held equivalent to a triple divorce (*Ḥāshiyah al-Dusūqī*).

In his *Aḥkām al-Qur'ān* (4, 295 and 296), Qāḍī Ibn al-'Arabī cites three rulings by Imām Mālik: (i) Forbidding one's wife for oneself is tantamount to one irrevocable divorce. (ii) This act is equivalent to a triple divorce. (iii) In the case of one's wife with whom his marriage has been consummated, it is unquestionably the same as a triple divorce. However, it is equal to a single divorce in the case of the wife with whom one's marriage has not been consummated. Ibn al-'Arabī's concluding statement is: "It is equal to a single divorce because if one uses the expression 'divorce' instead of 'forbidding' and does not specify the number of divorce, it will result in only a single divorce being reckoned."

Three rulings are ascribed to Imām Aḥmad ibn Ḥanbal on this issue: (i) Forbidding one's wife for himself or declaring lawful things as forbidden for himself in an absolute sense constitutes *ẓihār*, irrespective of whether *ẓihār* was his intention or not. (ii) This act is akin to divorce, and thus it brings into force a triple divorce, even though one may have intended only a single divorce. (iii) This act amounts to taking an oath, except if one's intention is divorce or *ẓihār*. Whatever one's intention, it will come into force. The first ruling, as cited above, is the most favoured Mālikī position on this issue (*al-Inṣāf*).

5. Allah is man's Guardian and Protector. He oversees all the affairs of man. He knows best what is in man's interest. His commands for man rest on perfect wisdom. The above verse states first that man is not independent. Rather, he is Allah's servant and Allah is the Lord. Therefore no one has the authority to alter the commands prescribed by Him. It is in man's own interest to refer all his affairs to Allah and to engage himself in worshipping and obeying Him. Before articulating the next point, it is

so after Allah revealed to the Prophet (that she had disclosed that secret), he made a part of it known to her and passed over a part of it. And when he told her about this [i.e., that she had disclosed the secret entrusted to her], she asked: "Who informed you of this?" He said: "I was told of it by He Who is All-Knowing, All-Aware."[6]

وَأَظْهَرَهُ ٱللَّهُ عَلَيْهِ عَرَّفَ بَعْضَهُۥ وَأَعْرَضَ
عَنۢ بَعْضٍۖ فَلَمَّا نَبَّأَهَا بِهِۦ قَالَتْ مَنْ أَنۢبَأَكَ
هَٰذَاۖ قَالَ نَبَّأَنِىَ ٱلْعَلِيمُ ٱلْخَبِيرُ ﴿٣﴾

---

emphasised that all the commands and laws enacted by Allah are based on perfect knowledge and wisdom. Out of His boundless knowledge and wisdom, He has declared things lawful or unlawful. Declaring things lawful or unlawful is not some haphazard act. Those who believe in Allah should realise that they are not all-knowing and all-wise. Rather, it is Allah Who is All-Knowing and All-Wise. It befits us to obey the commands laid down by Him.

6. Several reports relate the secret which the Prophet (peace be upon him) had shared with one of his wives, and which was disclosed by her to another of his wives. In our opinion, it is improper to pursue that secret. For Allah, in this verse, warns one of the Prophet's wives against her misconduct of disclosing a secret. How will it be proper for us to make efforts to ascertain and publicise the same secret? Moreover, it may be noted that the purpose for which this verse was revealed, it is not at all important to know what the secret was. Had it been relevant, Allah Himself would have mentioned it. The true purpose for which this incident is narrated in the Qur'ān is to warn one of the Prophet's wives against her misconduct of having disclosed what her illustrious husband had confided to her in private. Had it been a strictly personal matter, as in the case of an ordinary husband and wife, there was hardly any need for Allah to inform the Prophet's wives about it through His direct revelation to him. Besides informing, this incident is recorded in the Qur'ān, the Book which is to be recited by people until the end of time. Why this matter merited such attention was the fact that it involved not the wife of an ordinary person, but the wife of a great personality to

(4) If the two of you turn in repentance to Allah (that is better for you), for the hearts of both of you have swerved from the Straight Path.[7] But if you support ▶

إِن تَتُوبَآ إِلَى ٱللَّهِ فَقَدْ صَغَتْ قُلُوبُكُمَا ۖ وَإِن تَظَٰهَرَا عَلَيْهِ

---

whom Allah had entrusted a very important mission; a person who was in constant struggle against the disbelievers, polytheists, and hypocrites. Under his leadership, a massive effort was in progress to replace Islam against unbelief. A myriad of discussions were held inside his house which, if leaked, could damage the cause championed by him. So, as this lapse was committed by one of the residents of the Prophet's home, she was reprimanded. Let it be clarified that she had not disclosed it to some stranger or enemy. She had shared it with one of the Prophet's co-wives. Yet, she is not only chided publicly but is mentioned in the Qur'ān in a reprimanding tone. This is done in order to instruct the Prophet's wives, and through them, the wives of responsible Muslims, not to be negligent in guarding their secrets. The verse disregards the issue altogether whether the secret disclosed by her was an important one and whether its disclosure posed any danger or not. A serious note, however, is taken of the disclosure of that secret. This is because if a weakness in keeping household secrets is found among the members of a very responsible family, and if one day an unimportant secret is disclosed, there is no guarantee that an important secret is not leaked out the next day. The higher a person's position of responsibility in the community, the more dangerous it becomes for secrets to leak out of his household. Regardless of whether a matter is important or not, once a person becomes careless in guarding secrets, it is likely that he will disclose important matters along with those that are unimportant.

7. The word *ṣaghw*, used in the verse (*faqad ṣaghat qulūbukumā*), stands for swerving and twisting. Both Shāh Walīullāh and Shāh Rafī' al Dīn have rendered it with reference to the deviance of the heart. Ibn Mas'ūd, Ibn 'Abbās, Sufyān al-Thawrī and Ḍaḥḥāk also interpret it with the swerving of the heart. Imām al-Rāzī explains it thus: "Reference is to their moving away from the path of the truth." Ālūsī's version is as follows: "It is obligatory on you (the Prophet's wives) to follow the Prophet (peace be upon him) in what he likes and dislikes. In this particular instance, their

one another against the Prophet,[8] then surely Allah is his Protector; and after that Gabriel and all ▶	فَإِنَّ ٱللَّهَ هُوَ مَوْلَىٰهُ وَجِبْرِيلُ

hearts deviated from the Prophet's way and followed the course which amounted to opposing him."

8. *Taẓāhur* in the verse *wa in Taẓāharā 'alayhi* stands for supporting one another against someone or for uniting against someone. Most scholars of the Qur'ān from the Indo-Pakistan subcontinent, such as Shāh Walīullāh, Shāh 'Abdul Qādir, Mawlānā Ashraf 'Alī Thānawī, and Mawlānā Shabbīr Aḥmad 'Uthmānī have given a more or less similar meaning. The verse is pointedly addressed to two ladies, to be more precise, the two respected wives of the Prophet (peace be upon him) because verses 1–5 of this *Sūrah* deal specifically with his wives. All this is clear from the context of the Qur'ān. This leads us to the next issue – the identity of these two wives and the matter which incurred Allah's wrath. These details appear in the works of *aḥādīth*. Bukhārī, Aḥmad, Muslim, Tirmidhī, and Nasā'ī have cited an extensive report on the authority of 'Abdullāh ibn 'Abbās, with slight variations. Ibn 'Abbās reports:

For a long time, I thought of asking 'Umar about the identity of the two holy wives of the Prophet (peace be upon him) who had united against the Prophet (peace be upon him) and regarding whom the Qur'ān says: "If the two of you turn in repentance to Allah (that is better for you), because the hearts of both of you have swerved from the straight path." (Verse 4 of *al-Taḥrīm*) However, I was too overawed to ask him this question. Once, as he set out on *Ḥajj*, I took the opportunity to accompany him. On the way back, while assisting him in performing *wuḍū'*, I got an opportunity to raise this question. To this he replied: "Those two were 'Ā'ishah and Ḥafṣah." He then elaborated: "We, the Quraysh, were accustomed to keep our wives under strict control. However, when we migrated to Madīnah we came into contact with such men who were under the control of their wives. Our wives became influenced by this scenario. One day, as I was angry with my wife, she answered me back. Her answering back infuriated me. She asked me why I felt angry over this. "By Allah, even the Prophet's wives sometimes did this. Some of them remain in an angry mood for the whole day". (Bukhārī's report is to the contrary, saying that the Prophet [peace be upon him] remained angry with her for the whole day.) Upon hearing this, I left my house and went to Ḥafṣah's residence (she was his daughter and the Prophet's wife). I asked her whether she answered back to the Prophet (peace be upon him). She replied in the affirmative. Then I asked her whether some of them (the Prophet's holy wives) continued the angry behaviour the whole day. (Bukhārī once again attributes this act to the Prophet [peace be upon him]). When she replied again in the affirmative, I told her: "Wretched and a loser is she among you who behaves in this manner! Have you become totally fearless that the Prophet's displeasure may not evoke Allah's wrath upon you, leading to your peril and destruction? Never argue with him. Nor should you ever demand anything from him. You are free to demand anything from what I have. Do not be deluded by this that 'Ā'ishah does the same. She is more charming and dearer to him than you are." Then I called on Umm Salamah who is my relative as well. I discussed this issue with her. She told me: "O Ibn al-Khaṭṭāb, you are a strange fellow. You interfere in every matter. How dare you meddle in the life of the Prophet (peace be upon him) and his wives." This discouraged me from pursuing the matter further. Then it so happened that an Anṣār neighbour of mine called on me at night. We used to join the Prophet's company by turn and exchanged our notes. It was the period when there was the impending danger of the attack by the Ghassanids. As he called me out at night, he told me that a tragedy had struck. I asked him whether the Ghassanids had launched the attack. He told me: "No, it is something much more serious. The Prophet (peace be upon him) has divorced his wives." I exclaimed: "Wretched and lost is Ḥafṣah! (Bukhārī says that 'Umar named both Ḥafṣah and 'Ā'ishah). I already had a premonition of the same." (Bukhārī, *K. al-Maẓālim, Bāb al-Ghurfah … K. al-Nikāḥ, Bāb Maw'iẓah al-Rajul …* and *al-Fatḥ al-Rabbānī, K. Faḍā'il al- Qur'ān*).

The report adds that the next morning 'Umar visited the Prophet (peace be upon him) and tried to assuage him. The above account is based on the reports cited by Aḥmad and Bukhārī. It is clear from the context that the Prophet's wives sometimes did not hesitate to answer back to the Prophet. 'Umar advised his daughter, who was one of the wives of the Prophet (peace be upon him), not to be impudent.

The reason Allah reprimanded the Prophet's wives so strongly in the Qur'ān is a point worth studying. Was that matter so serious? Moreover, why did 'Umar take it so seriously that he first reprimanded his daughter and then called on other wives of the Prophet (peace be upon him) and warned them against Allah's displeasure? Above all, was the Prophet (peace be upon him) so sensitive that he used to get angry with his wives over trivial matters? Was he so irritable and enraged over his wives' minor

righteous believers and the angels are all his supporters.[9] (5) Maybe if he were to divorce you, your Lord might grant him in exchange wives better than you[10] – those ▶

وَصَـٰلِحُ ٱلْمُؤْمِنِينَ ۖ وَٱلْمَلَـٰٓئِكَةُ بَعْدَ ذَٰلِكَ ظَهِيرٌ ﴿٤﴾ عَسَىٰ رَبُّهُۥٓ إِن طَلَّقَكُنَّ أَن يُبْدِلَهُۥٓ أَزْوَٰجًا خَيْرًا مِّنكُنَّ

---

mistakes that on one occasion he even severed his ties with them and retired to his apartment? On studying the above, one must opt for either of these two scenarios. He may have such an overwhelming regard for his wives that he may show little concern about the attitude of Allah and His Messenger. Or he may concede that, at that particular point of time, the Prophet's wives had behaved so improperly that the Prophet (peace be upon him) was justified in taking such an extreme measure. Moreover, not only he but Allah too, warned them harshly against their impudence.

9. The Prophet's wives are warned that if they entered in league against him, they would only hurt themselves because he enjoyed Allah's complete protection and support. Moreover, Gabriel, Allah's other angels, and all the righteous believers stood by him. How then would their joining together against him be able to change anything?

10. This shortcoming did not apply to 'Ā'ishah and Ḥafṣah only, but to some of the Prophet's other wives who also shared some blame. Therefore, after admonishing these two, the other wives are also reprimanded. The Qur'ān does not throw any light on the exact nature of the lapses committed by them. However, some *ḥadīth* reports do shed some light, which are narrated as below.

Bukhārī (*K. al-Tafsīr, Sūrah al-Taḥrīm*) reproduces Anas's report that 'Umar related: "The mutual jealousy of the Prophet's wives caused offence to the Prophet (peace be upon him). On learning this, I told them: 'It is likely that if he divorces you, Allah will grant him better wives than you.'" On the authority of Anas, Ibn Abī Ḥātim cites 'Umar's following statement: "I learned about some discord between the Prophet (peace be upon him) and his wives. I visited each of them and asked them to give up offending him, otherwise Allah will grant him better wives than them. When I called on the last one (who, according to Bukhārī, was Umm Salamah), she responded saying: 'Does the Prophet (peace be upon him) not suffice for admonishing women that you too have taken to reproving them?' This silenced me. After a little while Allah sent down the above verse." (*Tafsīr Ibn Kathīr,* 8, 165)

Muslim (*K. al-Ṭalāq, Bāb fī al-Īlā'*) relates 'Abdullāh ibn 'Abbās's report which he heard from 'Umar: "When the Prophet (peace be upon him) turned away from his wives, I joined him in his mosque. I found all those present there with gloomy faces. They told one another of this happening." Then 'Umar narrated about his visit and advice to 'Ā'ishah and Ḥafṣah. He called on the Prophet (peace be upon him) and submitted: "Why are you upset over this matter? If you divorce them, Allah is with you, as are all the angels, including Gabriel and Michael. Abū Bakr, the believers, and I, are with you too."

I thank Allah that seldom it happened that whenever I made some observation while reposing trust in Allah, it was not followed by the sending down of some divine revelation, which endorsed my humble reflections. In this case too, the opening verses of *Sūrah al-Taḥrīm* were revealed. I then asked the Prophet (peace be upon him) whether he had divorced his wives, to which he replied in the negative. It was then, while standing at the gate of the Prophet's mosque, that I proclaimed in a loud voice that the Prophet (peace be upon him) had not divorced his wives."

Several reports feature in the *ḥadīth* collections by Bukhārī (*K. Ṭalāq*) and Aḥmad (*Musnad*, 1, 33 and 34), narrated by Anas, Ibn 'Abbās, 'Ā'ishah, and Abū Hurayrah to the effect that the Prophet (peace be upon him) had vowed not to have any relations with his wives for a period of one month. He stayed upstairs during this period. At the expiry of 29 days, Gabriel visited him and told him that its duration has been completed.

In his *'Umdat al-Qārī* (19, 249) Ḥāfiẓ Badr al-Dīn al-'Aynī has quoted 'Ā'ishah saying that the above incident had divided the Prophet's wives into two camps. To one belonged 'Ā'ishah, Ḥafṣah, Sawdah, and Ṣafīyah. The other camp included Zaynab, Umm Salamah, and other wives.

The above reports point to the situation of the Prophet's domestic life at the time. It necessitated Allah's intervention. All this was done to reform the conduct of the Prophet's respected wives. Although they were the best women of the day, they were, after all, human beings, and not altogether free from human weakness. At times, they found it hard to bear with the poverty that rocked their lives. Unable to restrain themselves, they asked the Prophet (peace be upon him) to provide them with proper resources for maintenance. The following verses 28–29 of *Sūrah al-Aḥzāb* were revealed in the same context:

> O Prophet, tell your wives: "If you seek the world and its embellishments, then come and I will make some provision for you

who truly submit to Allah,[11] are full of faith, obedient,[12] ▶	مُسۡلِمَـٰتٖ مُّؤۡمِنَـٰتٖ قَـٰنِتَـٰتٖ

and release you in an honourable way. But if you seek Allah and His Messenger and the abode of the Hereafter, then surely Allah has prepared a great reward for those of you who do good." (See also *Towards Understanding the Qur'ān*, vol. 9, *Sūrah al-Aḥzāb* 33: n. 41, p. 43 and also the Introduction to the *Sūrah*, pp. 18–19).

Overcome at times by their feminine nature, they committed acts which are fairly common in daily life. However, Allah had granted them a privileged position by virtue of being the Prophet's wives. Their mistakes did not befit their exalted status. In view of the apprehension that their shortcomings may disturb the peace of the Prophet's domestic life, which may, in turn, have its adverse effect on his noble mission entrusted to him by Allah, the Qur'ānic verses under discussion were revealed for reforming them. These awaken the Prophet's wives to their status and their role and responsibility entailed by their association with the Prophet (peace be upon him). The opening part of this verse: "May be if he were to divorce you, your Lord might grant him in exchange wives better than you," (verse 5 of *Sūrah al-Taḥrīm*) must have shaken them. It served as an effective warning for them. The very thought that Allah will grant the Prophet (peace be upon him) better wives than them must have been intolerable to them, for in that eventuality, they would have lost their privileged position of being the mothers of the Muslims. In the face of such a dire warning, any misconduct on their part, which could incur Allah's displeasure, was unthinkable. This explains why the note of warning directed at them occurs at only two places (i.e. in *Sūrahs al-Aḥzāb* and *al-Taḥrīm*) in the Qur'ān.

11. When both the expressions *Muslim* and *M'umin* are used at the same place, the former refers to one who acts on divine commands and the latter to the one blessed with firm faith. Thus the first and foremost feature of Muslim wives is that they truly submit to Allah, His Messenger and His faith. Moreover, in their morals and manners, habits, conduct and attitude they faithfully observe the divine teachings.

12. It is open to two sets of meanings and both of these are intended here. First, they are obedient to Allah and His Messenger, and next, they obey their husbands.

disposed to repentance,[13] and given to worship[14] and fasting[15] – both previously wedded ones and virgins. (6) Believers, guard yourselves and your kindred against a Fire whose fuel is ▶	تَٰٓئِبَٰتٍ عَٰبِدَٰتٍ سَٰٓئِحَٰتٍ ثَيِّبَٰتٍ وَأَبْكَارًا ۝ يَٰٓأَيُّهَا ٱلَّذِينَ ءَامَنُوا۟ قُوٓا۟ أَنفُسَكُمْ وَأَهْلِيكُمْ نَارًا وَقُودُهَا

13. When the expression *tā'ib* is used for someone, it does not refer to his seeking repentance only once. Rather, it stands for one who is repentant over his lapses, whose conscience keeps pricking him, and who is always aware of his weaknesses and vulnerability. In recognition of all this, his mind and heart are filled with repentance and shame. Such a person is not likely to become arrogant and selfish. On the contrary, he is most likely to be tender-hearted and forbearing.

14. A devout person, unlike a non-worshipper, can never disregard God. A God-conscious person contributes much to making a woman an excellent wife, for being a worshipper she follows the limits set by Allah, discharges her duty towards everyone, and keeps her faith strong and fresh. She is more likely not to have the courage and inclination to disobey any divine command.

15. The expression *sā'iḥāt*, as employed in this verse, is construed by many Companions and most of the Successors as "those who fast." *Siyāḥat* (travelling) is used in the context of fasting in view of the fact that in ancient times ascetics and dervishes were generally travellers, without having proper provision for their journey. They starved until someone offered them something to eat. Taken in this sense, not eating anything or fasting is a trait of dervishes. Until the appointed time of the sunset, a fasting person too does not eat anything. In his *tafsīr* on verse 12 of *Sūrah al-Tawbah* (12, 15), Ibn Jarīr has cited 'Ā'ishah's following observation: "The *siyāḥat* of this community consists in fasting." This implies that the virtuous wives are not those who fast only during Ramaḍān, they also observe *nafl* fasts.

Allah's statement directed at the Prophet's wives that if the Prophet (peace be upon him) were to divorce them Allah will grant him better wives in their place, does not imply that they were devoid of good qualities. Rather, they are urged to give up their incorrect behaviour which displeased the Prophet (peace be upon him), and are also asked to devote themselves heart and soul to developing excellent qualities.

human beings and stones,[16] a Fire held in the charge of fierce and stern angels who never disobey what He has commanded them, and always do what they are bidden.[17] (7) (It will then be said): "Unbelievers, make no excuses today. You are being recompensed for nothing else but your deeds."[18]

ٱلنَّاسُ وَٱلْحِجَارَةُ عَلَيْهَا مَلَٰٓئِكَةٌ غِلَاظٌ
شِدَادٌ لَّا يَعْصُونَ ٱللَّهَ مَآ أَمَرَهُمْ وَيَفْعَلُونَ
مَا يُؤْمَرُونَ ﴿٦﴾ يَٰٓأَيُّهَا ٱلَّذِينَ كَفَرُوا۟
لَا تَعْتَذِرُوا۟ ٱلْيَوْمَ ۖ إِنَّمَا تُجْزَوْنَ مَا كُنتُمْ
تَعْمَلُونَ ﴿٧﴾

---

16. This verse indicates that a person is required, first of all, to strive to guard himself against God's chastisement. Over and above that, he should also do whatever possible to raise members of his family who are under his care as righteous people so that they win God's pleasure. But if they are inclined to follow a course that is likely to land them in Hellfire, he should try, as far as he can, to prevent them from proceeding along that path. He should not be concerned only about their prosperity in the world. Rather, his priority should be to ensure that they do not end up as fuel for Hellfire. Bukhārī (*K. al-Aḥkām, Bāb Qawl Allāh ta'ālā Aṭī'ū Allāh wa Aṭī'ū al-Rasūl*) has cited this *ḥadīth* on Ibn 'Umar's authority: "The Prophet (peace be upon him) said: "Each one of you is like a shepherd, who will be accountable for those under his care. By this token, a ruler, being the master, is answerable regarding his subjects. A male is the head of his family and is responsible for them. A woman is in charge of her husband's house and children. She will be held accountable regarding them."

As for the words, "whose fuel is human beings and stones", they probably signify coal. Ibn Mas'ūd, Ibn 'Abbās, Mujāhid, Imām Muḥammad al-Bāqir, and al-Suddī are of the opinion that brimstone will be the fuel of Hellfire.

17. They will faithfully execute the sentence awarded to every culprit and will not take pity on anyone.

18. The tone of both verses carries a serious warning for the Muslims. The first verse asked Muslims to guard themselves and their family members against the horrible punishment of Hellfire. The next one

(8) Believers, turn to Allah in sincere repentance;[19] maybe your Lord will expunge your evil deeds and admit you to the Gardens ▸	يَـٰٓأَيُّهَا ٱلَّذِينَ ءَامَنُوا۟ تُوبُوٓا۟ إِلَى ٱللَّهِ تَوْبَةً نَّصُوحًا عَسَىٰ رَبُّكُمْ أَن يُكَفِّرَ عَنكُمْ سَيِّـَٔاتِكُمْ وَيُدْخِلَكُمْ جَنَّـٰتٍ

specifies what will be said to the disbelievers when punishment will be meted out to them in the Hereafter. Implicit in it is the message for Muslims that they should shun such misconduct which could place them in the rank of the disbelievers in the Hereafter.

19. The expressions employed in the above verse are *tawbatan naṣūḥā*. *Nuṣḥ*, in Arabic terminology connotes sincerity and wishing well for others. So, the reference is to one's sincere repentance, without even an iota of hypocrisy. In doing so, one acts sincerely towards his own self, for his repentance over his sins will protect him against an ignominious end in the Hereafter. By seeking forgiveness, he mends the dents caused in his faith. Likewise, after his sincere penitence, he turns out to be a role model for others to reform their lives. All these connotations are conveyed by its literal meaning. As to its meaning in the parlance of *Sharī'ah*, the following *ḥadīth*, narrated by Ibn abī Ḥātim, on the authority of Zirr ibn Ḥubaysh is quite instructive: "I requested Ubayy ibn Ka'b to explain the meaning of *tawbatan naṣūḥ*. He replied that once he had made the same request to the Prophet (peace be upon him) and in reply he told: "It means that you should repent when you commit a mistake. You should seek Allah's forgiveness for the guilt in the state of shame and do not repeat the same misdeed ever." (*Tafsīr* of Ibn Kathīr, 8, 169) A similar interpretation of the above term is on record on the authority of 'Umar, 'Abdullāh ibn Mas'ūd and 'Abdullāh ibn 'Abbās. In a report, 'Umar defines its meaning: "After his repentance, one should not even think of repeating his misdeed, what to say of repeating it." (*Tafsīr* of Ibn Jarīr al-Ṭabarī, 23, 106–108)

Once, when 'Alī observed a bedouin uttering the expressions of repentance and seeking forgiveness at a fast speed, he exclaimed: "This appears to be the repentance of a liar." The bedouin then asked what the right method of repentance is? 'Alī replied: "Repentance involves the following six points: (i) One should be repentant over his misdeed. (ii) One should fulfil the duties neglected by him. (iii) One should return to the owner what is usurped by him. (iv) One should tender his apology to the person he has offended. (v) One should resolve never to commit that

beneath which rivers flow.[20] This will be on the Day when Allah will not disgrace the Prophet and those who ▶	تَجْرِى مِن تَحْتِهَا ٱلْأَنْهَـٰرُ يَوْمَ لَا يُخْزِى ٱللَّهُ ٱلنَّبِىَّ وَٱلَّذِينَ ءَامَنُوا۟ مَعَهُۥ

misdeed again. (vi) One should surrender himself wholly to the obedience to Allah. His mind and soul steeped in sinful pleasures should undergo the hardships arising from the obedience to Allah." (al-Zamakhsharī, *al-Kashshāf*, 6, 162)

Some more points should be borne in mind regarding repentance. First, one should repent over his misdeed, realising that it was an act of disobedience to Allah. Otherwise just resolving not to do something, which is hazardous to health or incurs some financial loss or leads to infamy, does not fall in the category of repentance. Second, one should repent as soon as he realises he has committed disobedience to Allah and compensate for it without delay in whatever form he deems fit. One should not defer his repentance. Third, if one repeatedly breaks his resolve by committing the same misdeed again and again, it amounts to taking repentance as a sport and betrays his insincerity. The real essence of repentance lies in a genuine regret for the misdeed. The repeated committing of the same misdeed points to the absence of any remorse on his part. Fourth, if out of his human frailty, he again commits the same misdeed which he had resolved not to do and for which he had genuinely sought repentance and forgiveness, he should repent again and make a stronger resolve never to repeat it. Fifth, one need not repent every time he recalls his misdeed. However, if his soul derives any pleasure from the thought of having indulged in some sin, he should consistently repent until he tends to feel genuinely sorry for having committed that sin. For one who sincerely repents out of the fear of Allah cannot even think of gloating over his disobedience to Allah. If he does so, it underscores that his heart is devoid of any fear of God. As for one who fantasises on the past sin, it indicates that God's fear has not taken any root in his heart.

20. The wording of the verse is worth reflecting. It does not say that repentance will necessarily result in Allah's pardon and entry into Paradise. Rather, it gives out hope that one's sincere repentance may lead to Allah's forgiveness of his evil deeds. In other words, it is not obligatory on Allah to accept the repentance of every sinner and admit him to Paradise instead of punishing him for his sins. It will be His

نُورُهُمْ يَسْعَىٰ بَيْنَ أَيْدِيهِمْ وَبِأَيْمَـٰنِهِمْ يَقُولُونَ رَبَّنَآ أَتْمِمْ لَنَا نُورَنَا وَٱغْفِرْ لَنَآ ۖ إِنَّكَ عَلَىٰ كُلِّ شَىْءٍ قَدِيرٌ ۝٨

have embraced faith and are with him;[21] their light will be running before them and on their right hands, and they will say: "Our Lord, perfect for us our light and forgive us. Surely You have power over everything."[22]

graciousness and favour, if He pardons a sinner and then rewards him. One should no doubt look forward to His pardon. However, he should not keep committing misdeeds out of his belief that his repentance will secure His pardon.

21. Allah will not deprive them of the reward of their good deeds. He will not provide the disbelievers and the hypocrites the opportunity to taunt the believers, that despite their sincere devotion to Allah, they had gained nothing. On the contrary, disgrace will be the lot of those who are rebellious and disobey Allah.

22. On studying this verse, in conjunction with verses 12–13 of *Sūrah al-Ḥadīd*, it emerges that the light will be focussing on the route ahead of the believers who will proceed from the grand assembly to Paradise. On the contrary, those doomed to Hell will stumble in the all-round darkness. Only the believers will be blessed with light, which will facilitate their movement. On listening to the agonising cries of the disbelievers groping in darkness, the hearts of the believers will be filled with the awe of Allah. While recalling their own lapses and shortcomings, they will apprehend that the light may be switched off and they might grope in the darkness like the sinners. They will therefore make this supplication: "O our Lord, forgive us our lapses and perfect for us our light, enabling us to reach Paradise." Ibn Jarīr (*Tafsīr*, 23, 109) has related the wording of 'Abdullāh ibn 'Abbās that the believers will supplicate that their light be not extinguished until they safely cross the bridge of *Ṣirāṭ*. More or less, the same stance is adopted by Ḥasan al-Baṣrī, Mujāhid, and Ḍaḥḥāk. Ibn Kathīr cites their remark (*Tafsīr*, 8, 170) as follows: "On noting that the hypocrites are deprived of light, the believers will invoke Allah that their light be perfected for them." (For further details see *Sūrah al-Ḥadīd* 57: 17).

(9) O Prophet, strive against the unbelievers and the hypocrites, and be severe with them.[23] Hell shall be their resort. What a grievous end!

(10) Allah has set forth for the unbelievers the parable of the wives of Noah and Lot. They were wedded to two of Our righteous servants, but each acted treacherously with her husband,[24] and their husbands could be of no avail to them against Allah. The two of them were told: "Enter the Fire with all the others who enter it." (11) Allah has set forth for the believers the parable of Pharaoh's wife. ▶

يَٰٓأَيُّهَا ٱلنَّبِيُّ جَٰهِدِ ٱلۡكُفَّارَ وَٱلۡمُنَٰفِقِينَ
وَٱغۡلُظۡ عَلَيۡهِمۡۚ وَمَأۡوَىٰهُمۡ جَهَنَّمُۖ وَبِئۡسَ
ٱلۡمَصِيرُ ٩ ضَرَبَ ٱللَّهُ مَثَلٗا لِّلَّذِينَ
كَفَرُواْ ٱمۡرَأَتَ نُوحٖ وَٱمۡرَأَتَ لُوطٖۖ كَانَتَا
تَحۡتَ عَبۡدَيۡنِ مِنۡ عِبَادِنَا صَٰلِحَيۡنِ
فَخَانَتَاهُمَا فَلَمۡ يُغۡنِيَا عَنۡهُمَا مِنَ ٱللَّهِ شَيۡـٔٗا
وَقِيلَ ٱدۡخُلَا ٱلنَّارَ مَعَ ٱلدَّٰخِلِينَ ١٠ وَضَرَبَ
ٱللَّهُ مَثَلٗا لِّلَّذِينَ ءَامَنُواْ ٱمۡرَأَتَ فِرۡعَوۡنَ

---

23. For details see *Towards Understanding the Qur'ān* vol. III, *Sūrah al-Tawbah* 9: n. 82, pp. 232–234).

24. The statement that "each acted treacherously" does not mean, God forbid, that the wives of the Prophets Noah and Lot succumbed to any act of indecency. What is meant is that instead of lending support to the efforts of their husbands – Noah and Lot (peace be upon them) – to uphold the Truth, they lent support to the opponents of the true faith. Ibn 'Abbās states: "No wife of any Prophet has ever been immoral. The two women acted treacherously regarding the faith. They did not embrace the faith of their husbands. Noah's wife used to inform her unbelieving community leaders about the movement of the believers. Likewise, Lot's wife used to pass on the information about the Prophet Lot's guests to the evildoers of her community." (Ibn Jarīr, *Tafsīr*, 23, 111–112).

She prayed: "My Lord, build for me a house with You in Paradise and deliver me from Pharaoh and his misdeeds;[25] and deliver me from the iniquitous people." (12) Allah has also set forth the parable of Mary, the daughter of ʿImrān,[26] who guarded her chastity,[27] and into whom We breathed of Our Spirit,[28] and who testified to the words of her Lord and His Books. She was among the obedient.[29]

إِذْ قَالَتْ رَبِّ ٱبْنِ لِى عِندَكَ بَيْتًا فِى
ٱلْجَنَّةِ وَنَجِّنِى مِن فِرْعَوْنَ وَعَمَلِهِۦ وَنَجِّنِى
مِنَ ٱلْقَوْمِ ٱلظَّـٰلِمِينَ ﴿١١﴾ وَمَرْيَمَ ٱبْنَتَ
عِمْرَٰنَ ٱلَّتِىٓ أَحْصَنَتْ فَرْجَهَا فَنَفَخْنَا فِيهِ
مِن رُّوحِنَا وَصَدَّقَتْ بِكَلِمَـٰتِ رَبِّهَا
وَكُتُبِهِۦ وَكَانَتْ مِنَ ٱلْقَـٰنِتِينَ ﴿١٢﴾

25. Her supplication was that she not be punished for Pharaoh's evil deeds.

26. It is possible that the name of Mary's father was 'Imrān, or that she was called "daughter of 'Imrān" because she belonged to the family of 'Imrān.

27. This refutes the Jews' allegation that Jesus's birth was, God forbid, the result of a sin committed by his mother. The Qur'ān (4: 156) refutes this charge and calls it a "monstrous calumny." (For details see *Towards Understanding the Qur'ān*, vol. II, *Sūrah al-Nisā'* 4: n. 190, p. 105.)

28. Mary conceived Jesus without any physical contact with any human being. It took place simply because God breathed into her womb a spirit from Himself. (For details see *Towards Understanding the Qur'ān*, vol. II, *Sūrah al-Nisā'* 4: nn. 212–213, pp. 116–117 and vol. V, *Sūrah al-Anbiyā'* 21: n. 89, p. 294.)

29. Our Introduction to this *Sūrah* states the rationale behind presenting these three women as role models.

Sūrah 67

Al-Mulk

(Dominion)

(Makkan Period)

Title

The expression *al-mulk* (dominion) featuring in the opening verse of this *Sūrah* constitutes its title.

Period of Revelation

There is no authentic report about the period of its revelation. However, it is fairly evident from its contents and style that it was revealed in the early Makkan phase.

Subject Matter and Themes

On the one hand, this *Sūrah* introduces in a concise manner the teachings of Islam and on the other, it eloquently warns those who were steeped in heedlessness. It is a feature of the early Makkan *Sūrahs* that they deal with the entire teachings of Islamic faith and the purpose of the Prophet Muḥammad's mission, albeit stated briefly, not at length. This is done with a view to persuading the addressees in a way that they grasp these truths gradually. The focus, however, is on waking up the heedless, on prompting them to ponder, and on arousing their dormant conscience.

The opening five verses aim at making man realise that the universe inhabited by him represents a well-organised and stable kingdom. Were one to look, he could not detect any flaw or shortcoming in its working. It is God Who has brought it into existence out of nothing, and it is He Who exercises absolute power and authority over its functioning and control. His power is boundless. Man is also told that he has not been created in such a well organised system in vain. He has been sent to this world on a test and trial. His good conduct alone will help him pass this test.

Verses 6–11 graphically describe the dreadful consequences of unbelief which man will face in the Hereafter. Mankind is informed that God has sent down His Messengers to warn them in this world against such consequences. If they do not listen to the Messengers and do not mend their ways, they will have to concede in the Hereafter that they really deserve the punishment which will be meted out to them.

Verses 12–14 emphasise the truth that God, being the Creator, is not unaware of the condition of His creatures. He knows very well all that man declares and conceals, including the thoughts and innermost feelings of his mind and heart. Therefore, the first and foremost moral principle is that man should shun all evil out of the fear of the Unseen God; no matter whether he may be caught or not for his evil deed by any authority in this world and whether he may or may not have any fear of loss in this world. Those who adopt such a conduct in this world will attain deliverance and a great reward in the Hereafter.

Verses 15–23 draw attention to the signs which mankind disregards as routine matters. Man is asked to reflect on these signs seriously. It is said that you look at the earth on which you walk routinely in comfort and from which you derive your livelihood; it is God Who has made the earth subservient to you, otherwise, you may be struck by an earthquake which may destroy you, or a violent storm which may annihilate you completely. Look at the birds flying above you, it is God Who holds them in the air. Look at the resources you have mobilised and accumulated on the earth. No one can save you if God were to afflict you with His punishment. Nor can anyone restore the means of sustenance for you if God takes these away. All these signs should suffice for you to realise the truth. However, you look at these signs like the unthinking animals who cannot draw any inference from their observations. You do not properly utilise your faculties of hearing, seeing, and discernment with which God has endowed you as a human being. As a result, you fail to see the right path.

Verses 24–27 explain that man will ultimately stand before his Lord. It is not a Messenger's assignment to inform you of the exact time and date of the Resurrection. His only duty is to warn you beforehand about its occurrence. You refuse to believe in the Messenger and insist on witnessing the Last Day of Resurrection in front of you. But when it does occur, and you see it with your own eyes, you will be astounded. On that Day, you will be told that this is exactly what you asked to be expedited.

Verses 28–29 refute the Makkan disbelievers' allegations against the Prophet Muḥammad (peace be upon him) and his Companions. They used to curse the Prophet (peace be upon him) and pray for his and the believers' destruction. In response, it is stressed that whether the people who are calling them to the right way are punished or rewarded, how will this affect their destiny? They should better think as to who will protect them from the scourge of God. They consider those who believe in God and have trust in Him as misguided. Soon they will come to know who, in reality, is misguided.

Finally, they are asked to ponder over the question that if water, on which their lives depend in the deserts and hills of Arabia, were to sink down into the depths of the earth and vanish, who other than God can restore this lifeline to them?

In the name of Allah, the Most Merciful, the Most Compassionate.

(1) Blessed is He[1] in Whose Hand is the dominion of the Universe,[2] and Who has power over everything;[3] (2) Who created death and life that He might try you as to which of you is better in deed.[4] ▶

بِسۡمِ ٱللَّهِ ٱلرَّحۡمَٰنِ ٱلرَّحِيمِ

تَبَٰرَكَ ٱلَّذِى بِيَدِهِ ٱلۡمُلۡكُ وَهُوَ عَلَىٰ كُلِّ
شَىۡءٖ قَدِيرٌ ١ ٱلَّذِى خَلَقَ ٱلۡمَوۡتَ وَٱلۡحَيَوٰةَ
لِيَبۡلُوَكُمۡ أَيُّكُمۡ أَحۡسَنُ عَمَلٗاۚ

1. The expression *tabāraka* is an intensive from of *barakah*. The latter connotes glory and greatness, growth and abundance, permanence and multitudes of goodness. It is used in its intensive form '*tabāraka*', signifying that God is infinitely blessed and great, and is superior to everyone beside Himself in His being, attributes, and accomplishments. He is the source of boundless blessings and goodness. Moreover, His perfect accomplishments are forever. (For further details see *Towards Understanding the Qur'ān*, vol. III, *Sūrah al-A'rāf* 7: n. 43. pp. 34–35; vol. VI, *Sūrah al-Mu'minūn* 23: n. 14, p. 88 and vol. VII, *Sūrah al-Furqān* 25: nn. 1 and 19, pp. 3–4 and 12–13).

2. As the expression *al-mulk* is employed here in an absolute sense, the reference is not to some dominion in a limited context. Rather, it stands for God's total control over all that exists. That "in Whose hand is the dominion" does not imply that He possesses a hand in a physical, literal sense. It is used metaphorically in order to convey the idea of His total control, in which no one has any share.

3. God can do whatever He pleases. There is no way to strip Him of His power or to prevent Him from doing what He wills.

4. The purpose underlying the whole system of mankind's life and death is to test and ascertain as to who are the best in their deeds. This brief sentence draws attention to several truths. First, it is God alone Who gives life and death. None other than Him can grant life. Nor can

He is the Most Mighty, the Most Forgiving;[5] (3) Who created the seven heavens one upon another.[6] You will see no incongruity in the Merciful One's creation.[7] ▶

وَهُوَ ٱلْعَزِيزُ ٱلْغَفُورُ ۝٢ ٱلَّذِى خَلَقَ سَبْعَ سَمَـٰوَٰتٍ طِبَاقًا ۖ مَّا تَرَىٰ فِى خَلْقِ ٱلرَّحْمَـٰنِ مِن تَفَـٰوُتٍ ۖ

anyone else bring about death. Secondly, man is granted free will, to choose between doing good or evil. Therefore, man's life and death is not without purpose. Man's Creator has placed him on the earth in order to test him. His life in this world represents the duration of his test while death signifies the end of its duration. Thirdly, because of the test, God has provided everyone with an opportunity to do good or evil. This will eventually establish what kind of person he is. Fourthly, God, being man's Creator, will adjudge who did good and who did evil. Those appearing in this test are not entitled to set the standards of good and evil. God, Who has set the test, will decide this as well. So, those aspiring for success in this test, should find out what criteria have been set by their Creator for good deeds. Fifthly, the word test itself alludes that man will be recompensed according to his performance in the test. Without the component of recompense, a test loses its meaning and purpose.

5. It is open to two meanings and both are intended. At one level, the message conveyed is that God, notwithstanding, being Most Irresistible and Overwhelming, is extremely Merciful and Affectionate towards His creatures. He is not a cruel and hard task master. The other meaning is that He has every power to punish the culprits. No one has the strength to escape His punishment. However, He forgives those who repent for their misdeeds, refrain from evil, and seek His forgiveness.

6. For details see *Towards Understanding the Qur'ān*, vol. I, *Sūrah al-Baqarah,* 2: n. 34, p. 58; vol. IV, *Sūrah al-Ra'd* 13: n. 2, pp. 219–220; *Sūrah al-Ḥijr* 15: n. 8, pp. 284–285; vol. VI, *Sūrah al-Ḥajj* 22: n. 113, p. 64, and *Sūrah al-Mu'minūn* 23: n. 15, p. 89; vol. IX, *Sūrah al-*Ṣāffāt 37: n. 5, p. 282 and *Sūrah al-Mu'min* 40: n. 90.

7. The word *tafāwut* means imbalance, incongruity, and lack of coordination. The verse asserts that one cannot detect any discordance, irregularity, or incoherence in the whole universe. There is nothing

Turn your vision again, can you see any flaw?[8] (4) Then turn your vision again, and then again; in the end your vision will come back to you, worn out and frustrated.

(5) We have adorned the lower heaven[9] with lamps,[10] and have made them a means to drive away the satans.[11] ▶

فَٱرْجِعِ ٱلْبَصَرَ هَلْ تَرَىٰ مِن فُطُورٍ ۝٣ ثُمَّ
ٱرْجِعِ ٱلْبَصَرَ كَرَّتَيْنِ يَنقَلِبْ إِلَيْكَ ٱلْبَصَرُ
خَاسِئًا وَهُوَ حَسِيرٌ ۝٤ وَلَقَدْ زَيَّنَّا ٱلسَّمَآءَ
ٱلدُّنْيَا بِمَصَٰبِيحَ وَجَعَلْنَٰهَا رُجُومًا لِّلشَّيَٰطِينِ

discordant in the universe created by God. All of its components are interconnected and stand out for their sense of proportion and balance.

8. The word *fuṭūr* denotes a crack, rift, fissure, cleaving, or breaking apart. The verse means that the whole universe is so well-knit together and everything in it, from a particle on earth to the enormous galaxies, is so coherent and so well connected that no matter how hard one might try, one can find neither any flaw nor any crack in the system. (For further details see *Sūrah Qāf* 50: n. 8)

9. "The lower heaven" denotes the heaven whose stars and planets can be observed with the naked eye, without recourse to any astronomical instrument. The farther heaven, however, can be seen only with tools such as a telescope. Then there are heavens still at a further distance to which man does not have access, even with the help of the most powerful astronomical instruments.

10. The use of the Qur'ānic expression, *maṣābīḥ*, highlights the glory of these heavenly lamps. The verse declares that it is not created by God as a dark, desolate universe. On the contrary, it is profusely adorned with stars whose brightness and lustre in the darkness of night baffles the onlooker.

11. This does not mean that the devils are struck with these stars. Nor does it imply that meteorites are there only for shooting the devils. What is emphasised is that the constant and consistent movement of countless meteors in space and their frequent raining, striking the earth

We have prepared for them the chastisement of the Blazing Fire.

(6) The chastisement of Hell awaits those who disbelieve in their Lord.[12] What a wretched destination! (7) When they will be cast into it, they will hear it roar[13] as it boils, (8) as though it will burst with rage. Every time ▶

وَأَعْتَدْنَا لَهُمْ عَذَابَ ٱلسَّعِيرِ ۝٥ وَلِلَّذِينَ
كَفَرُوا۟ بِرَبِّهِمْ عَذَابُ جَهَنَّمَ ۖ وَبِئْسَ ٱلْمَصِيرُ
۝٦ إِذَآ أُلْقُوا۟ فِيهَا سَمِعُوا۟ لَهَا شَهِيقًا وَهِىَ
تَفُورُ ۝٧ تَكَادُ تَمَيَّزُ مِنَ ٱلْغَيْظِ ۖ كُلَّمَآ

with tremendous speed, obstruct the earthly devils from ascending to the heavens. If they ever try, the meteorites drive them away. The above point is made because the soothsayers claimed and the Arabs believed that they exercised control over the devils or maintained some rapport with them. Further, they asserted that the devils bring them news of the unseen, enabling them to foretell the destiny of people. The Qur'ān therefore repeatedly rules out the ascent of the devils to the heavens and their eavesdropping. (For details see *Towards Understanding the Qur'ān*, vol. IV, *Sūrah al-Ḥijr* 15: nn. 9–12, pp. 285–286 and vol. IX, *Sūrah al-Ṣāffāt* 37: nn. 6–7, pp. 282–283.)

As to the true nature of these meteorites, nothing can be said with certainty as human knowledge and research so far seems insufficient. In the light of the available information, and on the basis of the observation of meteors fallen on earth, scientists opine that these are found wandering in outer space and, at times, are drawn by earth's gravity. (For details see *Encyclopaedia Britannica*, 1967 edition, vol. XV, Entry "Meteorites".)

12. The chastisement of Hell will be the fate of all the men and jinns who disbelieve in their Lord. (For the detailed meaning of "disbelieving in the Lord", see *Towards Understanding the Qur'ān*, vol. I, *Sūrah al-Baqarah* 2: n. 161, pp. 130–131; vol. II, *Sūrah al-Nisā'* 4: n. 178, p. 102; vol. V, *Sūrah al-Kahf* 18: n. 39, pp. 108–109 and *Sūrah al-Mu'min* 40: n. 3.)

13. The Qur'ānic expression *shahīq*, as used in the verse, stands for the braying of a donkey. This might refer to the sound of Hell itself, or to the sound rising from it because of the crying and screaming of those

a multitude is cast into it, its keepers will ask them: "Did no warner come to you?"[14] (9) They will say: "Yes, a warner came to ▶

أُلْقِيَ فِيهَا فَوْجٌ سَأَلَهُمْ خَزَنَتُهَآ أَلَمْ يَأْتِكُمْ
نَذِيرٌ ۝٨ قَالُوا۟ بَلَىٰ قَدْ جَآءَنَا نَذِيرٌ

who have already been flung into it. The latter meaning is reinforced by verse 106 of *Sūrah Hūd* which speaks of "the sighing and groaning" of the wretched ones in the Hellfire. The former is nonetheless supported by verse 12 of *Sūrah al-Furqān* which states that from a place afar the sinners will hear the raging and roaring of the Hellfire. It would be thus correct to assume that the roar will be both of Hellfire itself and of those cast inside it.

14. The keepers of Hell will not ask them this question with a view to ascertaining whether a warner from God had come to them or not. This question is rather aimed at convincing them that no injustice has been committed in hurling them into the Hellfire. They would like the culprits to openly admit that God had not kept them in the dark about the truth. Messengers were sent for this reason and they had clearly told them about the ultimate reality and the straight way. Likewise, they had eloquently warned that any deviation from the straight way would land them in Hellfire, the truth which now stares them in the face. Since they did not listen to the Messengers, they deserve the punishment now being meted out to them.

The Qur'ān recurrently emphasises the truth that God has not subjected man to a test about which he is unaware. He has not been left misguided about following or transgressing from the straight way. On the contrary, he has been fully instructed about the path he should follow and for this, God has devised an elaborate system for man's guidance. As part of the same divine dispensation, Messengers and Scriptures were sent down. Man's test therefore consists in his believing or disbelieving in the Messengers and Scriptures. He is being tested to ascertain whether he follows the straight path or pursues his own desires and fancies while disregarding divine guidance. Thus, Messengership is a clinching argument and evidence against man, as his fate hinges on his believing or disbelieving in Messengers. After the advent of Messengers, no person can plead that he was in the dark about the truth or that he was harshly tested while he was ignorant of it, and he is being punished despite his us, but we gave the lie to him and said: 'Allah has revealed nothing. You are surely in huge error.'[15] (10) They will say: 'If we had only listened and understood,[16] we would not be among the inmates of the Blazing Fire.'" (11) Thus will they confess their sins.[17] Damned are these inmates of the Blazing Fire.

فَكَذَّبْنَا وَقُلْنَا مَا نَزَّلَ ٱللَّهُ مِن شَىْءٍ إِنْ
أَنتُمْ إِلَّا فِى ضَلَٰلٍ كَبِيرٍ ﴿٩﴾ وَقَالُوا۟
لَوْ كُنَّا نَسْمَعُ أَوْ نَعْقِلُ مَا كُنَّا فِىٓ
أَصْحَٰبِ ٱلسَّعِيرِ ﴿١٠﴾ فَٱعْتَرَفُوا۟ بِذَنۢبِهِمْ
فَسُحْقًا لِّأَصْحَٰبِ ٱلسَّعِيرِ ﴿١١﴾

---

innocence. The above point features in the Qur'ān at several places. Some instances in point are *Towards Understanding the Qur'ān*, vol. I, *Sūrah al-Baqarah* 2: 213, n. 230, vol. II, *Sūrah al-Nisā'* 4: 41–42 and 165, nn: 64 and 208, pp. 40 and 115; *Sūrah al-An'ām* 6: 130–131, nn 98–100, pp. 274–275; vol. V, *Sūrah Banī Isrā'īl* 17: 15, n. 17, p. 30; *Sūrah Ṭā Hā* 20: 134; vol. VII, *Sūrah al-Qaṣaṣ* 28: 47, 59 and 65 nn. 66 and 83, pp. 226–227 and 237; *Sūrah Fāṭir* 35: 37 and *Sūrah al-Mu'min* 40: 50 n. 66.)

15. Not only you yourselves but also those who believed in and followed you are misguided and in gross error.

16. Regretfully, they will realise that as genuine seekers of truth they should have listened to and followed the Messengers' teachings or they should have acted on reason in reflecting on their message. It is worth noting that in the above verse, listening is given precedence to understanding because the first and foremost step for a seeker of truth is to listen attentively to the Messenger's teachings or to study the message if it is available in its written form. The next stage is of abiding by it. Without the guidance of the Messengers and acting on reason alone one cannot grasp the truth.

17. The word *dhanb* (sin) is used here in its singular form. It refers to their fundamental sin which made them worthy of Hell; their denial of Messengers and their refusal to obey them. All other sins flowed as its consequences.

(12) Surely forgiveness and a mighty reward[18] await those who fear Allah without seeing Him.[19] (13) Whether you speak in secrecy or ▶

إِنَّ ٱلَّذِينَ يَخۡشَوۡنَ رَبَّهُم بِٱلۡغَيۡبِ لَهُم
مَّغۡفِرَةٞ وَأَجۡرٞ كَبِيرٞ ١٢ وَأَسِرُّواْ قَوۡلَكُمۡ

18. "Fearing Allah without seeing Him" lies at the core of Islamic ethics. Avoiding an evil because one personally takes it as evil, or because it is universally branded as evil, or out of fear of any loss in the world, or any apprehension of danger by any worldly power, is not a sound basis for ethics and morality, for one may err in his judgement. Or, guided by his own peculiar notions he may take some evil as good and *vice versa*. As to the secular concepts of good and evil, these are not consistent and are liable to change. Moral philosophers have failed to reach consensus about any universal or permanent criteria about morals, not only now but in the past too. Avoidance of some harm is not a tenable ground for the ethical code. If one shuns evil simply because it may harm him personally in this world, he may commit the same when he does not apprehend any harm. Likewise, the fear of being caught out by some worldly authority cannot ensure one's proper moral behaviour, for it is common knowledge that worldly authorities are neither omnipotent nor omniscient. Numerous crimes may be committed, without these ever coming into their knowledge. Then there are numerous ways and means for avoiding and evading detection and punishment. Secular laws cannot embrace all the crimes. Most of the evils are beyond their purview, including those which are worse in degree than the cognisable offences. This explains why Islam, being the true faith, has raised an elaborate superstructure of ethics on the fundamental principle that all evil be shunned out of the fear of God, even though one cannot see Him physically. God watches man in all circumstances and no one can escape from His grip. God has instructed man in a broad, universal moral code, spelling out what is good and what is evil. Shunning evil and doing good in accordance with this code and out of the fear of Allah carries real weight in Islam. If one does not commit evil or does good for any other consideration, he will not get any reward for this in the Hereafter. For such actions are akin to a structure raised on sand, without any substance or stability.

19. There are certainly two consequences of fearing God without seeing Him. The first is that one's lapses committed owing to human weakness will be forgiven, provided that these were not prompted by

aloud, (it is all the same to Allah). He even knows the secrets that lie hidden in the breasts of people.[20] (14) Would He not know, He Who has created,[21] when He is All-Subtle,[22] All-Aware?

(15) He it is Who made the earth subservient to you. So traverse in its tracks and partake of the sustenance He has provided.[23] ▶

أَوِ ٱجْهَرُواْ بِهِۦٓ إِنَّهُۥ عَلِيمٌۢ بِذَاتِ ٱلصُّدُورِ ﴿١٣﴾ أَلَا يَعْلَمُ مَنْ خَلَقَ وَهُوَ ٱللَّطِيفُ ٱلْخَبِيرُ ﴿١٤﴾ هُوَ ٱلَّذِى جَعَلَ لَكُمُ ٱلْأَرْضَ ذَلُولًا فَٱمْشُواْ فِى مَنَاكِبِهَا وَكُلُواْ مِن رِّزْقِهِۦ

one's sheer disregard of God. The second is that one will get great reward for his good deeds done out of his sincere belief in God.

20. This address is directed at everyone, whether believers or disbelievers. Believers are exhorted that they should lead their lives with the constant thought that all their actions, both open and secret, their intentions, and the ideas crossing their minds are fully known to God. By the same token, it carries a note of warning for the disbelievers that no matter what they do in sheer disregard of God, they cannot escape God's punishment.

21. An alternative translation could be: "Would He not know His own creatures?" This reinforces the fact that how is it possible that the Creator is unaware of the condition of His creatures. The creatures may be ignorant of their own condition. However, this does not hold true of the Creator, for it is He Who has shaped every sinew and fibre of the hearts and minds of His creation. Again, it is He Who allows every creature to continue breathing and to use his body parts. Given this, how can anything of yours remain hidden from Him?

22. *al-Laṭīf*, as used in the Qur'ānic text, stands for one who acts subtly and who knows the hidden truths.

23. The earth has not become subservient to man on its own. Nor does the food, which sustains man, grow of its own accord. Out of His

To Him will you be resurrected.[24] (16) Do you feel secure that He Who is in the heaven[25] will not cause the earth to cave in with you, and then suddenly it will begin to ▶

وَإِلَيْهِ ٱلنُّشُورُ ﴿١٥﴾ ءَأَمِنتُم مَّن فِى ٱلسَّمَآءِ أَن يَخْسِفَ بِكُمُ ٱلْأَرْضَ فَإِذَا هِىَ

creative power and infinite wisdom, God has created the earth in such a way that it enables man to flourish. Again, it is God Who has made the magnificent earth so calm and tranquil that man traverses in its tracks comfortably. He has provided such abundant sustenance for man to live in peace and bounty. If man is not negligent, and acts on the basis of reason, he would realise the profound thoughtfulness behind God creating the earth as a suitable habitat for man and for providing in it immeasurable sustenance for him. (For details see *Towards Understanding the Qur'ān*, vol. VII, *Sūrah al-Naml* 27: nn. 73, 74 and 81, pp. 171–173 and 176; vol. IX, *Sūrah Yā Sīn* 36: nn. 29 and 32, pp. 256–257 and 258–259; *Sūrah al-Mu'min* 40: nn. 90–91; *Sūrah al-Zukhruf* 43: n. 7; *Sūrah al-Jāthiyah* 45: n. 7 and *Sūrah Qāf* 50: n. 18.)

24. While man traverses the earth and subsists on the sustenance bestowed by God, he should not lose sight of the fact that one day he will ultimately appear before God.

25. This does not mean that God literally lives in the heavens. The present verse reflects the fact that when man wants to turn to God, he instinctively looks up to the heavens. Furthermore, when he prays to God, he raises his hands towards the heaven. Likewise, when he is overpowered with affliction and feels helpless, he again turns upwards to the heavens to convey his grievance to God; or when a misfortune suddenly befalls him, he tends to say that it has descended on him from heaven. In the same way, when he receives something in an extraordinary way, he says that it has come from the heavens. Likewise, the Scriptures revealed by God are called heavenly books. Abū Dāwūd cites a *ḥadīth*, on the authority of Abū Hurayrah (K. *al-Aymān wa al-Nudhūr, Bāb fī al-Raqabah al-Mu'minah*), that: "Once someone called on the Prophet (peace be upon him) along with a black slave girl, saying that it has become obligatory on him to free a believing slave. He asked the Prophet (peace be upon him) if he could free that slave-girl for this purpose. The Prophet

rock violently? (17) Do you feel secure that He Who is in the heaven will not let loose upon you a storm of stones?[26] Then shall you know what My warning is like![27] (18) Those who came before them also gave the lie (to the Messengers): ▶

تَمُورُ ﴿١٦﴾ أَمْ أَمِنتُم مَّن فِي ٱلسَّمَآءِ أَن
يُرْسِلَ عَلَيْكُمْ حَاصِبًا فَسَتَعْلَمُونَ كَيْفَ
نَذِيرِ ﴿١٧﴾ وَلَقَدْ كَذَّبَ ٱلَّذِينَ مِن قَبْلِهِمْ

(peace be upon him) asked her: "Where is Allah?" In reply she pointed her finger above. Then he asked her: "who am I?" She first pointed to him and then to the heavens above. What she meant was that God had sent him down. Upon noting this, he directed: "Set her free, she is a believer". Almost a similar report features in *al-Muwaṭṭa'*, Muslim's and Nasā'ī's *ḥadīth* collections. Regarding Khawlah bint Tha'labah, 'Umar told people that she was a person whose complaint reached the seven heavens. (A detailed report about this is included in note 2 on *Sūrah al-Mujādilah*.) All this indicates that it is part of man's nature that when he thinks of God, he associates Him with the heavens above, rather than with the earth below. Accordingly, the Qur'ān speaks of God Who is in the heavens. This should not, however, give rise to the notion that the Qur'ān locates Him in the heavens, for verse 3 of *Sūrah al-Mulk* declares that it is God Who has created the seven heavens, one upon another. Of similar thrust is verse 115 of *Sūrah al-Baqarah*, proclaiming: "To whichever direction you turn, you will be turning to God."

26. The truth highlighted here is that man's very survival and safety on earth depends wholly on God's grace. Man cannot enjoy his life on earth through his own strength, for God takes care of all the needs of man and ensures his safety and security. At any moment, at His single gesture, a devastating earthquake may turn man's habitat into his burial place, or a strong storm can cause such a terrible calamity that it will bring towns and villages to the ground. Equally vulnerable is man to other disastrous natural calamities such as a storm.

27. Reference is made to the warning delivered by the Prophet (peace be upon him) to the Makkan disbelievers through the Qur'ān. They are asked to give up their disbelief and polytheism. If they refuse to believe

then how awesome was
My chastisement![28] (19)
Have they not seen birds
above them spreading and
closing their wings, with
none holding them except
the Merciful One?[29] He
oversees everything.[30] (20)
Which is your army that will
come to your aid against
the Merciful Lord?[31] But
the unbelievers are in utter
delusion. (21) Who shall
provide for you if He with-
holds His sustenance? ▶

فَكَيْفَ كَانَ نَكِيرِ ﴿١٨﴾ أَوَلَمْ يَرَوْا۟ إِلَى ٱلطَّيْرِ
فَوْقَهُمْ صَٰٓفَّٰتٍ وَيَقْبِضْنَ ۚ مَا يُمْسِكُهُنَّ
إِلَّا ٱلرَّحْمَٰنُ ۚ إِنَّهُۥ بِكُلِّ شَىْءٍۭ بَصِيرٌ ﴿١٩﴾
أَمَّنْ هَٰذَا ٱلَّذِى هُوَ جُندٌ لَّكُمْ
يَنصُرُكُم مِّن دُونِ ٱلرَّحْمَٰنِ ۚ إِنِ
ٱلْكَٰفِرُونَ إِلَّا فِى غُرُورٍ ﴿٢٠﴾ أَمَّنْ
هَٰذَا ٱلَّذِى يَرْزُقُكُمْ إِنْ أَمْسَكَ رِزْقَهُۥ ۚ

---

in the call to monotheism presented to them, God's punishment will overtake them.

28. This alludes to the destruction of earlier communities for their crime of having rejected their Messengers.

29. Each and every bird flying in the air manages to do so, thanks to God's grace and protection. For it is He Who has created birds in a mould that they can fly. Furthermore, He instructed them how to fly. Again, it is He Who has subjected winds to such laws which facilitate the flight of bodies heavier than air. The Merciful God holds every flying bird in the air. Otherwise, whenever Allah withdraws this protection, they are liable to crash to the ground.

30. Not only birds, but all that exists in the universe owe their survival to God's mercy and care, for He alone provides every being with the means essential for his existence. It is He Who ensures the supply of basic necessities to all of His creatures.

31. An alternative translation would be: "Who is there other than the Merciful Lord Who comes to your aid as would your own army?" Our translated version, however, fits in more with the context of the next verse.

Nay; but they persist in rebellion and aversion. (22) Who is better guided: he who walks grovelling on his face,[32] or he who walks upright on a Straight Path? (23) Say: "He it is Who has brought you into being, and has given you hearing and sight, and has given you hearts to think and understand. How seldom do you give thanks!"[33]

بَل لَّجُّواْ فِي عُتُوّٖ وَنُفُورٍ ﴿٢١﴾ أَفَمَن يَمۡشِي
مُكِبًّا عَلَىٰ وَجۡهِهِۦٓ أَهۡدَىٰٓ أَمَّن يَمۡشِي
سَوِيًّا عَلَىٰ صِرَٰطٖ مُّسۡتَقِيمٖ ﴿٢٢﴾ قُلۡ هُوَ
ٱلَّذِيٓ أَنشَأَكُمۡ وَجَعَلَ لَكُمُ ٱلسَّمۡعَ
وَٱلۡأَبۡصَٰرَ وَٱلۡأَفۡـِٔدَةَۚ قَلِيلٗا مَّا تَشۡكُرُونَ ﴿٢٣﴾

32. It brings to mind the image of cattle with their heads cast down, trudging along the track on which they have been put.

33. Man is asked to reflect. He is not created like cattle, therefore he should not have blindly followed the errors prevalent in the world. He should better consider the way pursued by him – whether it is right or wrong. Man is endowed with the faculty of hearing in order to distinguish between good and bad. He is not supposed to ignore altogether the person who explains to him the distinction between good and evil. Nor is he expected to persist in error by way of clinging to false notions he already had in his mind. He is blessed with eyes so as not to follow others blindly. Rather, he should observe the signs scattered from the earth to the heavens, which unmistakably underscore the Oneness of God, which is the Prophet's core message. These signs in the universe do not suggest any multiplicity of gods or the absence of God. Man is endowed with a heart and mind so that he may reflect on his course of action. He is not supposed to imitate whatever someone has introduced in this world. He should better judge as to what is sound and what is not. God has endowed human beings with knowledge and intelligence, sight and hearing so that they might arrive at the truth. But they are ungrateful, in so far as they use these faculties for all kinds of purposes, except the one for which they were supposed to be used – to know the truth. (For details see *Towards Understanding the Qur'ān*, vol. IV, *Sūrah al-Naḥl* 16: nn. 72 and 73, pp. 350–351; vol. VI, *Sūrah al-Mu'minūn* 23: nn. 75 and 76,

(24) Say: "Allah it is Who multiplied you in the earth and to Him you will be mustered."[34] (25) They say: "If you are truthful, tell us when will this promise (of the Hereafter) be fulfilled?"[35] (26) Say: "Allah alone knows about that; and I am no more than a plain warner."[36] ▶

قُلْ هُوَ ٱلَّذِى ذَرَأَكُمْ فِى ٱلْأَرْضِ وَإِلَيْهِ
تُحْشَرُونَ ﴿٢٤﴾ وَيَقُولُونَ مَتَىٰ هَـٰذَا ٱلْوَعْدُ
إِن كُنتُمْ صَـٰدِقِينَ ﴿٢٥﴾ قُلْ إِنَّمَا ٱلْعِلْمُ عِندَ
ٱللَّهِ وَإِنَّمَآ أَنَا۠ نَذِيرٌ مُّبِينٌ ﴿٢٦﴾

pp. 118–119; vol. VIII, *Sūrah al-Sajdah* 32: nn. 17 and 18, pp. 165–166 and *Sūrah al-Aḥqāf* 46: n. 31.)

34. All men will be resurrected after their death, from every nook and corner of earth, and presented before God.

35. Their query was not aimed at finding out the time or date of the Resurrection. They were not ready to believe in the doctrine of the Hereafter, even if they were informed of its date and timing. On the contrary, they regarded this happening as impossible and illogical. They raised this question only with a view to rejecting this belief. For them, it was something improbable and hence they asked the Prophet (peace be upon him) to specify its date. They rather demanded that the spectacle of the Resurrection be witnessed by them and this alone would convince them. Let it be clarified that rational arguments alone can persuade one of this doctrine of the Hereafter. The Qur'ān therefore advances several arguments for it. As to its exact date, only an ignorant person can raise this question. Were it to be revealed, it will not make any difference. The disbeliever might say "I will believe in it when it does occur on your specified date, but how could I believe now that it will definitely occur on that very day". (For details see *Towards Understanding the Qur'ān*, vol. VIII, *Sūrah Luqmān* 31: n. 63, pp. 150–151; vol. IX, *Sūrah al-Aḥzāb* 33: n. 116, p. 106; *Sūrah Saba'* 34: nn. 5 and 48, pp. 152 and 189 and *Sūrah Yā Sīn* 36: n. 45, p. 265.)

36. The Prophet's reply to the disbelievers was simple: the Last Day is imminent and this should suffice for alerting people. God alone knows when it will happen, and the Prophet (peace be upon him) does

(27) When they will see it near at hand, the faces of all those who had denied it will be distraught,[37] and then they will be told: "This is the doom which you used to ask for."

(28) Say to them: "Did you ever consider: whether Allah destroys me and those that are with me, or shows mercy to us, who can protect the unbelievers from a grievous chastisement?"[38] (29) Say to them: "He is Merciful, and it is in Him that we believe, ▶

فَلَمَّا رَأَوْهُ زُلْفَةً سِيٓـَٔتْ وُجُوهُ ٱلَّذِينَ
كَفَرُوا۟ وَقِيلَ هَـٰذَا ٱلَّذِى كُنتُم بِهِۦ
تَدَّعُونَ ﴿٢٧﴾ قُلْ أَرَءَيْتُمْ إِنْ أَهْلَكَنِىَ
ٱللَّهُ وَمَن مَّعِىَ أَوْ رَحِمَنَا فَمَن
يُجِيرُ ٱلْكَـٰفِرِينَ مِنْ عَذَابٍ أَلِيمٍ
﴿٢٨﴾ قُلْ هُوَ ٱلرَّحْمَـٰنُ ءَامَنَّا بِهِۦ

---

not have this knowledge. As a warner, he is not obliged to possess this information. Let us illustrate the above further with this analogy: Only God knows when a particular person will die. However, it is in everyone's knowledge that all living beings will die one day. We should be concerned only about our preparation for the Last Day. It is immaterial as to when it will happen.

37. Their condition will be akin to that of a culprit sentenced to capital punishment on his way to his execution.

38. When the Prophet (peace be upon him) embarked on his mission in Makkah and the members of different Quraysh families started embracing Islam, the people of many a household began to curse him and his Companions. They even resorted to the use of magic and charms in their bid to exterminate him. They also hatched conspiracies designed to assassinate him. It was in this context that they were told that it was not important for them whether the Prophet (peace be upon him) died, or continued to live. They should rather be concerned with thinking about how they will save themselves from God's chastisement.

and it is in Him that we put all our trust.[39] Soon will you know who is in manifest error." (30) Say to them: "Did you even consider: if all the water that you have (in the wells) were to sink down into the depths of the earth, who will produce for you clear, flowing water?"[40]

وَعَلَيْهِ تَوَكَّلْنَا فَسَتَعْلَمُونَ مَنْ هُوَ فِي
ضَلَالٍ مُّبِينٍ ﴿٢٩﴾ قُلْ أَرَءَيْتُمْ إِنْ أَصْبَحَ
مَاؤُكُمْ غَوْرًا فَمَن يَأْتِيكُم بِمَاءٍ مَّعِينٍ ﴿٣٠﴾

39. The believers have firm faith in God whereas the disbelievers deny Him. The former repose full trust in Him while the latter rely on their allies, their resources and their gods other than the One True God. Given this, only the former, not the latter, deserve God's mercy.

40. Is there any other than God that has power to bring back the water which sinks down in to the depths of the earth? Since there is no one to do so, a fact recognised by the disbelievers as well, they should consider as to who deserves worship – God, or their idols who have no power to restore it. They should reflect deeply and ask their conscience who is in manifest error – the believers or the polytheists?

Sūrah 68

Al-Qalam

(The Pen)

(Makkan Period)

Title

This *Sūrah* has two titles – *Nūn* and *al-Qalam*. Both these words appear in the opening verse of the *Sūrah*.

Period of Revelation

It is one of those *Sūrahs* which were sent down in the early Makkan phase. However, it emerges from its contents that it must have been revealed at the time when the disbelievers' hostility towards the Prophet (peace be upon him) had increased intensively.

Subject Matter and Themes

Three themes are taken up in this *Sūrah*: (i) a response to the opponents' allegation; (ii) warning and advice to the opponents; and (iii) exhortation to the Prophet (peace be upon him) to practise perseverance and constancy.

At the outset, the Prophet (peace be upon him) is told that the disbelievers accuse him of being a mad person. However, the Book presented by him and his sublime morals and manners suffice to refute their allegation. Soon everyone will see who is wise and who is insane. He should not therefore feel the pressure of the storm of opposition directed against him. It is part of the disbelievers' strategy to force him into compromise.

Without naming, a prominent enemy of Islam who was a familiar figure in Makkah is presented in order to open everyone's eyes. At the same time, the Makkans were well aware of the Prophet's excellent conduct. His exemplary character and morals were in contrast with those possessed by the Makkan chiefs who were to the fore in opposing him.

Verses 17–33 present the parable of the orchard owners who were ungrateful to Allah, though they were blessed by His bounties. They did not listen to the advice of the best person amongst them. Eventually they lost the bounty granted to them. They realised the truth only after they had lost all that they had. This analogy warns the Makkans that the Prophet's advent in their midst constitutes a trial for them as it was for the owners of the orchard. If they refuse to follow the Prophet (peace be upon him) they will undergo punishment in this world and a more tormenting punishment is in store for them in the Hereafter.

Verses 34–47 constitute an extensive warning against the disbelievers. At places they are addressed directly, and at others indirectly, as the message is directed to the Prophet (peace be upon him). Only such will prosper in the Hereafter who, marked by the fear of God, lead their lives in this world. It is an irrational proposition that the obedient ones and culprits be recompensed alike by God. The disbelievers are totally deluded in assuming that God will recompense them as they think. They do not have any authority to support their whims. They refuse to surrender themselves to God. As a result, they will not be able to prostrate before God, even if they wish so on the Day of Judgement. They will meet a disgraceful end. They cannot escape God's punishment in that they are guilty of denying the Qur'ān. The respite granted to them has misled them. As they are not immediately punished for the rejection of truth, they mistakenly think that they are on the right path. However, they are on the way of self-destruction, even without realising it. They do not have any valid or sound ground for opposing the Prophet (peace be upon him), for he is a selfless preacher. He does not seek any reward from mortals. The disbelievers do not have any specific knowledge for rejecting his claim to Messengership or for dismissing his teachings as false.

In conclusion, the Prophet (peace be upon him) is directed to bear with all the hardships in the cause of preaching faith until God decides the matter. He should avoid the impatience betrayed by the Prophet Jonah (peace be upon him), which led to his ordeal.

In the name of Allah, the Most Merciful, the Most Compassionate.

بِسْمِ ٱللَّهِ ٱلرَّحْمَٰنِ ٱلرَّحِيمِ

(1) *Nūn.* By the pen and what the scribes write.[1] (2) By your Lord's Grace, you are not afflicted with madness,[2] ▶

نٓ ۚ وَٱلْقَلَمِ وَمَا يَسْطُرُونَ ﴿١﴾ مَآ أَنتَ بِنِعْمَةِ رَبِّكَ بِمَجْنُونٍ ﴿٢﴾

1. The leading commentator of the Qur'ān, Mujāhid, says that the word "pen" here signifies the pen with which the Qur'ān was being inscribed. From this it automatically follows that what was being inscribed was the Qur'ān.

2. Both the pen and the Book are invoked in the oath to assert that the Prophet (peace be upon him) is not afflicted with any kind of madness. In other words, the Qur'ān which is being recorded by the scribes of revelation is a weighty rejoinder to the disbelievers' slander that the Prophet (peace be upon him), God forbid, is a mad person. Before he laid his claim to Prophethood, the Makkans looked upon him as the best person in their city and reposed extreme trust in his honesty, integrity, and wisdom. However, as he presented the Qur'ān before them, they began to accuse him of being a mad person. To put it another way, for them the Qur'ān was the cause behind his madness. Accordingly, it is asserted that the Qur'ān itself suffices to refute this slanderous allegation. Since the Qur'ān stands out as a literary masterpiece; embodying eloquence, stylistic features, and sublime contents, its presentation by him is the proof of the bestowal of the divine favour upon him. It has nothing to do with madness. Let it be borne in mind that while these words are apparently addressed to the Prophet (peace be upon him), the real purpose of the statement is to refute the disbelievers' slanderous utterances, imputing madness to him. This should not be misconstrued by anyone in the sense that this verse was revealed to comfort and reassure the Prophet (peace be upon him) that he does not suffer from madness. He did not have any such misperception about himself, hence on this allegation there was no need to rest his mind with any such assurance. The thrust of the verse is that the Qur'ān, because of which they are accusing its presenter of

(3) and surely yours shall be a never-ending reward,[3] (4) and you are certainly on the most exalted standard of moral excellence.[4] (5) So you will soon see, and they too will see, (6) which of you is afflicted with madness. (7) Surely your Lord knows well those who have strayed from His Way just as He knows well those who are on the Right Way. (8) Do not, then, yield to those who reject the Truth, decrying it as false; ▶

وَإِنَّ لَكَ لَأَجْرًا غَيْرَ مَمْنُونٍ ﴿٣﴾ وَإِنَّكَ
لَعَلَىٰ خُلُقٍ عَظِيمٍ ﴿٤﴾ فَسَتُبْصِرُ وَيُبْصِرُونَ
﴿٥﴾ بِأَييِّكُمُ ٱلْمَفْتُونُ ﴿٦﴾ إِنَّ رَبَّكَ هُوَ
أَعْلَمُ بِمَن ضَلَّ عَن سَبِيلِهِۦ وَهُوَ أَعْلَمُ
بِٱلْمُهْتَدِينَ ﴿٧﴾ فَلَا تُطِعِ ٱلْمُكَذِّبِينَ ﴿٨﴾

---

madness, is itself sufficient refutation of such slanderous statements. (For details see *Sūrah al-Ṭūr* 52: 22.)

3. It is emphasised that the Prophet's reward will be boundless and that it will never cease. This is because he strove to direct people to the right way, but in return had to suffer bitter and heart-rending taunts from many of them. Admirably, the Prophet (peace be upon him) disregarded all this, patiently performing his duty with unabated dedication.

4. This sentence carries two meanings: (i) Since he is on the most exalted standard of moral excellence, he has been enduring all manner of hardship during his mission of guiding and reforming mankind. Otherwise, a person with weak character and conduct could not have performed this duty. (ii) In addition to the Qur'ān, the Prophet's excellent conduct and noble character is also a clear proof that the charge of madness that was directed at him was totally false. This is due to madness and high morals being mutually inconsistent. A mad person is imbalanced in his outlook and temperament. In contrast, a person with high morals and manners displays his sound mind and pleasant nature. He is endowed with a balanced, moderate mind. The Makkans were not unfamiliar with the Prophet's morals and manners. Hence the Qur'ānic allusion to his

excellent moral standard suffices to make every reasonable Makkan think that it was patently wrong and brazen to charge such a balanced, decent person with madness. This frivolity was not harmful for the Prophet but was harmful for the detractors themselves because in their zeal, they were uttering something that could not be considered as credible or tenable by any sensible person. The same applies to some scholars and researchers of our time who impute epilepsy and madness to the Prophet (peace be upon him). Copies of the Qur'ān and a detailed account of the Prophet's life and career are within everyone's reach. Those who ascribe madness to the bearer of such a unique book as the Qur'ān, and who was on the most exalted standard of moral excellence, betray their own foolishness in their blind opposition to him.

'Ā'ishah (may Allah be pleased with her) has paid a glowing tribute to the Prophet's excellent morals and character in remarking that his conduct was the full reflection of the Qur'ān. Imām Aḥmad (*Musnad*, 6, 54, 91 and 111), Muslim (*K. Ṣalāt al-Musāfirīn wa qaṣrihā, Bāb Jāmi' Ṣalāt al-Layl …*) Abū Dāwūd (*K. al-Taṭawwu', Bāb Fī Ṣalāt al-Layl*), Nasā'ī (*K. Qiyām al-Layl, Bāb Qiyām al-Layl wa Taṭaww' al-Nahār*), Ibn Mājah (*K. al-Aḥkām, Bāb al-Ḥukm fī man kasara shay'ā*), Dārimī (*K. al-Ṣalāt, Bāb Ṣifat Ṣalāt al-Rasūl*) and Ibn Jarīr all have cited the above report (*Tafsīr*, 23, 150), though with some minor variations. What is meant is that the Prophet (peace be upon him) not only introduced the Qur'ānic teachings to everyone, he was an embodiment of the teachings of the Qur'ān. He acted on all that the Qur'ān enjoins and shunned all that it forbids more than anybody else. The moral teachings emphasised in the Qur'ān were fully reflected in his conduct. By the same token, he had none of the traits which the Qur'ān disapproves. Another *ḥadīth* on the authority of 'Ā'ishah runs thus: "The Prophet (peace be upon him) never hit a servant or raised his hand on a female. He did not physically hurt anyone except in *Jihād* in the cause of Allah. Never did he take revenge for the wrongs done personally to him. No doubt he took action against those who had violated what Allah has sanctified. He took revenge only for Allah's sake. Given an option, he always chose the less difficult course of action, provided that it did not entail any sin. He kept himself away from any act if it contained any hint of some evil or sin." (*Musnad* of Imām Aḥmad, 6, 32, 114 and 116) Anas reports: "During my ten years' close association with the Prophet (peace be upon him), he never resented any action of mine. He never asked me as to why I had done something. Nor did he ever chide me for having failed to do something." (Bukhārī *K. al-Adab, Bāb Ḥusn al-Khulq* and Muslim *K. al-Faḍā'il, Bāb Kāna Rasūl Allāh Aḥsan al-Nās Khuluqan*.)

(9) they would wish you to be pliant so that they too may be pliant.[5] (10) And do not yield to any contemptible swearer,[6] (11) the fault-finder who goes around slandering, (12) the hinderer of good,[7] the transgressor, the sinful; (13) the coarse-grained, and above all mean[8] and ignoble;[9] ▶

وَدُّوا لَوْ تُدْهِنُ فَيُدْهِنُونَ ﴿٩﴾ وَلَا تُطِعْ
كُلَّ حَلَّافٍ مَّهِينٍ ﴿١٠﴾ هَمَّازٍ مَّشَّاءٍ بِنَمِيمٍ
﴿١١﴾ مَّنَّاعٍ لِّلْخَيْرِ مُعْتَدٍ أَثِيمٍ ﴿١٢﴾ عُتُلٍّ بَعْدَ
ذَٰلِكَ زَنِيمٍ ﴿١٣﴾

5. The disbelievers approached the Prophet (peace be upon him) with the offer that if he would slacken a bit in his drive to preach his teachings, they would tone down their opposition to him. Another nuance of the offer was that if the Prophet (peace be upon him) were to modify his religious stance in deference to the disbelievers' beliefs and practices, they would be willing to come to terms with him.

6. The word *mahīn* is used of a contemptible, degraded, and mean person. In fact, the main characteristic of such a person is that he swears profusely and frequently, out of his own realisation that everyone takes him to be a liar. By this logic, he tries to convince others of his credibility. His self-esteem is low and he is looked down upon by everyone in society.

7. On the Qur'ānic text words *"Mannā'in lil khayr"* (the hinderer of good) are used. *Al-Khayr* connotes both wealth and goodness. Taken in the former sense, the reference is to the person who is extremely miserly and stingy, not willing to give even a single penny to anyone. In its latter sense, it stands for one who creates a hindrance in every good work and thus, is very active in obstructing Islam.

8. *'Utull* is used to describe a person who has a sound physique and wealth, yet he is ill-mannered, quarrelsome and cruel.

9. *Zanīm* is employed in the Arabic idiom for a person born out of wedlock claiming to be a member of a family, though he does not belong to it. According to Sa'īd ibn Jubayr and Sha'bī, it is used also for someone notorious for his evildoing.

(14) (who so acts) simply because he has wealth and sons,[10] (15) and whenever Our verses are rehearsed to him, he says: "These are fairy-tales of times gone by." (16) Soon shall We brand him on his snout.[11]

(17) We have put them [i.e., the Makkans] to test even as We put to test the ▶

أَن كَانَ ذَا مَالٍ وَبَنِينَ ﴿١٤﴾ إِذَا تُتْلَىٰ عَلَيْهِ
ءَايَـٰتُنَا قَالَ أَسَـٰطِيرُ ٱلْأَوَّلِينَ ﴿١٥﴾ سَنَسِمُهُۥ
عَلَى ٱلْخُرْطُومِ ﴿١٦﴾ إِنَّا بَلَوْنَـٰهُمْ كَمَا بَلَوْنَآ

The Qur'ān commentators differ in identifying the person alluded to in the above verses. For some, the allusion is to Walīd ibn Mughīrah, for others to Aswad ibn 'Abd Yaghūth. Some identify him as Akhnas ibn Shurayq. Others have named different figures. However, the Qur'ān has only spelled out the despicable traits of this person, without naming him. It appears that this person was such a familiar figure in Makkah that there was hardly any need to name him. His portrait sufficed for his identification.

10. This statement can relate to the themes that both precede and follow it. In the first instance, it would mean that the Prophet (peace be upon him) should not yield to such a person simply because he has abundance of wealth and children. In the second instance, these words would mean that this person has become exceedingly arrogant because he has plenty of wealth and children. It is because of such arrogance that when the revelation is recited to him, he says: "These are the tales of times gone by."

11. Such a person considered himself to be possessed of extraordinary prestige and eminence. To controvert this arrogance, his nose is called a "snout". To say that "We shall brand him on his snout" means that God will disgrace him both in this world and the Hereafter, and will do so in such a way that the disgrace he is subjected to will endure forever.

owners of the orchard[12] when they vowed that they would gather the fruit of their orchard in the morning, (18) without making any allowance (for the will of Allah).[13] (19) Thereupon a calamity from your Lord passed over it while they were asleep, (20) and so by morning the orchard lay as though it had been fully harvested. (21) At daybreak they called out to one another: (22) "Hurry to your orchard[14] if you would gather its fruit." (23) So off they went, whispering to one another: (24) "No destitute person shall enter it today." (25) They went forth early,[15] believing that ▶

أَصۡحَٰبَ ٱلۡجَنَّةِ إِذۡ أَقۡسَمُواْ لَيَصۡرِمُنَّهَا
مُصۡبِحِينَ ﴿١٧﴾ وَلَا يَسۡتَثۡنُونَ ﴿١٨﴾ فَطَافَ
عَلَيۡهَا طَآئِفٞ مِّن رَّبِّكَ وَهُمۡ نَآئِمُونَ ﴿١٩﴾
فَأَصۡبَحَتۡ كَٱلصَّرِيمِ ﴿٢٠﴾ فَتَنَادَوۡاْ
مُصۡبِحِينَ ﴿٢١﴾ أَنِ ٱغۡدُواْ عَلَىٰ حَرۡثِكُمۡ إِن
كُنتُمۡ صَٰرِمِينَ ﴿٢٢﴾ فَٱنطَلَقُواْ وَهُمۡ
يَتَخَٰفَتُونَ ﴿٢٣﴾ أَن لَّا يَدۡخُلَنَّهَا ٱلۡيَوۡمَ
عَلَيۡكُم مِّسۡكِينٞ ﴿٢٤﴾ وَغَدَوۡاْ عَلَىٰ حَرۡدٖ

12. It is worth-pointing out that verses 32–44 of *Sūrah al-Kahf* relate a similar parable of the two owners of vineyards to teach a similar lesson.

13. The owners of the orchard were exceedingly confident about their power and authority. Hence they swore that they would gather the fruit of their orchard the next morning, without feeling any need to say: "We shall do so, if God so wills."

14. It appears that there was a field for farming in between the trees.

15. The expression *'alā ḥard* carries several meanings – of obstructing, not giving something, acting on a premeditated decision and for doing something at the earliest.

they had the power (to gather the fruit). (26) But as soon as they beheld the orchard, (they cried out): "We have certainly lost the way; (27) rather, we are utterly ruined."[16] (28) The best among them said: "Did I not say to you: why do you not give glory to (your Lord)?"[17] (29) They cried out: "Glory be to our Lord! Certainly we were sinners." (30) Then they began to reproach one another.[18] (31) They said: "Woe to us! We had indeed transgressed. (32) Maybe our Lord will give us a better orchard in its place; to our Lord do ▶

قَـٰدِرِينَ ﴿٢٥﴾ فَلَمَّا رَأَوْهَا قَالُوٓاْ إِنَّا لَضَآلُّونَ
﴿٢٦﴾ بَلْ نَحْنُ مَحْرُومُونَ ﴿٢٧﴾ قَالَ أَوْسَطُهُمْ
أَلَمْ أَقُل لَّكُمْ لَوْلَا تُسَبِّحُونَ ﴿٢٨﴾ قَالُواْ
سُبْحَـٰنَ رَبِّنَآ إِنَّا كُنَّا ظَـٰلِمِينَ ﴿٢٩﴾ فَأَقْبَلَ
بَعْضُهُمْ عَلَىٰ بَعْضٍ يَتَلَـٰوَمُونَ ﴿٣٠﴾
قَالُواْ يَـٰوَيْلَنَآ إِنَّا كُنَّا طَـٰغِينَ ﴿٣١﴾
عَسَىٰ رَبُّنَآ أَن يُبْدِلَنَا خَيْرًا مِّنْهَآ إِنَّآ إِلَىٰ رَبِّنَا

16. On looking at their orchard, they did not believe first that it was their own orchard. That is why they exclaimed: "We have certainly lost the way." A little later when the truth dawned on them, they cried out: "We are utterly ruined."

17. That person had warned them not to forget God when they were swearing an oath that they would definitely pluck fruits from their garden the next day. He asked them to glorify God and say: "God willing". However, they disregarded his exhortation altogether. He advised them the same when they were resolving not to share any fruit with the destitute. He counselled them not to have such an evil intention and to fear God. Yet they persisted in their resolve.

18. They took to blaming one another for the loss, stating that "under your misleading counsel we have disregarded God and committed evil."

we penitently turn." (33) Such is the chastisement; and the chastisement of the Hereafter is assuredly even greater, if only they knew.

(34) Surely[19] the God-fearing shall have Gardens of bliss with their Lord. (35) What! Shall We treat those who have submitted (to Our command) like those who have acted as criminals? (36) What is the matter with you? How ill do you judge![20] ▶

رَٰغِبُونَ ۝٣٢ كَذَٰلِكَ ٱلْعَذَابُ ۖ وَلَعَذَابُ
ٱلْءَاخِرَةِ أَكْبَرُ ۚ لَوْ كَانُوا۟ يَعْلَمُونَ ۝٣٣
إِنَّ لِلْمُتَّقِينَ عِندَ رَبِّهِمْ جَنَّٰتِ ٱلنَّعِيمِ ۝٣٤
أَفَنَجْعَلُ ٱلْمُسْلِمِينَ كَٱلْمُجْرِمِينَ ۝٣٥
مَا لَكُمْ كَيْفَ تَحْكُمُونَ ۝٣٦

19. This is a rejoinder to the Makkan nobility who teased the Muslims by saying that they enjoyed a great many blessings in the world, thereby indicating that they were God's favourites. Conversely, the Muslims' lot was a miserable one, which only proved that God was angry with them. They further argued that if there were life after the present one, it would be they, the disbelievers, who would enjoy bliss in much the same way that they did in the present world. As for the Muslims, they would suffer in the Hereafter. The present verses as well as the verses that follow refute this claim.

20. It is patently illogical that God will not differentiate between those who obeyed Him and those who rebelled against Him. The disbelievers are asked why they suffer from the delusion that this universe is ruled by some blind force that does not draw any line of demarcation between the devout and the culprits. There are some who faithfully follow divine commands and shun all evil. In contrast, there are some who brazenly indulge in every type of sin and commit all sorts of crimes and excesses, without ever thinking of God. They are acutely aware of their opulence and the adversity of the believers. However, they are blind to the vast difference in the morals and conduct of believers and disbelievers. That is why they unhesitatingly pass judgement that the believers will be treated by God like the culprits, whereas the disbelievers will be rewarded with Paradise.

(37) Or do you have a Book[21] wherein you read (38) that (in the Hereafter) you shall have all that you choose for yourselves? (39) Or have We sworn a covenant with you which We are bound to keep till the Day of Resurrection, (a covenant requiring that whatever you ordain for yourselves shall be yours)? (40) Ask them: "Which of them can guarantee that?[22] (41) Or has something been guaranteed by any of those whom they associate with Allah in His Divinity?" If so, let them bring forth their associates, if they are truthful.[23]

(42) On the Day when the dreadful calamity will ▶

أَمۡ لَكُمۡ كِتَٰبٞ فِيهِ تَدۡرُسُونَ ٣٧ إِنَّ
لَكُمۡ فِيهِ لَمَا تَخَيَّرُونَ ٣٨ أَمۡ لَكُمۡ
أَيۡمَٰنٌ عَلَيۡنَا بَٰلِغَةٌ إِلَىٰ يَوۡمِ ٱلۡقِيَٰمَةِ إِنَّ
لَكُمۡ لَمَا تَحۡكُمُونَ ٣٩ سَلۡهُمۡ أَيُّهُم
بِذَٰلِكَ زَعِيمٌ ٤٠ أَمۡ لَهُمۡ شُرَكَآءُ فَلۡيَأۡتُواْ
بِشُرَكَآئِهِمۡ إِن كَانُواْ صَٰدِقِينَ ٤١ يَوۡمَ

21. i.e., the Book revealed by God.

22. *Za'īm* in Arabic refers to a guarantor or spokesperson of a community. The disbelievers are asked to identify their representative, if any, who claims that God has made such a promise and obligation for them.

23. There is no basis whatsoever for the disbelievers' above stance. It is against reason and no Book of God contains any such promise. Nor can anyone among the disbelievers claim that God has pledged to do so. None of their idols can guarantee that they will get admitted to Paradise. Given this, what has deluded them into thinking so?

unfold,[24] when people will be summoned to prostrate themselves, and yet they will not be able to prostrate. (43) Their eyes shall be downcast and ignominy shall overwhelm them. For when they were safe and sound, they were summoned to prostrate themselves, (and they refused).[25]

(44) So leave Me, (O Prophet), to deal with him[26] who gives the lie to this ▶

يُكْشَفُ عَن سَاقٍ وَيُدْعَوْنَ إِلَى ٱلسُّجُودِ
فَلَا يَسْتَطِيعُونَ ﴿٤٢﴾ خَٰشِعَةً أَبْصَٰرُهُمْ
تَرْهَقُهُمْ ذِلَّةٌ ۖ وَقَدْ كَانُوا۟ يُدْعَوْنَ
إِلَى ٱلسُّجُودِ وَهُمْ سَٰلِمُونَ ﴿٤٣﴾ فَذَرْنِى
وَمَن يُكَذِّبُ بِهَٰذَا ٱلْحَدِيثِ ۖ

24. As to the Qur'ānic statement, *yawma yukshafu 'an sāq*, some Companions and Successors maintain that, according to Arabic idiom, such an expression figuratively describes hard times or a calamity. 'Abdullāh ibn 'Abbās endorses the above interpretation and cites some examples from Arabic poetry. However, another report, based on the authority of the same 'Abdullāh ibn 'Abbās and Rabī' ibn Anas, holds that the reference is to the unfolding of the truth. (*Tasfīr* of al-Ṭabarī, 23, 186-196 and *Tafsīr* of Ibn Kathīr, 8, 199) In other words, the allusion is to the Day of Judgement when all truths will become manifest and everyone's record of deeds will be made public.

25. On the Day of Judgement, it will be made public knowledge as to who was a devout person and who was not. For this reason, all mankind will be summoned to prostrate before God. The devout ones, habitual of prostrating, will immediately fall into prostration. However, those who had refused to bow down to God throughout their lives will be unable to prostrate. They will not be able to make even a false exhibition of their devotion to God. They will remain standing, overtaken by disgrace and remorse.

26. The Prophet (peace be upon him) is advised not to worry about the disbelievers' ultimate end. God will deal with them.

Discourse. We shall draw them little by little (to their undoing) in a way that they will not know.[27] (45) I am giving them a respite. Great is My scheme![28]

(46) Or are you asking them for some compensation so that they feel burdened with debt?[29] (47) Or do they have any knowledge of the Unseen which they ▶

سَنَسْتَدْرِجُهُم مِّنْ حَيْثُ لَا يَعْلَمُونَ ﴿٤٤﴾
وَأُمْلِى لَهُمْ ۚ إِنَّ كَيْدِى مَتِينٌ ﴿٤٥﴾
أَمْ تَسْـَٔلُهُمْ أَجْرًا فَهُم مِّن مَّغْرَمٍ
مُّثْقَلُونَ ﴿٤٦﴾ أَمْ عِندَهُمُ ٱلْغَيْبُ

27. The disbelievers do not realise how God leads them to loss and destruction. For that purpose, those who oppose the truth and do injustice in this life may be blessed by God with all material bounties, including good health, wealth, children, and other worldly gains. This deludes them into believing that they are on the right track and there is nothing wrong with their deeds. Thus, they become steeped in their opposition to truth and indulgence in injustice and rebellion. It does not occur to them that the bounties bestowed upon them are not some sort of reward, but in fact a means of their destruction.

28. *Kayd* refers to a secret move or scheme. In itself such a move is not evil. It is blameworthy when this scheme aims at harming someone unjustly. It is perfectly all right if a scheme is drawn against someone who deserves to be punished.

29. The question is apparently put to the Prophet (peace be upon him). However, it is actually directed against his opponents who had crossed all limits. They are asked whether God's Messenger wants any material benefit from them in return. Why are they so enraged? They know it well that he is a selfless person. His message is in their own interest. They are totally free not to accept his message. Then why are they becoming so violently furious over the message he is giving? (For further details see *Sūrah al-Ṭūr* 52: 31.)

are now writing down?[30] (48) So bear with patience until the Judgement of your Lord comes,[31] and do not be like the man in the fish[32] (i.e., Jonah) who called out, choking with grief:[33] ▶

فَهُمْ يَكْتُبُونَ ۝٤٧ فَاصْبِرْ لِحُكْمِ رَبِّكَ
وَلَا تَكُن كَصَاحِبِ الْحُوتِ إِذْ نَادَىٰ
وَهُوَ مَكْظُومٌ ۝٤٨

30. This second question too, though addressed to the Prophet (peace be upon him), is aimed at his detractors. They are asked whether they have gained some knowledge of the Unseen. How then does it make them so confident to think that he is not God's Messenger and the truths related by him and his message? Why are they so dogmatic and insistent in rejecting him as false? (For further details see *Sūrah al-Ṭūr* 52: 32.)

31. It will take some time for God to declare the Prophet's victory and his opponents' defeat. Until then, he should bear with perseverance all the hardships and afflictions he may encounter in the cause of preaching faith.

32. The directive is that one should not behave with the impatience that was displayed by the Prophet Jonah (peace be upon him), for, it was on account of the Prophet Jonah's impatience that he was consigned to the belly of a fish. The exhortation is immediately followed by the advice to the Prophet (peace be upon him) that he should not be like the Prophet Jonah (peace be upon him). This underscores the assumption that the latter had committed some act impatiently before the divine decree was issued. As a result, he incurred God's displeasure. (For details see *Towards Understanding the Qur'ān*, vol. IV, *Sūrah Yūnus* 10: 98, n. 99, pp. 66–67; vol. V, *Sūrah al-Anbiyā'* 21: 87–88, nn. 82–85, p. 292; vol. IX, *Sūrah al-Ṣāffāt* 37: 139–148, nn. 78–85, pp. 316–321).

33. It is clarified in *Sūrah al-Anbiyā'* that while inside the belly of the fish and in the darkness of the sea, the Prophet Jonah (peace be upon him) had cried out: "There is no god but You. Glory be to You! Indeed, I have done wrong." (*Sūrah al-Anbiyā'* 21: 87) God listened to his supplication and rescued him from his grief. (Ibid. 21: 87–88)

(49) had his Lord not bestowed His favour upon him, he would have been cast upon that barren shore[34] (and would have remained there) in disgrace. (50) But his Lord exalted him, and included him among His righteous servants.

(51) When the unbelievers hear this Exhortation, they look at you as though they would knock you off your feet with their (hostile) glances.[35] They say: "Surely he is afflicted with madness"; (52) although this is nothing but an Exhortation (to goodness) for everyone in the world.

لَّوۡلَآ أَن تَدَٰرَكَهُۥ نِعۡمَةٞ مِّن رَّبِّهِۦ لَنُبِذَ
بِٱلۡعَرَآءِ وَهُوَ مَذۡمُومٞ ﴿٤٩﴾ فَٱجۡتَبَٰهُ رَبُّهُۥ
فَجَعَلَهُۥ مِنَ ٱلصَّٰلِحِينَ ﴿٥٠﴾ وَإِن يَكَادُ
ٱلَّذِينَ كَفَرُواْ لَيُزۡلِقُونَكَ بِأَبۡصَٰرِهِمۡ
لَمَّا سَمِعُواْ ٱلذِّكۡرَ وَيَقُولُونَ إِنَّهُۥ لَمَجۡنُونٞ
﴿٥١﴾ وَمَا هُوَ إِلَّا ذِكۡرٞ لِّلۡعَٰلَمِينَ ﴿٥٢﴾

34. On studying this verse together with verses 142–146 of *Sūrah al-Ṣāffāt*, it appears that when he was placed in the belly of the fish, he was under divine reproach. However, as he prayed to and glorified Allah and confessed his fault, he was rescued from the belly of the fish and was delivered to a bare tract of land, though he was in ill health. However, he was no longer under divine reproach. Out of His mercy, God caused a creeping plant to grow there, providing him with both shade and food.

35. Reference is to the disbelievers' menacing looks. Verses 73–77 of *Sūrah Banī Isrā'īl* portray a similar scene of the Makkan disbelievers' fury and hostility against the Prophet (peace be upon him).

Sūrah 69

Al-Ḥāqqah

(The Indubitable Event)

(Makkan Period)

Title

The opening word of the *Sūrah* constitutes its title.

Period of Revelation

It is one of the early Makkan *Sūrahs*. From its contents, it emerges that it must have been revealed at a time when the opposition to the Prophet (peace be upon him) had begun, although it was not yet very intense. This report features in the *Musnad* of Imām Aḥmad (1, 17) on the authority of 'Umar which reads as follows: "Before my acceptance of Islam, I set out to tease the Prophet (peace be upon him). One day however, before I arrived he was already inside the *Ḥaram*. He was then reciting *Sūrah al-Ḥāqqah* in the prayer. I stood right behind him and listened to his recitation. While I was amazed at the glory and eloquence of the Qur'ān, the thought struck me that he really is a poet, as is alleged by the Quraysh. At that precise moment, he recited the verse: 'This is the speech of an honourable Messenger, not the speech of a poet' (verses 40–41 of *Sūrah al-Ḥāqqah*). I told myself that if he is not a poet, he must be a soothsayer. It was then that he recited this verse: 'Nor is this the speech of a soothsayer. Little do you reflect! It has been revealed by the Lord of the universe' (verses 42–43 of *Sūrah al-Ḥāqqah*). Upon listening to this, I felt deeply drawn towards Islam." It is evident from 'Umar's report that this *Sūrah* had been revealed much before his acceptance of Islam, for he did not embrace Islam until long after the above incident. He was struck by the truth of Islam on several occasions. The decisive moment, however, came when he was inside his sister's house. It was on listening to the Qur'ān there that he did accept Islam. (For details see Introduction to *Sūrah al-Wāqi'ah.*)

Subject Matter and Themes

The opening part of the *Sūrah* deals with the Hereafter, and the latter part affirms that the Qur'ān is the Word of God and that the Prophet Muḥammad (peace be upon him) is true in his claim to Prophethood.

The opening verses stress that the occurrence of the Resurrection (*Qiyāmah*) and the Hereafter (*Ākhirah*) are inevitable and bound to happen. Verses 4–12 illustrate the accursed end of earlier communities as a result of their disbelief in the Hereafter. They were subjected to divine punishment. Verses 13–17 portray the spectacle of the Day of Resurrection. Verses 18–27 spell out the purpose for which God has devised the Afterlife for mankind. On the Day of Judgement, all human beings will appear before their Lord, all of their actions will come out in the open, and everyone will receive his/her record of deeds. Those who had led their lives in accordance with the belief that they have to render their account to their Lord, and who had done good in preparation for reward in the Hereafter, will be extremely pleased with their record of deeds, and will be blessed with the eternal abode of Paradise. In contrast, those who had not discharged their duty to God and to fellow human beings, will not have anyone to save them from God's punishment. They will be consigned to the terrible punishment of Hellfire.

The later part of the *Sūrah,* while addressing the Makkan disbelievers, refutes their allegation that the Qur'ān is the product of the mind of a poet or a soothsayer. It is the Word of God, presented by His Messenger. He is not authorised to add to or delete even a word from it. Were he to interpolate anything of his own, God will sever his life vein. It is truly the Book of God. Those who reject it as false will eventually regret their disbelief.

In the name of Allah, the Most Merciful, the Most Compassionate.

(1) The indubitable event![1] (2) And what is that indubitable event?[2] (3) And what do you know what that indubitable event is? (4) The Thamūd[3] and the ʿĀd denied the (possibility of a) sudden calamity,[4] calling it false. ▶

بِسۡمِ ٱللَّهِ ٱلرَّحۡمَٰنِ ٱلرَّحِيمِ

ٱلۡحَآقَّةُ ﴿١﴾ مَا ٱلۡحَآقَّةُ ﴿٢﴾ وَمَآ أَدۡرَىٰكَ
مَا ٱلۡحَآقَّةُ ﴿٣﴾ كَذَّبَتۡ ثَمُودُ وَعَادُۢ بِٱلۡقَارِعَةِ ﴿٤﴾

---

1. Literally, *al-Ḥāqqah* denotes something that is bound to take place without a doubt. The significance of using this for the Resurrection and at the outset of the *Sūrah* is to convey to the disbelievers that their denial of the inevitable event, howsoever vehement, will fail to avert its occurrence.

2. These two questions, asked in quick succession, are aimed at alerting and drawing the attention of the addressees. They should better realise the significance of the contents of this message and listen with the attention that it deserves.

3. Since the Makkan disbelievers rejected the Resurrection and dismissed its tidings mockingly, they are warned that, irrespective of their rejection and denial, the Last Day is bound to happen. They are further told that its rejection has a deep bearing on the morals of the nation and their future. It is fairly evident, from the history of earlier communities, that those who rejected the belief of the Hereafter, mistaking this worldly life as the only life, and denied their appearance and accountability before God, landed themselves into moral degeneration. Ultimately divine penalty exterminated them from the earth.

4. *Al-qāri'ah* literally means rapping, striking, and thumping. This terminology has been used for the Resurrection (*Qiyāmah*), which emphasises that it will be an extremely horrendous and dreadful event.

(5) Then the Thamūd were destroyed by an awesome upheaval;[5] (6) and the ʿĀd were destroyed by a furiously raging wind-storm (7) which He let loose upon them for seven nights and eight days in succession; so that (if you had been there) you might have seen people lying prostrate, as though they were uprooted trunks of hollowed palm trees. (8) Do you now see any trace of them?

(9) Pharaoh and those before him and the people of the overturned habitations[6] all engaged in the same great sin. (10) They did not follow the Messenger of their Lord, and so He seized them with a severe grip.

فَأَمَّا ثَمُودُ فَأُهْلِكُوا بِالطَّاغِيَةِ ٥ وَأَمَّا عَادٌ
فَأُهْلِكُوا بِرِيحٍ صَرْصَرٍ عَاتِيَةٍ ٦
سَخَّرَهَا عَلَيْهِمْ سَبْعَ لَيَالٍ وَثَمَانِيَةَ أَيَّامٍ
حُسُومًا فَتَرَى الْقَوْمَ فِيهَا صَرْعَىٰ كَأَنَّهُمْ
أَعْجَازُ نَخْلٍ خَاوِيَةٍ ٧ فَهَلْ تَرَىٰ لَهُم
مِّن بَاقِيَةٍ ٨ وَجَاءَ فِرْعَوْنُ وَمَن قَبْلَهُ
وَالْمُؤْتَفِكَاتُ بِالْخَاطِئَةِ ٩ فَعَصَوْا
رَسُولَ رَبِّهِمْ فَأَخَذَهُمْ أَخْذَةً رَّابِيَةً ١٠

5. *Al-ṭāghiyah* is described as *al-rajfah* in verse 78 of *Sūrah al-A'rāf; al-ṣayḥah* in verse 67 of *Sūrah al-Hūd* and *ṣā'iqah* in verse 17 of *Sūrah Ḥā Mīm al-Sajdah*. All these expressions refer to an astonishing upheaval.

6. This is an allusion to the settlements and dwellings of the people of the Prophet Lot (peace be upon him) which, as mentioned in verse 82 of *Sūrah Hūd* and verse 74 of *Sūrah al-Ḥijr*, were completely razed to the ground.

(11) Verily when the water rose to great heights,[7] We bore you upon a floating vessel (i.e. the Ark)[8] (12) so that We might make it an instructive event for you, and retentive ears might preserve its memory.[9]

(13) So when the Trumpet is blown with a single blast[10] ▶

إِنَّا لَمَّا طَغَا ٱلْمَآءُ حَمَلْنَـٰكُمْ فِى ٱلْجَارِيَةِ ﴿١١﴾ لِنَجْعَلَهَا لَكُمْ تَذْكِرَةً وَتَعِيَهَآ أُذُنٌ وَٰعِيَةٌ ﴿١٢﴾ فَإِذَا نُفِخَ فِى ٱلصُّورِ نَفْخَةٌ وَٰحِدَةٌ ﴿١٣﴾

7. This refers to the Flood in the days of the Prophet Noah (peace be upon him) which, for their serious offences, drowned a whole community except the believers among them.

8. The whole human race that exists today consists of the descendants of those who boarded the ark several thousands of years ago. Hence it is said that "God bore you upon a floating ark." In other words, mankind survives to this day because God had rescued the believers and drowned only the disbelievers in the deluge.

9. Reference is made to the retentive ears that facilitate taking a lesson which penetrates to the heart. The obvious allusion is to the attentive listeners who do not disregard the truth. They remember this instructive event and draw a lesson. They realise that the rejection of the Hereafter or God's Messengers incurs devastating consequences.

10. Before studying the later verses, it should be borne in mind that at places the Qur'ān states the three different phases of Resurrection which will unfold in quick succession. At others, the Qur'ān provides a coherent narrative, combining all these phases together. For example, verse 87 of *Sūrah al-Naml* refers first to the blowing of the trumpet. All human beings will rise on hearing its dreadful sound. Then they will witness the harrowing spectacle of the end of the present order of the universe, which is graphically described in verses 1–2 of *Sūrah al-Ḥajj*, 49–50 of *Sūrah Yā Sīn* and 1–6 of *Sūrah al-Takwīr*. Verses 67–70 of *Sūrah al-Zumar* relate the

(14) and the earth and the mountains are carried aloft and are crushed to bits at one stroke, (15) on that Day shall that indubitable event come to pass; (16) when the sky will be rent asunder, the grip holding it together having loosened on that Day, (17) and the angels will stand on the sides, with eight of them bearing aloft the Throne of your Lord on that Day.[11] (18) That will be the Day when you shall be brought forth (before Allah) and no secret of yours shall remain hidden.

وَحُمِلَتِ ٱلْأَرْضُ وَٱلْجِبَالُ فَدُكَّتَا دَكَّةً
وَٰحِدَةً ﴿١٤﴾ فَيَوْمَئِذٍ وَقَعَتِ ٱلْوَاقِعَةُ ﴿١٥﴾
وَٱنشَقَّتِ ٱلسَّمَآءُ فَهِىَ يَوْمَئِذٍ وَاهِيَةٌ ﴿١٦﴾
وَٱلْمَلَكُ عَلَىٰٓ أَرْجَآئِهَا ۚ وَيَحْمِلُ عَرْشَ
رَبِّكَ فَوْقَهُمْ يَوْمَئِذٍ ثَمَٰنِيَةٌ ﴿١٧﴾ يَوْمَئِذٍ
تُعْرَضُونَ لَا تَخْفَىٰ مِنكُمْ خَافِيَةٌ ﴿١٨﴾

---

devastating effects of the second and third blowing of the trumpet. The former will bring about the death of all human beings while the latter will cause their resurrection and appearance before God. Verses 102–112 of *Sūrah Ṭā Hā*, 101–103 of *Sūrah al-Anbiyā'*, 51–53 of *Sūrah Yā Sīn* and 20–22 of *Sūrah Qāf* refer to only the third blowing of the trumpet. (For details see *Towards Understanding the Qur'ān*, vol. V, *Sūrah Ṭā Hā* 20: n. 78, pp. 223–224; vol. VI, *Sūrah al-Ḥajj* 22: n. 1, pp. 5–6 and vol. IX, *Sūrah Yā Sīn* 36: nn. 46–47, pp. 265–266.)

11. This is one of the ambiguous verses (*mutashābihāt*) of the Qur'ān, of which no precise meaning can be offered. We can neither know as to what the divine throne is, nor can we understand how eight angels will bear it aloft on the Day of Judgement. However, it is inconceivable that Allah will be sitting on His throne and that eight angels will literally bear him aloft on the Day of Judgement, for the verse does not specify this. In light of the Qur'ānic description of God elsewhere, it cannot be assumed that He will be sitting on a particular spot or that any creature will carry

(19) On that Day, he whose Record is given to him in his right hand[12] will say: "Lo! Read my Record![13] ▶	فَأَمَّا مَنْ أُوتِيَ كِتَـٰبَهُۥ بِيَمِينِهِۦ فَيَقُولُ هَآؤُمُ ٱقْرَءُوا۟ كِتَـٰبِيَهْ ﴿١٩﴾

Him, for He transcends the body, direction and place. Any attempt to overstretch the import of this verse is tantamount to jeopardising one's faith. However, this point should be understood well, that for conveying a palpable idea of God's kingship and dominion, the Qur'ān has employed the same imagery which is associated with the worldly kings. It has drawn upon the same terms which are usually used for the description of a king and his kingdom. By this analogy alone, man can gain some idea of God's dominion. Such terms are readily comprehensible to the human mind. However, it will be incorrect to take these expressions literally.

12. As one's record will be given to him in his right hand, it will signify that his account is clean and clear. He will appear before God not as a criminal, but as a righteous person. It is likely that at the time of the handing over of records, he himself will collect it in his right hand. From his death, up to the moment of his appearance in the grand assembly, he will receive such treatment, convincing him that God will reward, not punish him. The Qur'ān clarifies that at the time of death, everyone realises his status as a culprit or as a righteous servant of God. Obviously, these two types of persons are treated differently from the time of their death to the Resurrection. A righteous person is treated as a guest and an evil person as a culprit under custody. On the Day of Judgement, which will inaugurate a new life for everybody, the disbelievers and the righteous will stand apart from each other. (For details see *Towards Understanding the Qur'ān*, vol. IV, *Sūrah al-Naḥl* 16: 28 and 32, n. 26, pp. 324–325; vol. V, *Sūrah Ṭā Hā* 20: 102, 103 and 124–126, nn. 79, 80 and 107, pp. 224–225 and 240–241; *Sūrah al-Anbiyā'* 21: 103, n. 98, p. 299; vol. VII, *Sūrah al-Furqān* 25: 24, n. 38, p. 20; *Sūrah al-Naml* 27: 89, n. 109, pp. 189–190; vol. IX, *Sūrah Saba'* 34: 51, n. 72, p. 202; *Sūrah Yā Sīn* 36: 26–27, nn. 22–23, pp. 253–254; *Sūrah al-Mu'min* 40: 45–46, n. 63: *Sūrah Muḥammad* 47: 27, n. 37; *Sūrah Qāf* 50: 19–23, nn. 22, 23 and 25.)

13. He will be delighted on getting his record in his right hand and will show it to his friends. Verse 9 of *Sūrah al-Inshiqāq* captures his state of mind thus: "He shall return to his people joyfully."

(20) Verily I was sure that I would be handed over my account."[14] (21) Then he shall find himself in a life of bliss; (22) in a lofty Garden (23) the clusters of whose fruit will be hanging low to be within reach (of the inmates of Paradise). (24) (They will be told): "Eat and drink with good cheer as a reward for the good deeds you did in the days that have passed by."

(25) As for him whose Record will be given to him in his left hand,[15] he will exclaim: "Would that I had never been given my Record,[16] ▶

إِنِّى ظَنَنتُ أَنِّى مُلَٰقٍ حِسَابِيَهْ ﴿٢٠﴾ فَهُوَ فِى
عِيشَةٍ رَّاضِيَةٍ ﴿٢١﴾ فِى جَنَّةٍ عَالِيَةٍ ﴿٢٢﴾ قُطُوفُهَا
دَانِيَةٌ ﴿٢٣﴾ كُلُوا۟ وَٱشْرَبُوا۟ هَنِيٓـًٔا بِمَآ أَسْلَفْتُمْ
فِى ٱلْأَيَّامِ ٱلْخَالِيَةِ ﴿٢٤﴾ وَأَمَّا مَنْ
أُوتِىَ كِتَٰبَهُۥ بِشِمَالِهِۦ فَيَقُولُ يَٰلَيْتَنِى لَمْ
أُوتَ كِتَٰبِيَهْ ﴿٢٥﴾

14. He will explain the reason behind his good fortune: that it lay in the fact that he was never heedless of the Hereafter and spent his entire life in believing that one day he will be made to stand before God and be called to render account by Him.

15. Verse 10 of *Sūrah al-Inshiqāq* states that a sinner will be given his record behind his back. This is likely to be because he would already be aware of his being a sinner and a culprit, and also of the contents of his ignoble record, so he will dejectedly collect his record in his left hand and will try to hide it behind his back so that no one may find out what he received.

16. A sinner would wish that he had not faced public humiliation in the grand assembly when he receives his record of deeds. His wish would be that he should have been punished for his misdeeds secretly.

(26) and had not known my account.[17] (27) Oh! Would that the death that came to me in the world had made an end of me![18] (28) My riches have not availed me, (29) and my authority has vanished."[19] (30) (A command will be issued): "Seize him and shackle him, (31) then cast him in the Fire, (32) then fasten him with a chain, seventy cubits long. (33) He would not believe in Allah, the Most Great; ▶

وَلَمْ أَدْرِ مَا حِسَابِيَهْ ﴿٢٦﴾ يَٰلَيْتَهَا كَانَتِ
ٱلْقَاضِيَةَ ﴿٢٧﴾ مَآ أَغْنَىٰ عَنِّى مَالِيَهْ ۜ ﴿٢٨﴾
هَلَكَ عَنِّى سُلْطَٰنِيَهْ ﴿٢٩﴾ خُذُوهُ فَغُلُّوهُ
﴿٣٠﴾ ثُمَّ ٱلْجَحِيمَ صَلُّوهُ ﴿٣١﴾ ثُمَّ فِى سِلْسِلَةٍ
ذَرْعُهَا سَبْعُونَ ذِرَاعًا فَٱسْلُكُوهُ ﴿٣٢﴾ إِنَّهُۥ
كَانَ لَا يُؤْمِنُ بِٱللَّهِ ٱلْعَظِيمِ ﴿٣٣﴾

---

17. Another possible meaning could be: "Would that I had known what accounting is!" This emphasises that the evildoers will be faced with something they had not imagined – that they will be required to render an account of all their deeds and that the whole record of their lives will be placed before them.

18. His wish would be that his death would have made a permanent end to him, not to be followed by any other life after death.

19. The word *sulṭān* connotes both a clinching argument and authority. In its former sense, the meaning would be that his resorting to any argument or pretext in this world will not work on the Day of Judgement. He will have no argument whatsoever to defend himself. Taken in the latter sense, the verse means that on that day, he will see that the power he once enjoyed in the world, which had made him exultant and arrogant, has vanished. Unaided by an army, or by those who once obeyed him, he will stand as a miserable and powerless creature, lacking even the ability to defend himself.

(34) nor would he urge the feeding of the poor.[20] (35) Today he has been left here friendless; (36) and has no food except the filth from the washing of wounds, (37) which only the sinners will eat."

(38) But no;[21] I swear by what you see, (39) and by what you do not see, (40) that this is the speech of an honourable Messenger,[22] ▶

وَلَا يَحُضُّ عَلَىٰ طَعَامِ ٱلْمِسْكِينِ ﴿٣٤﴾
فَلَيْسَ لَهُ ٱلْيَوْمَ هَٰهُنَا حَمِيمٌ ﴿٣٥﴾ وَلَا طَعَامٌ
إِلَّا مِنْ غِسْلِينٍ ﴿٣٦﴾ لَّا يَأْكُلُهُۥٓ
إِلَّا ٱلْخَٰطِـُٔونَ ﴿٣٧﴾ فَلَآ أُقْسِمُ
بِمَا تُبْصِرُونَ ﴿٣٨﴾ وَمَا لَا تُبْصِرُونَ ﴿٣٩﴾
إِنَّهُۥ لَقَوْلُ رَسُولٍ كَرِيمٍ ﴿٤٠﴾

---

20. Let alone feeding a hungry person himself, he was not even moved enough to ask others to do so.

21. i.e., the reality is quite different from what they fancy.

22. "The honourable Messenger" is the Prophet Muḥammad (peace be upon him) while in verse 19 of *Sūrah al-Takwīr,* the same appellation is used for Gabriel (may peace be on him). In the verse under study, the assertion about the Prophet (peace be upon him) is followed by the statement that the Qur'ān is not the product of the mind of some poet or soothsayer. Needless to add, the Makkan disbelievers accused the Prophet (peace be upon him), not the angel Gabriel, of being a poet or a soothsayer. In *Sūrah al-Takwīr* however, the remark about the honourable message-bearer is followed by this description: "One mighty and held in honour with the Lord of the Throne; there he is obeyed, and held trustworthy. He (the Prophet) indeed saw the message-bearer on the clear horizon." (*al-Takwīr* 81: 19–23) Almost a similar description of Gabriel features in verses 5–10 of *Sūrah al-Najm*.

It nonetheless raises the question that in what sense can the Qur'ān be referred to as the word of the Prophet (peace be upon him) and Gabriel? The answer is that people received the Qur'ān from the tongue of the Prophet (peace be upon him) who, in turn, received it from the tongue of Gabriel. The Qur'ān is thus the word of the Prophet (peace be upon him) as

(41) not the speech of a poet. Little do you believe![23] (42) Nor is this the speech of a soothsayer. Little do you reflect! (43) It has been revealed by the Lord of the Universe.[24] (44) And if he [i.e., the Prophet] had forged this Discourse and thereafter ascribed it to Us,▶

وَمَا هُوَ بِقَوْلِ شَاعِرٍ ۚ قَلِيلًا مَّا تُؤْمِنُونَ ﴿٤١﴾
وَلَا بِقَوْلِ كَاهِنٍ ۚ قَلِيلًا مَّا تَذَكَّرُونَ ﴿٤٢﴾
تَنزِيلٌ مِّن رَّبِّ ٱلْعَـٰلَمِينَ ﴿٤٣﴾ وَلَوْ تَقَوَّلَ
عَلَيْنَا بَعْضَ ٱلْأَقَاوِيلِ ﴿٤٤﴾

well as of Gabriel. It is therefore clarified later that the Qur'ān is indeed the Word of the Lord of the universe, which is conveyed through the agency of the Prophet (peace be upon him) and Gabriel. The word *Rasūl* (Messenger) itself signifies that it is not directly from them, rather, as Messengers they presented the Qur'ān on behalf of the Lord of the universe.

23. "That they believe little" in Arabic is an idiom that points to their lack of faith. Alternatively, it might mean that at times on listening to the Qur'ān, they instinctively exclaim that it is not the product of the human mind. However, they soon relapse into their disbelief and obstinately refuse to believe in the Qur'ān.

24. While swearing by all that the disbelievers see and what they do not see, it is emphasised that the Qur'ān is not the word of a poet or a soothsayer. It is the Word of the Lord of the universe, conveyed through an honourable, noble Messenger. Let us now focus on the oath taken in the verse. The disbelievers could easily discern all this:

i. The Qur'ān was being presented by someone whom every Makkan knew to be a noble, trustworthy person and there was nothing hidden about him. It was common knowledge that he was of the highest moral standard in his society. He was the best among his people. Such a decent person was not likely to invent such a flagrant lie as to attribute something falsely to God and to parade his own ramblings as the Word of God.
ii. The Makkan disbelievers knew full well that he had no personal motive or gain behind presenting the Qur'ān. On the contrary,

he was sacrificing his interests in the cause of this mission, for he had abandoned his profession of trade. He had given up all personal comforts and joys. He was reviled by those who used to hold him in great esteem. Not only he himself, but his family, his children included, had been subjected to all manner of hardships. He had been undergoing an ordeal, never expecting any personal gain in return.

iii. They recognised that the members of their own society who embraced faith at his hands were completely transformed overnight. No poet or soothsayer had ever achieved this feat. They were incapable of morally transforming anyone. Nor could they inspire anyone to withstand all sorts of hardships for their sake.

iv. They were fully aware of the limitations of the sayings of a poet or a soothsayer. Only a blindly obstinate person could dismiss the Qur'ān as poetry or soothsaying. (For details see *Towards Understanding the Qur'ān*, vol. V, *Sūrah al-Anbiyā'* 21: n. 7, pp. 252–254; vol. VII, *Sūrah al-Shu'arā'* 26: nn. 142–145, pp. 126–129; *Sūrah al-Ṭūr* 52: n. 22.)

v. They realised that no one among them throughout Arabia could match the Qur'ān in its eloquence and stylistic features. There was simply no comparison with the Qur'ān.

vi. It was in their knowledge that the Prophet's own literary skills were vastly different from those of the Qur'ān. No native Arabic speaking person who listened to the Qur'ān and to the Prophet's own speech could ever assume that the Qur'ān and the Prophet's speech were the product of the same source.

vii. Even a day prior to the Prophet's declaration of his Messengership, the Makkans had never heard him discussing the issues and truths which he presented as the contents of the Qur'ān. They knew well that he did not have access to any source of knowledge. Even if his detractors alleged that he had borrowed the contents of the Qur'ān from someone, no Makkan would have bought this story. (For details see *Towards Understanding the Qur'ān*, vol. IV, *Sūrah al-Naḥl* 16: n. 107, pp. 366–367 and vol. VII, *Sūrah al-Furqān* 25: n. 12, pp. 7–10.)

viii. They witnessed the functioning of the vast universe which exhibited the operation of extensive and well-coordinated laws. There was no ground whatsoever for vindicating polytheism and for rejecting the belief of the Hereafter, the notions to

(45) We would surely have seized him by the right hand, (46) and then severed his life vein; (47) and not one of you would have been able to withhold Us from doing so.[25] ▶

لَأَخَذْنَا مِنْهُ بِٱلْيَمِينِ ﴿٤٥﴾ ثُمَّ لَقَطَعْنَا
مِنْهُ ٱلْوَتِينَ ﴿٤٦﴾ فَمَا مِنكُم مِّنْ أَحَدٍ عَنْهُ
حَـٰجِزِينَ ﴿٤٧﴾

which the Arabs of the day subscribed. On the contrary, they could observe all around them the overwhelming evidence for monotheism and the Hereafter, which are the bulwarks of the message of the Qur'ān.

The Makkan disbelievers were unable to perceive that Allah alone is the Creator, Master, and Ruler of this universe and that all human beings are His servants. They failed to see that there is no god other than Him and that the Resurrection is bound to happen. They could not reconcile themselves to the truth that God had appointed Muḥammad (peace be upon him) as His Messenger and had sent down the Qur'ān to him.

On the basis of all that the Makkan disbelievers could and could not see, the oath is taken for vindicating the above truths.

25. The true purpose of the statement is to stress that the Prophet (peace be upon him) had no authority whatsoever to alter the revelation. If he did so, he would be liable to God's severe chastisement. The tone and tenor of the statement brings to mind how a king might react on learning that his official had forged a document and had ascribed it to him. It should not be surprising if such persons are subjected to a grievous punishment such as a beheading. Some people put forward an altogether false assertion on the basis of this verse. They claim that if anyone declared that he was a Prophet and his life-vein was not then immediately severed, it would prove that his claim was true. The fact, however, is that what is said in this verse pertains to Prophets and not to false claimants of prophethood, for as we know, there have been claimants even to Godhead who lived long years despite the absolute falsity of their claims. Their longevity was no proof that their claim to Godhead was true. (For further details see *Towards Understanding the Qur'ān*, vol. IV, *Sūrah Yūnus* 10: n. 23, pp. 21–24.)

(48) Surely it is a Good Counsel[26] for the God-fearing. (49) We certainly know that some among you will give the lie to it, (50) and surely it will be a cause of regret for the unbelievers.[27] (51) Certainly it is a Truth of absolute certainty. (52) So glorify the name of your Lord Most Great.

وَإِنَّهُۥ لَتَذْكِرَةٌ لِّلْمُتَّقِينَ ﴿٤٨﴾ وَإِنَّا لَنَعْلَمُ
أَنَّ مِنكُم مُّكَذِّبِينَ ﴿٤٩﴾ وَإِنَّهُۥ لَحَسْرَةٌ عَلَى
ٱلْكَـٰفِرِينَ ﴿٥٠﴾ وَإِنَّهُۥ لَحَقُّ ٱلْيَقِينِ ﴿٥١﴾
فَسَبِّحْ بِٱسْمِ رَبِّكَ ٱلْعَظِيمِ ﴿٥٢﴾

26. The Qur'ān is good counsel for those who are keen on avoiding the dire consequence of following the wrong path. (For details see *Towards Understanding the Qur'ān*, vol. I, *Sūrah al-Baqarah* 2: n. 3.)

27. The disbelievers will eventually regret their rejection of the Qur'ān.

Sūrah 70

Al-Maʿārij

(The Ascending Steps)

(Makkan Period)

Title

Its title is taken from the word *ma'ārij* which occurs in verse 3 of this *Sūrah*.

Period of Revelation

In light of its contents, it seems that it must have been sent down in the same period in which *Sūrah al-Ḥāqqah* was revealed.

Subject Matter and Themes

This *Sūrah* admonishes and delivers a note of warning to those disbelievers who used to mock the tidings about the Resurrection, the Hereafter, Paradise, and Hell. They used to challenge the Prophet (peace be upon him) to expedite the chastisement of the Resurrection, if he was true, and if they deserved to be consigned to Hellfire. The whole *Sūrah* constitutes a response to their above challenge.

At the outset, it is affirmed that as the disbelievers seek the divine punishment to be expedited, they are destined to undergo it. Once it overwhelms them, no one will be able to protect them from it. However, it will strike them only at its appointed time. It might take some time, but they are bound to be recompensed for their disbelief. The Prophet (peace be upon him) is advised to have patience and bear with their mocking. The divine chastisement is imminent and at hand, though they regard it as a far off, remote happening.

The disbelievers are told that the Resurrection, which they take as the butt of their mockery, is something formidable and horrendous. The sinners will undergo a real ordeal then. Exasperated, they will be more than willing to offer their wives, children and kith, and kin as ransom in order to escape divine punishment. However, nothing will help them in averting their recompense.

Mankind is clearly told that on the Day of Judgement, everyone's fate will be decided while taking into account their belief, conduct, and record of deeds. Those who disregarded the truth in this world, amassed a huge amount of wealth, and withheld it from those in need will deserve Hellfire. In contrast, those who feared the chastisement of God, firmly believed in the Afterlife, regularly offered prayers, discharged the rights of the poor and needy out of their wealth, shunned immoral and evil deeds, did not betray trusts, kept their word, and testified to the truth will get an honourable place in Paradise.

Finally, the Makkan disbelievers who thronged to mock at the Prophet (peace be upon him) are warned that if they do not give up, God will replace them with other people. The Prophet (peace be upon him) is advised not to bother about their ridiculing him. If they are determined to face disgrace in the Hereafter, he should allow them to indulge in their vain pursuits. Soon will they confront their abhorrent end.

In the name of Allah, the Most Merciful, the Most Compassionate.

بِسۡمِ ٱللَّهِ ٱلرَّحۡمَٰنِ ٱلرَّحِيمِ

(1) A beseecher besought the visitation of chastisement,[1] (2) (a chastisement meant) for the unbelievers, one which none can avert; (3) a chastisement from Allah, the Lord of the ascending steps,[2] ▶

سَأَلَ سَآئِلُۢ بِعَذَابٖ وَاقِعٖ ١ لِّلۡكَٰفِرِينَ
لَيۡسَ لَهُۥ دَافِعٞ ٢ مِّنَ ٱللَّهِ ذِي ٱلۡمَعَارِجِ ٣

1. As to the opening words of the *Sūrah, sa'ala sā'il*, some commentators of the Qur'ān take these in the sense of asking a question. For them, the thrust of the verse is that someone asked the question about the promised divine punishment, as to who it will befall. To this, God replies that His chastisement will befall the disbelievers. However, most of the commentators construe the question in the sense of the disbelievers' throwing a challenge about divine punishment. Nasā'ī and other *ḥadīth* scholars have cited the following report narrated by 'Abdullāh ibn 'Abbās. Ḥākim bears out the authenticity of this report. Naḍr ibn Ḥārith Kaladah had demanded: "O God! If this indeed be the Truth from You, then rain down stones upon us from heavens, or bring upon us a painful chastisement." (*Sūrah al-Anfāl* 8: 32) [*Tafsīr* of al-Ṭabarī, 11, 144–145 and *Tafsīr* of Ibn Kathīr, 4, 48] At several other places, the Qur'ān has recounted this challenge thrown by the Makkan disbelievers, that they asked the Prophet (peace be upon him) to bring upon them the chastisement which he used to warn them of (For further details see *Sūrah Yūnus* 10: 46–48; *Sūrah al-Anbiyā'* 21: 36–41; *Sūrah al-Naml* 27: 67–72; *Sūrah Saba'* 34: 26–30; *Sūrah Yā Sīn* 36: 45–52 and *Sūrah al-Mulk* 67: 24–27).

2. *Ma'ārij* is the plural of *mi'rāj* which means the ascending steps or a staircase. That Allah is the Lord of the ascending steps underscores His exalted glory, for even the angels have to ascend considerably to gain access to Him, a point elaborated in verse 4 of this *Sūrah*.

(4) by which the angels and the Spirit[3] ascend to Him[4] in one Day the duration of which is fifty thousand years.[5] ▶

تَعْرُجُ ٱلْمَلَـٰٓئِكَةُ وَٱلرُّوحُ إِلَيْهِ فِى يَوْمٍ كَانَ مِقْدَارُهُۥ خَمْسِينَ أَلْفَ سَنَةٍ ﴿٤﴾

---

3. The word *rūḥ* (the spirit) denotes here Gabriel who is mentioned independently from the angels on account of his high position. Other Qur'ānic descriptions of Gabriel are as follows: "Indeed this is a revelation from the Lord of the universe which the truthful spirit has carried down to your heart." (*Sūrah al-Shu'arā'* 26: 192–194), and "Say: 'Whoever is an enemy to Gabriel (should know that) he revealed this (Qur'ān) to your heart by Allah's leave.'" (*Sūrah al-Baqarah* 2: 97). On studying the above, it is clear that the spirit here stands for the archangel Gabriel.

4. By the nature of things, any statement about ascension to God belongs to the category of ambiguous Qur'ānic statements (*mutashābihāt)* whose meaning cannot be determined precisely. To take this particular case, it is evident that we do not fully know the reality of the angels, nor their nature of ascent to God. Nor can our minds comprehend what "the ascending steps" are like. Similarly, we cannot even imagine that God lives (literally) in a particular place, for the Supreme Being transcends all limitations of time and space.

5. Verse 47 of *Sūrah al-Ḥajj* proclaims: "They ask you to hasten the punishment. Allah shall most certainly not fail His promise; but a day with your Lord is as a thousand years of your reckoning." Likewise, it is stated in verse 5 of *Sūrah al-Sajdah*: "God governs from the Heaven to the earth and then the record (of this governance) goes up to Him in a day whose measure is a thousand years in your reckoning." But in the verse under study, in response to a disbeliever's challenging demand that God's chastisement visit them, one day of God's reckoning is stated to measure fifty thousand years. In order to grasp the two statements, it is necessary that we relinquish our own restricted scales of measurement when we speak of time with reference to God. When we speak of a hundred or even fifty years with reference to human beings, that is a fairly long time span. But when we speak of time durations with reference to God, each chunk of time consists of a thousand or fifty thousand years; and even these figures are for purposes of illustration only. Divine plans

(5) So, (O Prophet), persevere with gracious perseverance.[6] (6) Verily they think that the chastisement is far off, (7) while We think that it is near at hand.[7] ▶	فَٱصْبِرْ صَبْرًا جَمِيلًا ۝٥ إِنَّهُمْ يَرَوْنَهُۥ بَعِيدًا ۝٦ وَنَرَىٰهُ قَرِيبًا ۝٧

span over thousands of years. Some of the plans related to this universe and galaxies may extend over millions or billions of years. One of the important divine plans is the creation of the human species on the earth with a particular time duration for their existence in the world. It is not in man's knowledge when this plan commenced, how much of its duration has already been covered, and when this will come to an end, which will mark the Resurrection. Likewise, man has no clue about the date when the grand assembly will be held in which all human beings born from the beginning until the Last Day will be gathered. They will stand before God and will be called to render their account. We are aware of only that part of this divine scheme of things which are passing before our eyes or that for which we have some historical record of in the past. It is simply beyond man's sense of understanding to grasp this divine scheme of things. Nor can we fathom the numerous considerations behind this divine plan. So, those who demand that this long term plan be abruptly abandoned and its last stage be hastened, they betray their own foolishness. More absurd is their stance, that if their demand is not met, it proves the falsity of any divine plan. (For further details see *Towards Understanding the Qur'ān*, vol. VI *Sūrah al-Ḥajj* 22: nn. 92–93, pp. 48–49 and vol. VIII, *Sūrah al-Sajdah* 32: n. 9, p. 162.)

6. That is, he should exercise the kind of perseverance that befits a dignified and gracious person.

7. It is open to two meanings: (i) While the disbelievers regard the Resurrection as improbable, in God's scheme it is near at hand. (ii) Whereas people take it as a far-off distant happening, for God it is close at hand and can occur at any moment.

(8) It shall befall on a Day[8] hereon the sky will become like molten brass,[9] (9) and the mountains will become like dyed tufts of wool,[10] (10) and no bosom friend will enquire about any of his bosom friends (11) although they shall be within sight of one another.[11] The guilty one would fain ransom himself from the torment of that Day by offering his children, ▶

يَوْمَ تَكُونُ ٱلسَّمَآءُ كَٱلْمُهْلِ ﴿٨﴾ وَتَكُونُ
ٱلْجِبَالُ كَٱلْعِهْنِ ﴿٩﴾ وَلَا يَسْـَٔلُ حَمِيمٌ
حَمِيمًا ﴿١٠﴾ يُبَصَّرُونَهُمْ ۚ يَوَدُّ ٱلْمُجْرِمُ لَوْ يَفْتَدِى
مِنْ عَذَابِ يَوْمِئِذٍۭ بِبَنِيهِ ﴿١١﴾

8. Some of the commentators of the Qur'ān take this day to be the one mentioned in verse 4, of which the duration is fifty thousand years. In other words, the reference is to the Day of Resurrection. However, the *Musnad* of Imām Aḥmad (3, 175) and *Tafsīr* of Ibn Jarīr (23, 253–254) contain the following report narrated by Abū Sa'īd al-Khudrī: "As this verse was discussed with the Prophet (peace be upon him) and amazement was expressed that it would be an exceptionally long day. Upon this the Prophet (peace be upon him) said: 'By Him Who has my life in His hand, for the believers it will be quite light. It will take them only as much time as is required for offering obligatory prayer.'" Had this report been supported by an authentic chain, it would have served as the best elucidation of the verse under discussion. However, its two narrators – Darrāj and his teacher, Abū al-Haytham, are reckoned weak in the chain.

9. That is, the sky will constantly change its colour.

10. As mountains are of various hues and colours, when these will be uprooted on the Day of Resurrection, they will look like dyed tufts of wool, flying in the air.

11. Although these culprits shall be within the sight of each other and witness one another's plight in the grand assembly, each one of them

(12) and his spouse and his brother, (13) and his kinsfolk who had stood by him, (14) and all persons of the earth, if only he could thus save himself. (15) By no means! It will be the fierce flame (16) that will strip off the scalp. (17) It shall insistently summon him who turned his back and retreated, (18) and amassed wealth and covetously hoarded it.[12]

(19) Verily man is impatient by nature:[13] ▶

وَصَـٰحِبَتِهِۦ وَأَخِيهِ ﴿١٢﴾ وَفَصِيلَتِهِ ٱلَّتِى
تُـْٔوِيهِ ﴿١٣﴾ وَمَن فِى ٱلْأَرْضِ جَمِيعًا ثُمَّ
يُنجِيهِ ﴿١٤﴾ كَلَّآ ۖ إِنَّهَا لَظَىٰ ﴿١٥﴾ نَزَّاعَةً لِّلشَّوَىٰ
﴿١٦﴾ تَدْعُوا۟ مَنْ أَدْبَرَ وَتَوَلَّىٰ ﴿١٧﴾ وَجَمَعَ
فَأَوْعَىٰٓ ﴿١٨﴾ ۞ إِنَّ ٱلْإِنسَـٰنَ خُلِقَ هَلُوعًا ﴿١٩﴾

---

will be so overwhelmed with his own misery that he will not care even about his bosom friend.

12. As in verses 33–34 of *Sūrah al-Ḥāqqah,* this verse too identifies the following two factors for his terrible loss in the Hereafter: (i) his rejection of truth and his refusal to accept faith, and (ii) his worldliness and miserliness which prompted him to amass and hoard wealth, and also dissuaded him from spending his wealth on any good cause.

13. Although the verse affirms that man is impatient by nature, the Qur'ān elsewhere exempts the believers and those who follow the straight way from such misconduct. This point is elaborated further in the proceeding verse. In other words, these innate human weaknesses are alterable. If one abides by divine guidance and mends his ways, he can overcome these natural predispositions. Conversely, if he lets his base-self act in an unbridled way, he is liable to entangle with more sinful acts. (For further details see *Towards Understanding the Qur'ān*, vol. V, *Sūrah al-Anbiyā'* 21: n. 41, p. 267; *Sūrah al-Zumar* 39: nn. 23 and 28 and *Sūrah al-Shūrā* 42: n. 75.)

(20) bewailing when evil befalls him, (21) and tight-fisted when good fortune visits him, (22) except those that pray,[14] (23) and are constant in their Prayer;[15] (24) and those in whose wealth there is a known right[16] ▶

إِذَا مَسَّهُ ٱلشَّرُّ جَزُوعًا ﴿٢٠﴾ وَإِذَا مَسَّهُ ٱلْخَيْرُ مَنُوعًا ﴿٢١﴾ إِلَّا ٱلْمُصَلِّينَ ﴿٢٢﴾ ٱلَّذِينَ هُمْ عَلَىٰ صَلَاتِهِمْ دَآئِمُونَ ﴿٢٣﴾ وَٱلَّذِينَ فِىٓ أَمْوَٰلِهِمْ حَقٌّ مَّعْلُومٌ ﴿٢٤﴾

14. One's offering prayer underscores his conviction in God, His Messenger, His Book, and his striving to act in accordance with his faith.

15. No laziness, laxity, preoccupation, or interest stops them from offering prayer punctually. When it is time for prayer, they abandon their preoccupations and promptly stand before God to worship Him. That "they are constant in prayer" is interpreted by 'Uqbah ibn 'Āmir in the sense that they offer prayers with full poise and total devotion. While performing prayers, they are not after fulfilling their obligation half-heartedly or in a hurry. Nor are they distracted by irrelevant things. Their condition during prayer is akin to the Arabic idiom of "still waters".

16. Verse 19 of *Sūrah al-Dhāriyāt* affirms: "In their wealth there is a rightful share for him who would ask and for the destitute." The present verses declare: "In their wealth there is a known right for those who ask and those who are dispossessed." Some construe "the known right" (*ḥaqqun ma'lūm*) as obligatory *Zakāh* whose *niṣāb* and rate have been fixed.

However, this view is unacceptable, because *Sūrah al-Ma'ārij* was revealed, according to the consensus view, in Makkah, whereas *Zakāh* as a religious duty, with its fixed quantum and rate, was promulgated in Madīnah. "The known right" therefore stands for a specific share they have fixed for the poor out of their wealth, and pay it as a right which they owe to the poor. This is the stance of 'Abdullāh ibn 'Abbās, 'Abdullāh ibn 'Umar, Mujāhid, Sha'bī and Ibrāhīm al-Nakha'ī.

'As to "those who ask" (*sā'il*), the reference is not to the professional beggars. Rather, it denotes a genuinely needy person who asks for help. As to "those who are dispossessed" (*maḥrūm*), the reference is to the unemployed, or those who struggle to earn a living but cannot meet their ends, or those

(25) for those that ask and those that are dispossessed, (26) those who firmly believe in the Day of Recompense,[17] (27) and fear the chastisement of their Lord[18] – (28) surely the chastisement of their Lord is a thing none can feel secure from – (29) and those who guard their private parts,[19] (30) except in regard to their spouses and those whom their right hands possess, for in regard to them they are not reproachable, ▶

لِّلسَّآئِلِ وَٱلْمَحْرُومِ ﴿٢٥﴾ وَٱلَّذِينَ يُصَدِّقُونَ
بِيَوْمِ ٱلدِّينِ ﴿٢٦﴾ وَٱلَّذِينَ هُم مِّنْ عَذَابِ رَبِّهِم
مُّشْفِقُونَ ﴿٢٧﴾ إِنَّ عَذَابَ رَبِّهِمْ غَيْرُ مَأْمُونٍ
﴿٢٨﴾ وَٱلَّذِينَ هُمْ لِفُرُوجِهِمْ حَـٰفِظُونَ ﴿٢٩﴾
إِلَّا عَلَىٰٓ أَزْوَٰجِهِمْ أَوْ مَا مَلَكَتْ
أَيْمَـٰنُهُمْ فَإِنَّهُمْ غَيْرُ مَلُومِينَ ﴿٣٠﴾

---

who are physically disabled because of a mishap or calamity and so are unable to earn anything. Once a God-conscious person learns about their condition, he does not wait for them to approach him for help. Rather, he helps them of his own volition. (For detail see *Sūrah al-Dhāriyāt* 51: n. 17.)

17. They do not regard themselves totally independent and unaccountable for all that they do in this life. On the contrary, they are always conscious of their answerability to God on the Day of Judgement.

18. They are not like the disbelievers who indulge in all sorts of sins, crimes, and wrongdoing without any fear of God. Rather, despite conforming to the code in morality and deed, they always fear God, apprehending that their shortcomings may exceed their good deeds in God's court, incurring divine punishment on them. (For details see *Towards Understanding the Qur'ān*, vol. VI, *Sūrah al-Mu'minūn* 23, n. 54, pp. 108–109; *Sūrah al-Dhāriyāt* 51: n. 19.)

19. That "they guard their private parts" signifies their shunning sex outside of marriage, indecency, and nudity. (For details see *Towards Understanding the Qur'ān*, vol. VI, *Sūrah al-Mu'minūn* 23: n. 6, p. 81;

(31) but any who seeks to go beyond that, it is indeed they who are the transgressors,[20] (32) and those who fulfil their trusts and their covenants,[21] (33) and those who are upright in their testimonies;[22] (34) and who take due care of their Prayer:[23] ▶	فَمَنِ ٱبْتَغَىٰ وَرَآءَ ذَٰلِكَ فَأُو۟لَـٰٓئِكَ هُمُ ٱلْعَادُونَ ﴿٣١﴾ وَٱلَّذِينَ هُمْ لِأَمَـٰنَـٰتِهِمْ وَعَهْدِهِمْ رَٰعُونَ ﴿٣٢﴾ وَٱلَّذِينَ هُم بِشَهَـٰدَٰتِهِمْ قَآئِمُونَ ﴿٣٣﴾ وَٱلَّذِينَ هُمْ عَلَىٰ صَلَاتِهِمْ يُحَافِظُونَ ﴿٣٤﴾

Sūrah al-Nūr 24: nn. 30 and 32, pp. 226 and 228–229 and vol. IX, *Sūrah al-Aḥzāb* 33: n. 62, p. 59.)

20. For details see *Towards Understanding the Qur'ān*, vol. VI, *Sūrah al-Mu'minūn* 23: n. 7, pp. 81–85.

21. "Trust" includes both kinds of trusts which God and fellow human beings repose in somebody. Likewise, "covenants" embrace both the types of pledges which one makes to God and to fellow human beings. Fulfilling these trusts and covenants is an essential trait of a believer. Anas (may Allah be pleased with him) relates in a *ḥadīth* that "whenever the Prophet (peace be upon him) addressed us, he used to remind us: 'Beware! One who does not keep his trust has no faith and one who does not fulfil his pledges has no religion.'" (Bayhaqī *Fī Shu'ab al-Īmān*)

22. They do not conceal or tamper with testimony.

23. This highlights the importance of prayer. The account of a believer with excellent conduct, who is declared worthy of Paradise, begins and ends with their outstanding trait of offering prayers. Their first and foremost characteristic is their devotion to prayer. Their regularity in offering prayer and their keenness on performing it at its appointed time are their other striking features. As to "their taking due care of their prayer", it includes the following: performing it at its prescribed time, ensuring the cleanliness of the body and clothes before commencing the prayer, performing *wuḍū'* (ablution) and washing the body parts thoroughly during ablution, paying due attention to all the components,

(35) all these shall live honourably in the Gardens.

(36) But what is the matter with the unbelievers who are hurrying towards you[24] (37) in crowds, both on the right and on the left? (38) Does everyone of them wish to enter the Garden of Bliss?[25] (39) By no means! They know that which We have created them from.[26] ▶

أُوْلَٰٓئِكَ فِي جَنَّٰتٖ مُّكۡرَمُونَ ٣٥ فَمَالِ
ٱلَّذِينَ كَفَرُواْ قِبَلَكَ مُهۡطِعِينَ ٣٦ عَنِ
ٱلۡيَمِينِ وَعَنِ ٱلشِّمَالِ عِزِينَ ٣٧ أَيَطۡمَعُ
كُلُّ ٱمۡرِيٕٖ مِّنۡهُمۡ أَن يُدۡخَلَ جَنَّةَ نَعِيمٖ ٣٨
كَلَّآۖ إِنَّا خَلَقۡنَٰهُم مِّمَّا يَعۡلَمُونَ ٣٩

both obligatory and desirable, observing all the norms related to prayer, and not bringing their prayers to a nought by disobeying God.

24. This refers to those disbelievers who, whenever they heard the Prophet (peace be upon him) reciting the Qur'ān or saw him inviting people to embrace his teachings, rushed towards him, subjecting him to ridicule and banter.

25. God's Paradise is exclusively for such servants of God whose traits are described in the above Qur'ānic passage. Those who are not even willing to listen to the call to truth and who exert themselves in stifling this call cannot enter Paradise. God has not made Paradise for such people. For a better understanding of these verses, they should be studied together with verses 34–41 of *Sūrah al-Qalam*, which contain a rejoinder to the Makkan disbelievers. The absurd notion of theirs is refuted, that even if there is any Life after Death, they will enjoy it in the Hereafter, and that those who believe in the Prophet (peace be upon him) will have a miserable life, similar to what they had been experiencing in Makkah.

26. This verse is open to two meanings. On studying it, in conjunction with the preceding verses, it may mean that it is true that all men are alike in that all of them have been created from the same substance. Were this to be taken as the criterion for admission to Paradise, everyone, be they pious or evil, just or unjust, criminals or innocent, should enter Paradise. However, common sense tells us that one's good conduct alone, and

(40) I swear[27] by the Lord of the easts and the wests[28] that We have the power (41) to replace them by others who would be better than they; and We shall certainly not be overpowered.[29] ▶

فَلَآ أُقۡسِمُ بِرَبِّ ٱلۡمَشَٰرِقِ وَٱلۡمَغَٰرِبِ إِنَّا لَقَٰدِرُونَ ۝٤٠ عَلَىٰٓ أَن نُّبَدِّلَ خَيۡرًا مِّنۡهُمۡ وَمَا نَحۡنُ بِمَسۡبُوقِينَ ۝٤١

---

nothing else, will decide whether he is eligible or not eligible for entering Paradise. On reading this verse, together with the subsequent verses, it may be taken as a warning to the disbelievers who regard themselves immune from the divine punishment and who laugh at the Prophet (peace be upon him) when he warns them about God's chastisement. Indeed, God is capable of punishing the disbelievers whenever He wills. He may resurrect them at His will at any time. They recognise that God has created them out of a small drop of sperm and allowed them to mature into adulthood with the power of moving around. Had they reflected on how they have been created, they would not have suffered from the delusion that they can ever escape God's grip or that He has no power to create them again.

27. i.e., what the disbelievers think is not the truth.

28. God has taken an oath here with reference to His own being. The words "easts" and "wests" are used in the plural with good reason. Each day of the year, the angle of the rising and setting of the sun varies. Furthermore, the angles at which it rises and sets in different parts of the earth also vary. In this sense, there is not one but many easts; there is not one but many wests. It is worth noting that in verse 28 of *Sūrah al-Shua'arā'* and verse 19 of *Sūrah al-Muzzammil*, God is spoken of as the Lord of the east and the west. For, like north and south, there are two opposing directions of east and west. In another sense, however, there are two easts and two wests. For as the sun sets in one hemisphere of the Earth, it rises in the other. Accordingly, in verse 17 of *Sūrah al-Raḥmān*, God is designated as the Lord of the two easts and two wests. (For further details see *Sūrah al-Raḥmān* 55: n. 17.)

29. This is the truth affirmed with reference to the oath invoking God as the Lord of the easts and the wests, He therefore exercises His absolute

(42) So leave them to engage in vain talk and to amuse themselves until they come face to face with the Day which they are promised, (43) the Day on which they will hastily come forth from their graves, as though they were hurrying on to the altars of their deities.[30] (44) Their eyes will be downcast and disgrace will overwhelm them. Such is the Day that they were promised.

فَذَرْهُمْ يَخُوضُوا۟ وَيَلْعَبُوا۟ حَتَّىٰ يُلَـٰقُوا۟
يَوْمَهُمُ ٱلَّذِى يُوعَدُونَ ﴿٤٢﴾ يَوْمَ يَخْرُجُونَ
مِنَ ٱلْأَجْدَاثِ سِرَاعًا كَأَنَّهُمْ إِلَىٰ نُصُبٍ
يُوفِضُونَ ﴿٤٣﴾ خَـٰشِعَةً أَبْصَـٰرُهُمْ تَرْهَقُهُمْ
ذِلَّةٌ ۚ ذَٰلِكَ ٱلْيَوْمُ ٱلَّذِى كَانُوا۟ يُوعَدُونَ ﴿٤٤﴾

---

control over the earth. It is not possible at all for man to flee from His grip. He may destroy man at His will and may replace mankind with other beings who would be better than they are.

30. The commentators of the Qur'ān have given various explanations for the Qur'ānic expression *nuṣub*. Some take it to mean deities in the sense that the disbelievers will rush to the designated place on the Day of Judgement, the way they rush today to the altars of their deities. Others however, take it as a mark signifying the end point of a race. All those racing try their best to reach that mark first.

Sūrah 71

Nūḥ

(Noah)

(Makkan Period)

Title

Nūḥ (Noah) is both the title and subject matter of this *Sūrah* for the entire *Sūrah* relates the account of the Prophet Noah (peace be upon him).

Period of Revelation

It is one of the early *Sūrahs* revealed in Makkah. However, the internal evidence of its contents indicate that it was sent down at a time when the Makkan disbelievers' opposition to the Prophet's mission had turned quite intense and bitter.

Subject Matter and Themes

The account of the Prophet Noah (peace be upon him) is not related here only for the sake of recounting his story. Rather, it aims at alerting the Makkan disbelievers that, if they treat the Prophet Muḥammad (peace be upon him) in the same manner as the Prophet Noah's community had behaved with him, and if they do not mend their ways, they will meet the same end which befell the Prophet Noah's community. Although the above point is not explicitly made in this *Sūrah*, it is implicit, especially in its circumstantial setting.

The opening verse spells out the assignment God had entrusted to the Prophet Noah (peace be upon him) when he was appointed to this august office.

Verses 2–4 recount briefly how he commenced his mission and the main features of his call. Verses 5–20 recapture the Prophet Noah's narrative, detailing the hardships he encountered during the long course of his preaching. Notwithstanding his best efforts to reform his community, he narrates how he encountered only their stiff and obstinate opposition.

The Prophet Noah's concluding submission features in verses 21–24. He pleads with God that his community has conclusively rejected his call and is under the spell of their chiefs who have manipulated a tremendous plot of deceit and misguidance. Therefore, it is time that they should be deprived of any grace or opportunity to attain divine guidance. This was not any show of impatience by the Prophet Noah (peace be upon him), but an expression of disappointment in that for centuries he had invited them to embrace the truth with great patience and received nothing but humiliating responses. After his utter frustration, he arrived at the conclusion that they were in no way willing to accept the truth. His assessment was fully in accord with divine dispensation. Verse 25 informs that God's chastisement descended on his community as punishment for their misdeeds.

The concluding verses of the Sūrah contain the Prophet Noah's supplication which he had made at the time the divine chastisement befell his community. He is seen seeking forgiveness for himself and all the believers. However, he pleads with God not to spare a single disbeliever, for they were completely devoid of any good. If any of them survived, he will beget none but utter disbelievers and sinners.

While studying this *Sūrah,* it will be rewarding to study also the Prophet Noah's account featuring at other places in the Qur'ān, as for example, in verses 59–64 of *Sūrah al-A'rāf*, 71–73 of *Sūrah Yūnus*, 25–49 of *Sūrah Hūd*, 23–31 of *Sūrah al-Mu'minūn*, 15–122 of *Sūrah Shu'arā'*, 14–15 of *Sūrah al-'Ankabūt*, 75–82 of *Sūrah al-Ṣāffāt* and 9–16 of *Sūrah al-Qamar*.

In the name of Allah, the Most Merciful, the Most Compassionate.

(1) We sent Noah to his people (and directed him): "Warn your people before a grievous chastisement comes upon them."[1] (2) Noah said: "My people, I have certainly been sent as a clear warner to you, (3) that you serve Allah and fear Him, and follow me;[2] (4) He will forgive your sins[3] and will grant you respite until an appointed ▶

بِسْمِ ٱللَّهِ ٱلرَّحْمَٰنِ ٱلرَّحِيمِ

إِنَّآ أَرْسَلْنَا نُوحًا إِلَىٰ قَوْمِهِۦٓ أَنْ أَنذِرْ قَوْمَكَ
مِن قَبْلِ أَن يَأْتِيَهُمْ عَذَابٌ أَلِيمٌ ۝١ قَالَ
يَٰقَوْمِ إِنِّى لَكُمْ نَذِيرٌ مُّبِينٌ ۝٢ أَنِ ٱعْبُدُوا۟
ٱللَّهَ وَٱتَّقُوهُ وَأَطِيعُونِ ۝٣ يَغْفِرْ لَكُم
مِّن ذُنُوبِكُمْ وَيُؤَخِّرْكُمْ إِلَىٰٓ أَجَلٍ مُّسَمًّى ۚ

1. It was the Prophet Noah's assignment to warn his people that if they do not mend their ways, their defiance and misconduct will bring upon them divine punishment. He was also to guide them to the path which will save them from God's punishment.

2. The Prophet Noah (peace be upon him) asked his people to accept the three above-mentioned directives: to serve God, to adopt piety, and to obey His Messenger. Serving God meant abandoning all false gods, and worshipping God alone as their only Lord, obeying His commands. Inculcating piety meant avoiding all those misdeeds which incur God's displeasure and leading life in a manner befitting a pious person. As to their following the Prophet Noah (peace be upon him), it required that they should abide by his commands which he proclaimed in his capacity as God's Messenger.

3. The verse does not say that God will forgive some of their sins. It implies that if they accept the three above-mentioned directives given to them, God will overlook all the sins they have committed in the past.

term.[4] Indeed when Allah's appointed term comes, it cannot be deferred;[5] if you only knew!"[6]

(5) He[7] said: "My Lord, I called my people by night and by day, (6) but the more I called, the farther they fled.[8] (7) And every time I called them so that You might forgive them,[9] ▸

إِنَّ أَجَلَ ٱللَّهِ إِذَا جَآءَ لَا يُؤَخَّرُ لَوْ كُنتُمْ
تَعْلَمُونَ ۝٤ قَالَ رَبِّ إِنِّى دَعَوْتُ قَوْمِى
لَيْلًا وَنَهَارًا ۝٥ فَلَمْ يَزِدْهُمْ دُعَآءِىٓ
إِلَّا فِرَارًا ۝٦ وَإِنِّى كُلَّمَا دَعَوْتُهُمْ لِتَغْفِرَ لَهُمْ

4. If they follow the above three mentioned directives, then God would grant them respite to live until the time He had determined for their natural death.

5. The expression "Allah's appointed term" signifies the time determined by God to send His scourge on a people. In this context, the Qur'ān has explicitly stated on many occasions that once God resolves to strike a nation down with His scourge, that nation will not be spared the scourge even if they embrace the faith at the last minute.

6. They should realise it well that after the Prophet Noah's delivery of the divine message to them, they are enjoying a period of respite for embracing faith. Once this moment is over, there is no way they can escape God's punishment. They should therefore accept the message at the earliest and not defer it to their peril.

7. Omitting the history of a long intervening period, the *Sūrah* goes straight to the last phase of the Prophet Noah's mission and brings to the fore his entreaty to God.

8. The more he invited them to embrace faith, the farther they moved away from him.

9. The inherent message here is that they should have given up their habit of disobedience and sought God's forgiveness. This was their only way to receive their deliverance.

they thrust their fingers into their ears and wrapped up their faces with their garments[10] and obstinately clung to their attitude, and waxed very proud.[11] (8) Then I summoned them openly, (9) and preached to them in public, and also addressed them in secret. (10) I said to them: "Ask forgiveness from your Lord; surely He is Most Forgiving. (11) He will shower upon you torrents from heaven, ▶

جَعَلُوٓاْ أَصَٰبِعَهُمْ فِىٓ ءَاذَانِهِمْ وَٱسْتَغْشَوْاْ
ثِيَابَهُمْ وَأَصَرُّواْ وَٱسْتَكْبَرُواْ ٱسْتِكْبَارًا ﴿٧﴾
ثُمَّ إِنِّى دَعَوْتُهُمْ جِهَارًا ﴿٨﴾ ثُمَّ إِنِّىٓ أَعْلَنتُ
لَهُمْ وَأَسْرَرْتُ لَهُمْ إِسْرَارًا ﴿٩﴾ فَقُلْتُ
ٱسْتَغْفِرُواْ رَبَّكُمْ إِنَّهُۥ كَانَ غَفَّارًا ﴿١٠﴾
يُرْسِلِ ٱلسَّمَآءَ عَلَيْكُم مِّدْرَارًا ﴿١١﴾

10. The reason that these disbelievers "wrapped up their faces with their garments" could be that owing to their disgust at his preaching, they could not even stomach looking at him and so kept their faces, including their eyes covered. Another reason for doing so could have been to prevent the Prophet Noah (peace be upon him) from recognising and communicating his teachings to them. The same was the attitude of the Makkan disbelievers towards the blessed Prophet (peace be upon him) in those days. Verse 5 of *Sūrah Hūd* recounts their attitude as follows: "Lo! They turn away their chests in order to conceal themselves from him. Surely when they cover themselves up with their garments, God still knows well what they cover and what they reveal. Indeed, He even knows the secrets hidden in the breasts of people." (For details see *Towards Understanding the Qur'ān*, vol. IV, *Sūrah Hūd* 11: nn. 5–6, pp. 81–82.)

11. Their arrogance consisted in their refusal to embrace the truth. Moreover, they considered it beneath their dignity to accept the advice of God's Messenger. In doing so, they behaved like an arrogant person who rudely responds to his well-wisher's counsel.

(12) and will provide you with wealth and children, and will bestow upon you gardens and rivers.[12] ▶	وَيُمْدِدْكُم بِأَمْوَٰلٍ وَبَنِينَ وَيَجْعَل لَّكُمْ جَنَّٰتٍ وَيَجْعَل لَّكُمْ أَنْهَٰرًا ﴿١٢﴾

12. This truth is affirmed at several places in the Qur'ān, that rebellion to God lands people into misery not only in the Hereafter but also in the life of this world. By the same token, if a community, far from betraying disobedience, embraces faith, piety, and obedience to God's commands, it benefits them not only in the Hereafter, but in this life too they are endowed with numerous bounties. It is recounted in verse 124 of *Sūrah Ṭā Hā*: "Whosoever turns away from My admonition shall have a straitened life. We shall raise him blind on the Day of Resurrection." Of similar thrust is verse 66 of *Sūrah al-Mā'idah*: "Had the People of the Book observed the Torah and the Gospel and all that had been revealed to them from their Lord, sustenance would have been showered over them from above and would have risen from beneath their feet." Verse 96 of *Sūrah al-A'rāf* affirms the same: "Had the people of those towns believed and been God-fearing, We would have certainly opened up to them blessings from the heavens and the earth." The Prophet Hūd (peace be upon him) told his people: "My people! Ask your Lord for forgiveness and turn to Him in repentance. He will shower abundant rains upon you from the heavens and will add strength to your strength." (*Sūrah Hūd* 11: 52) The Makkans were given the same advice by the Prophet (peace be upon him): "You may seek forgiveness of your Lord and turn to Him in repentance whereupon He will grant you a fair enjoyment of life until an appointed term." (*Sūrah Hūd* 11: 3) The Prophet (peace be upon him) is on record advising the Quraysh: "If you believe in this true word, you will turn into the rulers of the Arabs and non-Arabs." (For details see *Towards Understanding the Qur'ān*, vol. II, *Sūrah al-Mā'idah* 5: n. 96, p. 177; vol. IV, *Sūrah Hūd* 11: nn. 3 and 57, pp. 77, 80 and 109; vol. V, *Sūrah Ṭā Hā* 20: n. 105, p. 237 and Introduction to *Sūrah Ṣād*.)

While acting on the above Qur'ānic directive, once during a famine, 'Umar went out to invoke Allah for sending rain but he sought only Allah's forgiveness. When someone queried as to why he did not make a specific supplication for rain, he replied: "I have knocked at the doors in the heavens wherefrom the rain is sent down." He then recited these verses of *Sūrah Nūḥ* which are presently under discussion. (*Tafsīr* of Ibn Jarīr al-Ṭabarī, 23, 293–294 and *Tafsīr* of Ibn Kathīr, 8, 232–233) Likewise,

(13) What is amiss with you that you do not look forward to the majesty of Allah[13] (14) when He has created you in stages?[14] (15) Do you not see how Allah has created seven heavens, one upon the other, ▸

مَّا لَكُمْ لَا تَرْجُونَ لِلَّهِ وَقَارًا ﴿١٣﴾ وَقَدْ خَلَقَكُمْ أَطْوَارًا ﴿١٤﴾ أَلَمْ تَرَوْا۟ كَيْفَ خَلَقَ ٱللَّهُ سَبْعَ سَمَـٰوَٰتٍ طِبَاقًا ﴿١٥﴾

---

when someone complained about drought to Ḥasan al-Baṣrī, he directed him to seek forgiveness from Allah. Another person present there related to him his problem of low income, a third one about his childlessness and a fourth one about the low yield of his fields. To each one of them he advised the same – seeking Allah's forgiveness. When people asked him why he gave the same reply to everyone for different complaints, he recited these verses of *Sūrah Nūḥ* in order to vindicate his stance. (*Kashshāf*, 6, 215)

13. People are generally cognisant that it is dangerous to say or do anything that is offensive to the majestic sensibilities of even the petty chiefs and nobles of this world, but they are hardly concerned with showing deference to God's majesty. In fact, they do a great deal that may offend Him – they rebel against Him, associate others with Him in His divinity, disobey His commands – and yet they are not at all afraid of His wrath that will befall them as a result of their misconduct.

14. God has brought man to the present stage of his existence through different phases of the creation process. Initially, he existed in the form of separate reproductive material in the bodies of his parents. Through divine command, there was the union of these reproductive materials, which led to conception. For nine months, the foetus went through various stages of growth. Finally, he received the human form and shape. He was endowed with all the faculties needed for leading life in the world. Then as a baby he was delivered by his mother. The process of growth continued as the baby passed through from one stage to another. He eventually grew into an adult and later an old man. All along, man is totally under God's control. Had He willed, he would not have been conceived in the first place. Or he would have been born as a blind, deaf, dumb, disabled or mentally deficient person. Or it could be a still birth. Even after birth,

وَجَعَلَ ٱلْقَمَرَ فِيهِنَّ نُورًا وَجَعَلَ ٱلشَّمْسَ
سِرَاجًا ﴿١٦﴾ وَٱللَّهُ أَنۢبَتَكُم مِّنَ ٱلْأَرْضِ
نَبَاتًا ﴿١٧﴾ ثُمَّ يُعِيدُكُمْ فِيهَا وَيُخْرِجُكُمْ
إِخْرَاجًا ﴿١٨﴾ وَٱللَّهُ جَعَلَ لَكُمُ ٱلْأَرْضَ
بِسَاطًا ﴿١٩﴾ لِّتَسْلُكُوا۟ مِنْهَا سُبُلًا فِجَاجًا
﴿٢٠﴾ قَالَ نُوحٌ رَّبِّ إِنَّهُمْ عَصَوْنِى وَٱتَّبَعُوا۟
مَن لَّمْ يَزِدْهُ مَالُهُۥ وَوَلَدُهُۥٓ إِلَّا خَسَارًا ﴿٢١﴾
وَمَكَرُوا۟ مَكْرًا كُبَّارًا ﴿٢٢﴾

(16) and has placed the moon in them as a light, and the sun as a radiant lamp? (17) And Allah has caused you to grow out of the earth so wondrously,[15] (18) and He will later cause you to return to it and will then again bring you out of it. (19) Allah has made the earth a wide expanse for you (20) so that you may tread its spacious paths."

(21) Noah said: "My Lord, they did not pay heed to what I said, and followed those (nobles) whose possession of wealth and children has led them to an even greater loss. (22) They contrived a plot of great magnitude.[16] ▶

man is liable to die at any time. At God's behest, he would have lost his life in an accident. Since man is so powerless and totally at God's mercy, how could he even think of being disrespectful, ungrateful, and rebellious, and do all those with impunity? Has he thought that he will never face any punishment for such heinous activities?

15. Here a similitude is drawn between man's creation out of different elements taken from the earth, and the growth of vegetation. There was a time when there was no vegetation on earth and then God caused vegetation to appear. In like manner, there was a time when man did not exist on earth and then God planted him on it.

16. Reference is to the plots *(makr)* contrived by the chiefs to mislead the people about the Prophet Noah's mission. Some of their objections

(23) They said: 'Do not abandon your deities; do not abandon Wadd, nor Suwāʿ, nor Yaghūth, nor Yaʿūq, nor Nasr.'[17] ▶	وَقَالُوا۟ لَا تَذَرُنَّ ءَالِهَتَكُمْ وَلَا تَذَرُنَّ وَدًّا وَلَا سُوَاعًا وَلَا يَغُوثَ وَيَعُوقَ وَنَسْرًا ﴿٢٣﴾

were: "We see you as merely a human being like ourselves." (*Sūrah al-A'rāf* 7: 63 and *Sūrah Hūd* 11: 27); "Nor do we find among those who follow you except the lowliest of our folk, those who follow you without any proper reason." (*Sūrah Hūd* 11: 27); "Had Allah wanted (to send any Messenger) He would have sent down angels." (*Sūrah al-Mu'minūn* 23: 24); Had he been a Messenger, he should have possessed God's treasures or access to the Unseen or would have been like an angel, free from all the human wants (*Sūrah Hūd* 11: 31); "He has nothing in him to suggest that he is any better than us." (*Sūrah Hūd* 11: 27); "He only desires to have superiority over people." (*Sūrah al-Mu'minūn* 23: 24); "He is a person who has been seized with a little madness." (*Sūrah al-Mu'minūn* 23: 25) Almost the same allegations were hurled by the Quraysh chiefs against the Prophet Muḥammad (peace be upon him) to mislead people.

17. Here only some deities of the Prophet Noah's people are mentioned whom the people of Arabia later on started worshipping. These and their shrines were scattered across the expanse of Arabia at the time of the advent of Islam. It is not unlikely that the survivors of the Flood may have related to their subsequent generations some account of these deities. When ignorance once again penetrated among their children, they made statues of the same idol and started worshipping those deities again.

Wadd was the deity of Banī Kalb ibn Wabrah, a branch of the Quḍā'ah tribe. They had erected its temple at Dūmat al-Jandal. In the ancient Arabian scrolls, it is mentioned as Waddam Abam. According to Kalbī, this idol had the form of an erroneous male figure. Members of the Quraysh tribe looked upon it as a deity and called it Wudd. It is not therefore surprising that one of the Arabs in history was named 'Abd Wudd.

Suwā' was the deity of the Ḥudhayl tribe and the idol was a female figure. Its temple was at Ruhāṭ, a place in the vicinity of Yanbū'.

Yaghūth was the deity of the An'um and Madhjiḥ tribes. The latter had installed its idol in a temple at Jurash, a town midway between Yemen

(24) They have misled many. So do not enable these evil-doers to increase in anything except straying (from the Right Way)."[18]

(25) And so they were drowned on account of their sins, and then cast into the Fire,[19] and did not ▶

وَقَدْ أَضَلُّوا۟ كَثِيرًا ۖ وَلَا تَزِدِ ٱلظَّـٰلِمِينَ
إِلَّا ضَلَـٰلًا ﴿٢٤﴾ مِّمَّا خَطِيٓـَٔـٰتِهِمْ أُغْرِقُوا۟
فَأُدْخِلُوا۟ نَارًا فَلَمْ

---

and Hijaz. It bore the form of a lion. From this, some of the Quraysh bore the name, 'Abd Yaghūth.

Ya'ūq was the deity of Khaywān, a branch of the Ḥamdān tribe in Yemen. It had the form of a horse.

Nasr was the deity of Āl-Dhū al-Kulā', a branch of the Humayr tribe. Its temple was located in Balkha', and bore the form of a vulture. In the ancient scrolls of Saba', it is referred to as Nasūr. This temple was known as Bayt-e-Nasūr and its devotees were called the people of Nasūr. Many temples of ancient Arabia had the image of a vulture engraved on their doors.

18. As already explained in the introduction to this *Sūrah,* the Prophet Noah (peace be upon him) did not invoke this curse simply out of impatience on his part. He did so after he had tried extremely hard to reform his people by constantly preaching his message for centuries and only then reached a point of utter desperation. In almost identical circumstances, the Prophet Moses (peace be upon him) had cursed the Pharaoh and his people thus: "Our Lord! Obliterate their riches and harden their hearts that they may not believe until they observe the painful chastisement." To this Allah responded: "The prayer of the two of you is accepted." (*Sūrah Yūnus* 10: 88–89) This curse was in accord with the divine plan, as in the case of the Prophet Noah (peace be upon him). The Qur'ān states: "It was revealed to Noah that no more of your people other than those who already believe, will ever come to believe. So, do not grieve over their deeds." (*Sūrah Hūd* 11: 36)

19. Not only were these culprits drowned, their souls were cast into the Fire immediately after their death. Exactly the same punishment

find any other than Allah, to come forth to their help.[20] (26) Noah said: "My Lord, do not leave out of these unbelievers even a single dweller on earth, (27) for certainly if You should leave them (alive), they will mislead Your servants, and will beget none but sinners and utter unbelievers. (28) My Lord, forgive me and my parents, and whoever enters my house as a believer, and forgive all believers, both men and women, and do not increase the wrong-doers in anything except perdition."

يَجِدُوا۟ لَهُم مِّن دُونِ ٱللَّهِ أَنصَارًا ﴿٢٥﴾ وَقَالَ
نُوحٌ رَّبِّ لَا تَذَرْ عَلَى ٱلْأَرْضِ مِنَ
ٱلْكَٰفِرِينَ دَيَّارًا ﴿٢٦﴾ إِنَّكَ إِن تَذَرْهُمْ
يُضِلُّوا۟ عِبَادَكَ وَلَا يَلِدُوٓا۟ إِلَّا فَاجِرًا كَفَّارًا
﴿٢٧﴾ رَّبِّ ٱغْفِرْ لِى وَلِوَٰلِدَىَّ وَلِمَن دَخَلَ
بَيْتِىَ مُؤْمِنًا وَلِلْمُؤْمِنِينَ وَٱلْمُؤْمِنَٰتِ
وَلَا تَزِدِ ٱلظَّٰلِمِينَ إِلَّا تَبَارًۢا ﴿٢٨﴾

---

was meted out to the Pharaoh and his people, as is mentioned in verses 45–46 of *Sūrah al-Mu'min* (for details see *Sūrah al-Mu'min* 40: n. 63). This verse affirms the existence of *barzakh* (the intermediary stage between this world and the Resurrection) and punishment therein.

20. They did not find any of their idols, whom they took as their patrons and protectors, to come forth to their aid. It served as a warning to the Makkan disbelievers that on being afflicted with divine punishment, their idols in whom they reposed so much trust, will not be of any avail.

Sūrah 72

Al-Jinn

(The Jinn)

(Makkan Period)

Title

Al-Jinn is both the title and subject matter of this *Sūrah,* for it relates at length the episode of the *jinn* listening to the Qur'ān and preaching Islam among the members of their species on their return.

Period of Revelation

Both Bukhārī (*K. al-Tafsīr, Sūrah al-Jinn*) and Muslim (*K. al- Ṣalāt, Bāb al-Jahr bi al-Qirā'ah*) have cited this report on the authority of 'Abdullāh ibn 'Abbās that once, while the Prophet (peace be upon him) was on his way to the 'Ukāẓ market along with some of his Companions, he led *Fajr* Prayer at Nakhlah. At that time, a group of *jinn* were passing by. They stopped on hearing the Qur'ān and listened to its recitation attentively. This incident is recounted within this *Sūrah.*

In light of the above report, most of the Qur'ān commentators take it as an event related to the Prophet's journey to Ṭā'if, which took place in the tenth year of his mission, three years before his migration to Madīnah. However, this assumption is not sound on several grounds. As to the incident involving the *jinn* listening to the Qur'ān during the Prophet's journey to Ṭā'if, it is recorded in verses 29–32 of *Sūrah al-Aḥqāf*. On studying those verses, it readily emerges that the *jinn* who had embraced the message of Islam then were already believers in the Prophet Moses (peace be upon him) and earlier Scriptures. On the contrary, verses 2–7 of this *Sūrah* indicate that these *jinn* were polytheists, who did not believe in the Resurrection and the institution of the Prophethood. Furthermore, it is on record that only Zayd ibn Ḥārithah had accompanied the Prophet (peace be upon him) during his journey to Ṭā'if. On this occasion, however, as informed by Ibn 'Abbās, he was accompanied by some of his Companions. Moreover, all the reports state that those *jinn* had listened to the Qur'ān when the Prophet (peace be upon him) had stayed at Nakhlah, on returning from Ṭā'if to Makkah. During this journey, the incident occurred when the Prophet (peace be upon him) was on his way from Makkah to 'Ukāẓ. On the basis of the above, it is safer to assume that *Sūrah al-Aḥqāf* and *Sūrah al-Jinn* describe two separate events which took place during the Prophet's two separate journeys and that these do not relate to the same incident.

As to the episode featuring in *Sūrah al-Aḥqāf*, the reports unanimously state that it happened in the tenth year of the Prophet's mission during his return journey from Ṭā'if. However, as to the date of the second episode, Ibn 'Abbās's report is silent over it. No other report provides any clue about the date when the Prophet (peace be upon him) visited 'Ukāẓ along with some of his Companions. On studying verses 8–10 of this *Sūrah* closely, however, it appears that this incident may have taken place in the early years of the Prophet's career, as these verses state that before the Prophet's advent, the *jinn* somehow got an opportunity to gather news from the heavens. However, all of a sudden they noted the entire heavenly space had been cordoned off by the angels and there was a downpour of meteorites from every side. This prevented them from finding any space to sneak or eavesdrop. As a result, they became curious to find out about the special event on earth which had occasioned such strict security.

Most probably several groups of *jinn* set out to ascertain the matter. One of these groups, on hearing the Prophet's recitation of the Qur'ān, assumed that the revelation of this new divine message had placed stringent restrictions and the gates of the heavens had been shut on them.

Nature of the Jinn

Before embarking upon the study of this *Sūrah*, it will be in order to discuss the nature of the *jinn* to avoid any misconceptions. In our times, many people suffer from the delusion that the *jinn* do not exist and that it is an outdated notion. This assumption of theirs does not rest on sound knowledge. Since they do not have any clinching argument for the non-existence of the *jinn* they cannot lay any such claim. Yet they insist, without any evidence, that nothing exists in the universe except that which is within the reach of their sense of perception. Let us not forget that man's sense of perception apprehends only an infinitesimal part of the universe like a drop in the ocean. If one insists that anything beyond the realm of the unseen is non-existent and what is existent must necessarily be perceivable betrays his own narrow outlook. Going by this flawed logic, man will have to deny not only the *jinn*, but also numerous other truths. Such a person will not believe even in the existence of God, what to say of other intangible things.

As to those Muslims who are under the influence of the above mindset, they cannot dare deny the Qur'ān, they seek to offer garbled versions of the plain, categorical Qur'ānic descriptions of the *jinn*, Iblīs, and Satan. For them, *jinn* are not some invisible creatures who enjoy their independent existence. At times, they equate them with man's animal instincts called Satan. Some others define them as uncivilised communities inhabiting forests and mountains. Some explain the above incident as the reference to some human beings who used to listen to the recitation of the Qur'ān secretly. However, the categorical and explicit Qur'ānic statements about the *jinn* do not admit any of the above flawed interpretations.

The Qur'ān repeatedly speaks of men and *jinn* as two separate creatures. The following Qur'ānic passages are instances in point:

Verses 38 of *Sūrah al-A'rāf*, 119 of *Sūrah Hūd*, 25 and 29 of *Sūrah Ḥā Mīm al-Sajdah*, 18 of *Sūrah al-Aḥqāf*, 56 of *Sūrah al-Dhāriyāt*, 6 of *Sūrah al-Nās and* the entire *Sūrah al-Raḥmān*, which leaves no room whatsoever for mistaking the *jinn* as members of the human species.

Verses 12 of *Sūrah al-A'rāf*, 26–27 of *Sūrah al-Ḥijr* and 14–15 of *Sūrah al-Raḥmān* proclaim expressly that man is created of clay whereas the *jinn* is created of fire.

Verse 27 of *Sūrah al-Ḥijr* clarifies that the *jinn* were created prior to man. This truth is reinforced by the account of the Prophet Ādam (peace be upon him) and Iblīs, which is related at seven places in the Qur'ān. It is consistently said in all the above Qur'ānic passages that Iblīs was already there when man was created. Verse 50 of *Sūrah al-Kahf* conclusively states that Iblīs was a *jinn*.

Verse 27 of *Sūrah al-A'rāf* declares that whereas the *jinn* are able to see human beings, the latter cannot see them.

Verses 16–18 of *Sūrah al-Ḥijr*, 6–10 of *Sūrah al-Ṣāffāt* and 5 of *Sūrah al-Mulk* inform that although the *jinn* may ascend to the heavens, they cannot go beyond a certain limit. If they try to ascend further or spy on what is going on in the heavens, they are stopped from proceeding any further. If they eavesdrop, meteorites pursue them. This refutes the misperception of the Arab polytheists about the *jinns'* access to the Unseen or divine dispensation. The same fallacious notion is demolished in verse 14 of *Sūrah Saba'*.

It is evident from verses 30–34 of *Sūrah al-Baqarah* and 50 of *Sūrah al-Kahf* that God has bestowed His vicegerency on man and that as a creature, man is superior to the *jinn*. It is an altogether different point that the *jinn* have been endowed with some extraordinary abilities, as one learns from verse 7 of *Sūrah al-Naml*. However, even some animals excel man in certain special abilities; this does not establish their superiority over man.

The Qur'ān informs that like man, the *jinn* have been granted free will to choose between obedience and rebellion to God and between faith and disbelief. The above is substantiated by the Qur'ānic account of Iblīs and of his description of some *jinn* embracing faith, as detailed in *Sūrah al-Aḥqāf* and *Sūrah al-Jinn*.

It is recurrently clarified in the Qur'ān that from the time of man's creation Satan had resolved to mislead man. Since then satans among the men and the *jinn* have been engaged in misdirecting humanity. They cannot compel man into sinning. However, they are quite capable of putting false notions into man's mind, of misleading him, and of presenting evil before him as something alluring and pleasant. This point is made clear from the following Qur'ānic passages: verses 117–120 of *Sūrah al-Nisā'*, 11–17 of *Sūrah al-A'rāf*, 22 of *Sūrah Ibrāhīm*, 30–42 of *Sūrah al-Ḥijr*, 98–100 of *Sūrah al-Naḥl* and 61–65 of *Sūrah Banī Isrā'īl*.

The Qur'ān states that in the age of *Jāhiliyyah*, the Arab polytheists regarded the *jinn* as God's partners, worshipped them, and ascribed divinity to them. Their beliefs feature in verses 100 of *Sūrah al-An'ām*, 40–41 of *Sūrah Saba'* and 158 of *Sūrah al-Ṣaffāt*.

The above account makes it abundantly clear that the *jinn* have their independent existence and that they are a distinct species, independent of human beings. The ignorant people entertain highly exaggerated and baseless notions about the *jinn* in view of the mystery surrounding them. Some went to the extent of even worshipping them. The Qur'ān, however, defines them fully in terms of what they are and what they are not.

Subject Matter and Themes

Verses 1–15 of this *Sūrah* relate the impact of the Qur'ān recitation upon a group of the *jinn*. On their return to their community, how did they convey to them the message of the Qur'ān? The Qur'ān has not reproduced in full their conversation with their community members. Rather, it has focused on only the salient points of this exchange. For this purpose, the style is not of a continuous conversation but a selected portion of the narrative. On studying these sentences carefully, one may easily grasp the rationale behind their inclusion in the Qur'ān, for the Qur'ān quotes only those statements of theirs which concern their acceptance of faith. Our explanatory notes will facilitate further the appreciation of this episode.

Verses 16–18 admonish mankind, asking them to give up polytheism and to follow the straight way consistently. It will bring to them numerous divine blessings. Otherwise, their rejection of the divine message will bring upon them God's severe punishment. Verses 19–22 reproach the Makkan disbelievers for their hostility towards the Prophet (peace be upon him) when he invites them to God's way. The job of the Messenger is to convey the divine message. He does not claim to have the power to benefit or harm anyone. Verses 24–25 further warn the disbelievers that notwithstanding their efforts to stifle the Prophet's voice, they will soon realise who enjoys power and success – they or the Prophet (peace be upon him). Whether that Day is far or near even the Prophet (peace be upon him) does not know when it will happen. However, the occurrence of that Day is inevitable. Finally, people are told that God alone knows all that is beyond the ken of man's perception. A Messenger possesses only such knowledge which God grants him, that which is essential for discharging his duty as the Messenger. Such knowledge is transmitted to him safely, protected against any external interference whatsoever.

In the name of Allah, the Most Merciful, the Most Compassionate.

بِسْمِ ٱللَّهِ ٱلرَّحْمَٰنِ ٱلرَّحِيمِ

(1) Say, (O Prophet), it was revealed to me that a band of *jinn* attentively listened to (the recitation of the Qur'ān)[1] and then (went back to their people) and said: (2) "We have indeed heard a wonderful Qur'ān[2] which guides to the Right Way;▶

قُلْ أُوحِىَ إِلَىَّ أَنَّهُ ٱسْتَمَعَ نَفَرٌ مِّنَ ٱلْجِنِّ فَقَالُوٓا۟
إِنَّا سَمِعْنَا قُرْءَانًا عَجَبًا ۝ يَهْدِىٓ إِلَى ٱلرُّشْدِ

---

1. This shows that the *jinn* on this occasion were not visible to the Prophet (peace be upon him). Nor did he know that they were listening to his recitation of the Qur'ān. Instead, he was informed of the incident later through revelation. In connection with this great incident, 'Abdullāh ibn 'Abbās has also stated that: "The Prophet (peace be upon him) did not recite the Qur'ān before the *jinn*, nor did he see them." See Muslim (*K. al-Ṣalāt, Bāb al-Jahr bi al-Qirā'ah*), Tirmidhī (*K. al-Tafsīr, Sūrah al-Jinn*), Aḥmad ibn Ḥanbal (*Musnad*, 23, 310), Ibn Jarīr al-Ṭabarī, (*Tafsīr*, 1, 252).

2. The *jinn* spoke of the Qur'ān as "*Qur'ānan 'Ajabā*" or the "wonderful reading" (the literal meaning of 'Qur'ān' is something that is read time and again), for prior to this they had no idea about it, and this was the first time they became overwhelmed by it, without realising that the recitation they were listening to was the Qur'ān itself. The intensive form of the Arabic word *'ajab* is employed here in order to underscore the feeling of amazement experienced by the *jinn*. What they meant was that in terms of its language and its contents, it was something unprecedented.

One thus learns that the *jinn* not only listen to human conversation, but understand their language thoroughly, though they may not be the master of all human languages. It is likely that they are familiar with the local languages of their respective regions. It is nonetheless clear that this particular group of *jinn* were so well versed in Arabic that they not only followed the lofty contents of the Qur'ān, they appreciated its inimitable stylistic features as well.

so we have come to believe in it, and we will not associate aught with Our Lord in His Divinity";[3] (3) and that "He – exalted be His Majesty – has not taken to Himself either a wife or a son";[4] (4) and that "the foolish among us[5] have been wont to say outrageous things about Allah"; ▶

فَـَٔامَنَّا بِهِۦ ۖ وَلَن نُّشْرِكَ بِرَبِّنَآ أَحَدًا ۝٢ وَأَنَّهُۥ تَعَـٰلَىٰ جَدُّ رَبِّنَا مَا ٱتَّخَذَ صَـٰحِبَةً وَلَا وَلَدًا ۝٣ وَأَنَّهُۥ كَانَ يَقُولُ سَفِيهُنَا عَلَى ٱللَّهِ شَطَطًا ۝٤

3. This brings to light the following points: (i) The *jinn* do not deny the existence of God and His Lordship, (ii) There are polytheists among them who like men take others as partners of God. This particular group of *jinn* that listened to the Qur'ān were among the polytheists. (iii) Messengers and divine scriptures have not been sent down among the *jinn*. The believing *jinn* are those who accept the divine message preached by the Messengers raised from among the human beings and the scriptures brought by them. The same fact is confirmed in verses 29–31 of *Sūrah al-Aḥqāf*, for those *jinn* who listened to the Qur'ān were among the followers of the Prophet Moses (peace be upon him). After listening to the Qur'ān, this particular group of *jinn* asked their community members to believe in the Qur'ān which confirms the previous scriptures. *Sūrah al-Raḥmān* also points to the same fact as its entire subject matter emphasises that the addressees of the Prophet's message are both the human beings and *jinn*.

4. From this event, two things could be deduced: (i) Either the group of *jinn* were from the Christian faith or followers of a certain religion that ascribed the spouse and children to God. (ii) Moreover, it appears that the Prophet (peace be upon him) was at that time reciting a Qur'ānic passage which alerted them to the error in their articles of faith. After listening to the Qur'ān, they realised that it is the height of ignorance and disrespect to ascribe a spouse and children to someone as majestic and exalted as God.

5. The word *safīhunā* ("the foolish among us") here could have both a singular and plural meaning. If we take the word "foolish" to refer to an individual, it would denote Iblīs. And if it is considered to be a plural, it would denote a group of foolish *jinn* who made such statements.

(5) and that "we had thought that men and *jinn* would never speak a lie about Allah",[6] (6) and that "some from among the humans used to seek protection of some among the *jinn*, and thus they increased the arrogance of the *jinn*";[7] (7) and that "they thought, even as you thought, that Allah would never raise anyone (as a Messenger)";[8] ▶

وَأَنَّا ظَنَنَّآ أَن لَّن تَقُولَ ٱلْإِنسُ وَٱلْجِنُّ عَلَى
ٱللَّهِ كَذِبًا ﴿٥﴾ وَأَنَّهُۥ كَانَ رِجَالٌ مِّنَ ٱلْإِنسِ
يَعُوذُونَ بِرِجَالٍ مِّنَ ٱلْجِنِّ فَزَادُوهُمْ رَهَقًا
﴿٦﴾ وَأَنَّهُمْ ظَنُّوا۟ كَمَا ظَنَنتُمْ أَن لَّن يَبْعَثَ
ٱللَّهُ أَحَدًا ﴿٧﴾

6. What misled them was their belief that no human being or *jinn* could dare to forge a lie about God. On listening to the Qur'ān, however, they realised that the foolish among them were liars as well.

7. Ibn 'Abbās reports that in the days of *Jāhiliyyah,* when the Arabs spent the night in a desolate valley, they cried aloud: "We seek protection from the *jinn* who is the owner of this valley." Several reports of that period bear out a similar message. For example, when their supply of water and fodder was exhausted, the nomad bedouins sent a member of their team to find out whether such a supply is available. On locating the place, before camping at this new place, they cried out: "We seek protection from the Lord of this valley against every adversity." Ibn Jarīr al-Ṭabarī (*Tafsīr*, 23, 322–324) and *Tafsīr* of Ibn Kathīr (8, 239). They believed that the *jinn* were in charge of all desolate places and if they stayed there without invoking their protection, they would be harmed by them. The believing *jinn* are alluding to this very thing in their observation that man, in spite of being God's vicegerent on earth, became so frightened of the *jinn* that they had to seek their protection, rather than the protection of God. This has increased the *jinn's* arrogance, wickedness and oppression of human beings. By this they also became more foolish and bold in their error and disbelief.

8. "That God would never raise anyone" is open to two possible meanings: (i) One meaning is that which we have mentioned in the

(8) and that "we tried to pry (the secrets of) the heaven, but we found it full of terrible guards and shooting meteors"; (9) and that "we would take up stations in the heaven to try to hear but anyone who now attempts to listen finds a shooting meteor in wait for him";[9] (10) and that "we do not know whether evil is intended for those on the earth, or whether their Lord intends to direct them to the Right Way";[10] ▶

وَأَنَّا لَمَسْنَا ٱلسَّمَآءَ فَوَجَدْنَٰهَا مُلِئَتْ
حَرَسًا شَدِيدًا وَشُهُبًا ﴿٨﴾ وَأَنَّا كُنَّا نَقْعُدُ
مِنْهَا مَقَٰعِدَ لِلسَّمْعِ ۖ فَمَن يَسْتَمِعِ ٱلْءَانَ يَجِدْ
لَهُۥ شِهَابًا رَّصَدًا ﴿٩﴾ وَأَنَّا لَا نَدْرِىٓ أَشَرٌّ
أُرِيدَ بِمَن فِى ٱلْأَرْضِ أَمْ أَرَادَ بِهِمْ
رَبُّهُمْ رَشَدًا ﴿١٠﴾

---

translation of the text, "They thought even as you thought, that Allah would never raise anyone (as a Messenger)." (ii) "God will not raise anyone after death". In keeping with the comprehensive meaning of the word it may be said that like the human beings, the community of *jinn* at that time also rejected the doctrines of Messengership and the Resurrection. However, the verse which follows indicates that the first meaning mentioned above is more pertinent. In this context, the believing *jinn* here are informing the polytheistic *jinn* that their conjecture that God will not raise any Messenger is completely wrong. The gates of heaven which have been shut upon them is the clear indication that the Messenger has already been sent by God.

9. This shows that these *jinn* noticed that strict measures had been taken in the heavens to prevent them from prying on any secrets of heaven. They therefore tried to find out what has happened or is about to happen on earth that required such strict secrecy to be maintained. However, the arrangements they found were too stringent to allow them any opportunity to eavesdrop, for whenever anyone makes such an attempt, a "shooting meteor is in wait for him." (verse 9)

10. One thus learns that such extraordinary arrangements are made in either of these two situations: (i) If God has decreed His punishment

(11) and that "some of us are upright and some of us are otherwise for we follow widely divergent paths";[11] (12) and that "we thought that we will neither be able to frustrate Allah on earth, nor frustrate Him by flight";[12] ▶

وَأَنَّا مِنَّا ٱلصَّٰلِحُونَ وَمِنَّا دُونَ ذَٰلِكَ ۖ
كُنَّا طَرَآئِقَ قِدَدًا ﴿١١﴾ وَأَنَّا ظَنَنَّآ أَن لَّن نُّعْجِزَ
ٱللَّهَ فِى ٱلْأَرْضِ وَلَن نُّعْجِزَهُۥ هَرَبًا ﴿١٢﴾

against the human beings in the scheme of God, the *jinn* should not get any inkling of this lest they may foretell this to their ally human beings. (ii) When God sends down His Messenger, extraordinary security measures are taken to ensure that no tampering is done by any devil. Nor can they learn beforehand what divine revelation is being conveyed to the Messenger. The *jinn* affirm that when they observed strict security in the heavens and saw the downpour of shooting meteors, it made them curious to ascertain whether God had suddenly afflicted some people with His punishment or had sent down His Messenger somewhere. While they were conducting this enquiry, they listened to the wonderful recitation which guided them to the straight way. Then they realised that God had not punished anyone. Rather, He had sent down His Messenger for guiding the creation to the straight path. (For details see *Towards Understanding the Qur'ān*, vol. IV, *Sūrah al-Ḥijr* 15: nn. 8–12, pp. 284–286; vol. IX, *Sūrah al-Ṣāffāt* 37: n. 7, p. 283 and *Sūrah al-Mulk* 67: n. 11.)

11. From the moral point of view, there are both good and evil among the *jinn*. In the dominion of belief, far from being the adherents of a single faith, they are divided and follow various religions. By stressing this, they persuaded their community members that they definitely stood in need of guidance. They could not dispense with this need.

12. The *jinn's* belief that they could neither frustrate God on earth nor flee from it led them to the path of success. They feared God and were also conscious that if they disobeyed, they would not be able to avert His chastisement. Therefore, when they heard God's Word which directed them to the right way, they did not have the audacity to cling to the erroneous beliefs that had been spread among them by the ignorant members of their society. They could not do so because they had come to know the truth.

(13) and that "when we heard the teaching of the Right Way we came to believe in it; he who believes in His Lord shall have no fear of suffering loss or being subjected to any injustice";[13] (14) and that "among us some are Muslims [those who have submitted to Allah], and some of us are deviant. So those who became Muslims found the Right Course; (15) but those who deviated from the Truth, will be the fuel for Hell."[14]

وَأَنَّا لَمَّا سَمِعْنَا ٱلْهُدَىٰٓ ءَامَنَّا بِهِۦ ۖ فَمَن يُؤْمِنۢ
بِرَبِّهِۦ فَلَا يَخَافُ بَخْسًا وَلَا رَهَقًا ﴿١٣﴾
وَأَنَّا مِنَّا ٱلْمُسْلِمُونَ وَمِنَّا ٱلْقَٰسِطُونَ ۖ
فَمَنْ أَسْلَمَ فَأُو۟لَٰٓئِكَ تَحَرَّوْا۟ رَشَدًا ﴿١٤﴾
وَأَمَّا ٱلْقَٰسِطُونَ فَكَانُوا۟ لِجَهَنَّمَ حَطَبًا ﴿١٥﴾

---

13. Injustice means rewarding someone less than what he deserves. It would be patently wrong if he is not given any reward at all and is punished more than what is due or to punish an innocent person. Believers have no fear of suffering any such loss or being subjected to any injustice by God.

14. This might prompt one to ask: "The *jinn*, according to the Qur'ān itself, are created out of fire. How then can Hellfire torment them?" In response, one can point to a parallel case. Man, according to the Qur'ān, is created out of the clay, and yet he is hurt if a lump of clay is hurled at him. True, man's body is composed of the elements from clay, yet his body assumes an independent and different entity of blood and flesh and is liable to be hurt by things made of the same elements. Similarly, though the *jinn* are created from fire, they have a body of their own which is subject to burning by fire. (For details see *Sūrah al-Raḥmān* 55: n. 15.)

(16) If[15] people were to keep firmly to the Right Way, We would have vouchsafed them abundant rain[16] (17) so that We might try them through this bounty.[17] Whoso turns away from the remembrance of his Lord,[18] He will cause him to suffer a grievous chastisement; (18) and that "mosques belong to Allah, so do not invoke anyone with Him";[19] ▶

وَأَلَّوِ ٱسْتَقَـٰمُوا۟ عَلَى ٱلطَّرِيقَةِ لَأَسْقَيْنَـٰهُم
مَّآءً غَدَقًا ﴿١٦﴾ لِّنَفْتِنَهُمْ فِيهِ ۚ وَمَن يُعْرِضْ
عَن ذِكْرِ رَبِّهِۦ يَسْلُكْهُ عَذَابًا صَعَدًا ﴿١٧﴾
وَأَنَّ ٱلْمَسَـٰجِدَ لِلَّهِ فَلَا تَدْعُوا۟ مَعَ ٱللَّهِ
أَحَدًا ﴿١٨﴾ وَأَنَّهُۥ لَمَّا قَامَ عَبْدُ ٱللَّهِ يَدْعُوهُ
كَادُوا۟ يَكُونُونَ عَلَيْهِ لِبَدًا ﴿١٩﴾

15. This marks the end of the observations of the *jinn* and the beginning of the comments of God the Almighty.

16. The same truth is highlighted in verse 12 of *Sūrah Nūḥ*, that if people seek Allah's pardon, He will bless them with plenty of rain. (For details see *Sūrah Nūḥ* 71: n. 12.) The abundance of rain typifies the abundance of divine bounty. For life depends upon water. Without water, there cannot be any habitat. Nor can the basic needs of human beings be met without it. The same holds true for the flourishing of industry which is contingent upon water.

17. The trial consists in watching whether they remain grateful or not after being blessed with divine bounties. It is also to be seen whether they properly utilise or abuse the blessings granted to them.

18. Turning away from the remembrance of his Lord means man's rejection of guidance and advice sent down by God or his outright refusal to listen to any remembrance of Him or to turn away from worshipping Him.

19. The Qur'ān commentators generally explain the Qur'ānic expression *masājid* as the place of worship. Taken in this sense, the verse means that no one other than God is to be worshipped there. According to Ḥasan al-Baṣrī, the entire earth is a place of worship. The verse thus indicates that polytheism should not be committed anywhere on God's

(19) and when Allah's servant[20] stood up to call on Him, they well-nigh swarmed him. (20) Say, (O Prophet): "I call on my Lord alone, and I do not associate aught with Him in His Divinity."[21] (21) Say: "Surely neither it is in my power to hurt you nor to bring you to the Right Way." (22) Say: "None can protect me from Allah, nor can I find a refuge apart from Him. (23) (My task is no more than) to deliver Allah's proclamation and His messages.[22] ▶

قُلْ إِنَّمَآ أَدْعُواْ رَبِّى وَلَآ أُشْرِكُ بِهِۦٓ أَحَدًا ﴿٢٠﴾
قُلْ إِنِّى لَآ أَمْلِكُ لَكُمْ ضَرًّا وَلَا رَشَدًا
﴿٢١﴾ قُلْ إِنِّى لَن يُجِيرَنِى مِنَ ٱللَّهِ أَحَدٌ
وَلَنْ أَجِدَ مِن دُونِهِۦ مُلْتَحَدًا ﴿٢٢﴾
إِلَّا بَلَـٰغًا مِّنَ ٱللَّهِ وَرِسَـٰلَـٰتِهِۦ

earth. His stance is premised on the Prophet's remark: "The entire earth has been made as a place of worship and attaining cleanliness for me." (*al-Kashshāf*, 6, 231) In the opinion of Sa'īd ibn Jubayr, *masājid* signifies man's body parts such as his hands, knees, feet, and forehead which are involved in prostration. (*Tafsīr* of Ibn Kathīr, 8, 244) The verse thus highlights that it is God Who has created these body parts and hence these should not be used for prostrating before anyone other than Him.

20. God's servant alludes to the Prophet Muḥammad (peace be upon him).

21. Calling upon God is not something outrageous which should anger anyone. What is detestable is to associate partners to His divinity. The Prophet (peace be upon him) is not guilty of this. Rather, the culprits are those who swarm and mob him for his 'crime' of mentioning God's name.

22. The Prophet (peace be upon him) lays no claim to his share in Godhead. He does not have any power to make or mar anyone's fate. He is simply a Messenger and his assignment consists only in conveying the divine message to mankind. It is God alone Who enjoys all power and

And whoever disobeys Allah and His Messenger, surely the Fire of Hell awaits him; therein he will abide in perpetuity."[23]

(24) (They shall not change their ways) until they see that against which they had been warned, and then they will know whose helpers are weaker and whose supporters are fewer in number.[24] (25) Say: "I know not whether what ▶

وَمَن يَعْصِ ٱللَّهَ وَرَسُولَهُۥ فَإِنَّ لَهُۥ نَارَ
جَهَنَّمَ خَـٰلِدِينَ فِيهَآ أَبَدًا ﴿٢٣﴾ حَتَّىٰٓ إِذَا
رَأَوْا۟ مَا يُوعَدُونَ فَسَيَعْلَمُونَ مَنْ أَضْعَفُ
نَاصِرًا وَأَقَلُّ عَدَدًا ﴿٢٤﴾ قُلْ إِنْ أَدْرِىٓ

authority. Far from benefiting or harming anyone, the Messenger does not have any power to benefit or harm himself. Were he to disobey God, he cannot escape His punishment. There is no help and support from anywhere except the protection and refuge of God alone. (For details see *Sūrah al-Shūrā* 42: n. 7.)

23. This does not imply that the eternal Hellfire is the punishment for every sin. Rather, it emerges from the context of this verse that one who rejects the call to monotheism presented by God and His Messenger, and refuses to give up his polytheism, will abide in perpetuity in the Hellfire.

24. Reference is to those of the Quraysh who were bent upon attacking the Prophet (peace be upon him) as soon as they heard him inviting people to God. They entertained a false notion about the strength of their band of supporters and the lack of strength of the Prophet (peace be upon him). They therefore succumbed to the illusion that they would easily prevail upon the Prophet (peace be upon him) and his small number of followers. The Qur'ān, however, tells them that soon there will be a worse time against which they are warned, when they will realise who is utterly helpless and friendless.

أَقَرِيبٌ مَّا تُوعَدُونَ أَمْ يَجْعَلُ لَهُۥ رَبِّىٓ أَمَدًا ﴿٢٥﴾ عَـٰلِمُ ٱلْغَيْبِ فَلَا يُظْهِرُ عَلَىٰ غَيْبِهِۦٓ أَحَدًا ﴿٢٦﴾ إِلَّا مَنِ ٱرْتَضَىٰ مِن رَّسُولٍ فَإِنَّهُۥ يَسْلُكُ مِنۢ بَيْنِ يَدَيْهِ وَمِنْ خَلْفِهِۦ رَصَدًا ﴿٢٧﴾

you are promised is near or whether my Lord will prolong its term.[25] (26) He is the Knower of the Unseen, and He does not disclose His Unseen to anyone[26] (27) other than to a Messenger whom He chooses (for the bestowal of any part of the knowledge of the Unseen),[27] whereafter He appoints guards who go before him and behind him,[28] ▸

25. It seems that it is a response to the disbelievers' comment which is not reproduced here. It is likely that in response to the message of the preceding verses, the disbelievers may have mockingly asked the Prophet (peace be upon him) as to when they will be struck with the dreadful divine punishment. The Prophet (peace be upon him) is instructed to give them this reply: "I am not privy to the date of punishment destined for you, nonetheless it will come at its appointed time. Only Allah knows whether it is imminent or He has set a distant term for it."

26. God alone has complete knowledge of the Unseen and He does not disclose it in full to anyone.

27. Messengers do not have access to the Unseen as such; but when God decides to designate anyone as His Messenger, He bestows upon him whatever portion of the truths of the Unseen He pleases.

28. The word "guards" denotes angels. The purpose of the verse is to affirm that when God communicates any knowledge of the truths belonging to the realm of the Unseen through revelation, He appoints angels to safeguard that knowledge. This is done to ensure that it reaches the Messengers safely, untarnished by adulteration. The same truth is enunciated in verses 8–9 of this *Sūrah* that, after the Prophet Muḥammad's advent, the *jinn* noticed strict secrecy in the heavens along with heavy

(28) so that He may know that they have delivered the messages of their Lord.[29] He encompasses in His knowledge their surroundings and keeps a count of all things."[30]	لِّيَعْلَمَ أَن قَدْ أَبْلَغُوا۟ رِسَـٰلَـٰتِ رَبِّهِمْ وَأَحَاطَ بِمَا لَدَيْهِمْ وَأَحْصَىٰ كُلَّ شَىْءٍ عَدَدًۢا ﴿٢٨﴾

security measures that had been taken to prevent their access to the heavens for eavesdropping.

29. This carries the following three meanings: (i) The Messenger may know that the angels have faithfully delivered to him the message of God. (ii) God may know that the angels have delivered safely His message to His Messenger, and (iii) God may know that the Messengers have properly conveyed His message to people. The wordings of the verse possibly imply all the above three meanings. Moreover, this verse also highlights the following two truths: (i) Messengers are endowed with the knowledge of only that portion of the Unseen that is needed by them to perform their mission as God's Messengers. (ii) God appoints angels not only to oversee that this knowledge reaches them in its pristine form, but also that the Messengers faithfully transmit it to His creatures without any changes.

30. God's power firmly encompasses the Messengers and the angels. Hence, if they deviate even slightly from God's directives, they will be instantly taken to task. A strict count is kept of every letter of God's message. Hence neither the Messengers nor the Prophets can tamper with even a single letter of His message.

Sūrah 73

Al-Muzzammil

(The Enwrapped One)

(Makkan Period)

Title

The word *al-muzzammil* occurring in the opening verse of this *Sūrah* constitutes its title. It is not related to the subject matter of the *Sūrah*.

Period of Revelation

The *Sūrah* comprises two sections which were revealed at different dates.

The consensus view is that its first section (verses 1–10) was revealed in Makkah. Both its subject matter and the reports of *aḥādīth* about its circumstantial setting support the above view. Reports are silent over the exact date of its revelation in the Makkan phase. However, internal evidence helps in dating it.

First, it instructs the Prophet (peace be upon him) to stand up in prayer by night to enable him to shoulder the onerous duty of prophethood and to discharge the responsibility befittingly. It is therefore obvious that this section must have been revealed in the early days of his prophethood while Allah was training him for his august office.

Secondly, it commands the Prophet (peace be upon him) to recite the Qur'ān in *Tahajjud* prayer by night, half of it (the night) or a bit more. This indicates that at least a substantial portion of the Qur'ān had been revealed by then, which could be recited in prayers spread over a few hours of the night.

Thirdly, the Prophet (peace be upon him) is directed to have patience and bear with the excesses committed by his detractors. The Makkan disbelievers on the other hand are seriously warned of divine punishment. It is thus clear that this section was revealed at a time when the Prophet (peace be upon him) had started preaching Islam publicly and the Makkans opposed him vehemently.

Many Qur'ānic scholars hold the view that the second section of the *Sūrah* was also sent down in Makkah. However, others emphasise that it was revealed in Madīnah, a point endorsed by its contents, for it speaks of fighting in the way of Allah. This particular command was not of course applicable in Makkah. Furthermore, it commands that *Zakāh* be paid as an obligatory duty. It is on record that *Zakāh* as a duty, with its prescribed rate, was promulgated in Madīnah and not in Makkah.

Subject Matter and Themes

Verses 1–7 ask the Prophet (peace be upon him) to prepare himself for discharging the great mission assigned to him. A practical way to achieve this is to stand up in prayer for half of the night or a little less or a little more of it.

Verses 8–14 exhort the Prophet (peace be upon him) to devote himself fully to Allah, the Lord of the universe. He should rest content, entrusting everything to Him. He should bear with the opposition of his opponents and not engage with them. He should leave their affairs with Allah; He Himself will deal with them.

Verses 15–19 warn the Makkan opponents of the Prophet (peace be upon him) that Allah has sent His Messenger among them in the same way He sent a Messenger to the Pharaoh. They should better consider the tragic end of the Pharaoh when he refused to believe in the Messenger's call. Suppose, if somehow one is spared divine punishment in this world, how could one escape Allah's chastisement on the Day of Resurrection for his disbelief?

The second section of the *Sūrah*, according to Sa'īd ibn Jubayr's report, was revealed ten years later. It announces a reduction in the command for *Tahajjud* prayer, contained in the opening verses of the *Sūrah* (*Tafsīr* of Ibn Jarīr al-Ṭabarī, 23, 361). The revised command is that one is free to offer this prayer as much as is convenient to him. However, Muslims must be very particular about offering the five daily obligatory prayers, paying *Zakāh* accurately, and spending their wealth sincerely in the way of Allah. Finally, Muslims are told that their good deeds in this world will not go to waste. These will constitute their asset, as the provision of a traveller who dispatches it in advance for his future residence. He will find this safe and secure with Allah in the Hereafter. It is not only much better than what they amass and hoard in this world, they will also receive a huge reward from Allah, in addition to the recompense for their good deeds.

In the name of Allah, the Most Merciful, the Most Compassionate.

(1) O you the (sleeping) enwrapped one![1] (2) Stand up in Prayer by night,[2] all but a small part of it;[3] (3) half of it, or reduce it a little; (4) or add to it a little; and recite the Qur'ān slowly and distinctly.[4] ▶

بِسْمِ ٱللَّهِ ٱلرَّحْمَٰنِ ٱلرَّحِيمِ

يَٰٓأَيُّهَا ٱلْمُزَّمِّلُ ۝١ قُمِ ٱلَّيْلَ إِلَّا قَلِيلًا ۝٢
نِّصْفَهُۥٓ أَوِ ٱنقُصْ مِنْهُ قَلِيلًا ۝٣ أَوْ زِدْ عَلَيْهِ
وَرَتِّلِ ٱلْقُرْءَانَ تَرْتِيلًا ۝٤

---

1. The wordings of this command to the Prophet (peace be upon him) suggest that he had at that time gone to bed or was lying in bed, wrapped up in a sheet intending to sleep, for the verse asks him to stand up in prayer by night. Instead of addressing him as the Prophet or Messenger, he is referred to as "the enwrapped one", which implies a delicate message that the days of enjoying sound, night long sleep are over for him. He is charged with an onerous duty which calls for total devotion to the mission and whose demands are different.

2. It may have these two meanings: (i) He should spend the night standing up in prayer while he should sleep for a little while. (ii) He is not required to stand up in prayer throughout the night. Rather, he should pray for a while and take rest in the night. However, the verses which follow seem to reinforce the former meaning. The same is borne out also by verse 26 of *Sūrah al-Dahr*: "Prostrate yourself before God at night and extol His glory during the long hours of the night."

3. This specifies the quantum of time for prayer to be devoted in the night. He is given the choice to spend half the night or a little less or a bit more in prayer. From the style of the verse it appears that to pray up to the middle of the night is preferable. This was set up as a criterion which could be increased or decreased according to convenience.

4. The Qur'ān should be recited slowly and distinctly. Each word is to be recited clearly with a pause at every verse. More importantly, one

(5) Behold, We shall cast upon you a Weighty Word.[5] ▶	إِنَّا سَنُلْقِى عَلَيْكَ قَوْلًا ثَقِيلًا ۝٥

should reflect over the contents of each and every verse in order to fully grasp the meaning of the divine message, which in turn, should move one's heart and mind. If a verse is about Allah's might and glory, it should fill one's heart with awe. If it describes His mercy, it should evoke gratitude from the depths of one's heart. Likewise, if a verse relates His wrath and punishment, one's heart should be filled with fear. Similarly, one should reflect over the verses commanding or forbidding something. The study of the Qur'ān is thus not restricted to its verbal recitation. It must be marked by reflection and soul searching. On being asked how the Prophet (peace be upon him) used to recite the Qur'ān, Anas replied: "He stretched each and every word during his recitation." He illustrated this by reciting *basmalah*. Bukhārī (*K. Faḍā'il al- Qur'ān, Bāb Madd al-Qirā'ah*). When Umm Salamah was asked the same question, she replied: "He recited every verse separately and paused at each verse. For example, after reciting verse 1 of *Sūrah al-Fātiḥah* he paused and likewise after reciting verse 2 he paused again." *Musnad* of Imām Aḥmad (1, 294) Abū Dāwūd (*K. al-Ḥurūf wa al-Qirā'ah*) and Tirmidhī (*Bāb Abwāb al-Qirā'ah*). In another report, she is credited with this version: "The Prophet (peace be upon him) used to recite each and every word of the Qur'ān clearly and distinctly." Tirmidhī (*Abwāb Faḍā'il al-Qur'ān*) and Nasā'ī (*K. Iftitāḥ wa Taz'īn al- Qur'ān bi al-Ṣawt*). Ḥudhayfah ibn al-Yamān says: "Once I joined the Prophet (peace be upon him) in the night prayer. I saw him reciting in this manner: when there was the occasion for exalting Allah, he glorified Him; when it demanded a supplication, he implored and sought His protection." Muslim (*K. Ṣalāt al-Musāfirīn, Bāb Istiḥbāb Taṭwīl al-Qirā'ah*) and Nasā'ī (*K. al-Iftitāḥ, Bāb Ta'awwudh al-Qārī*). Abū Dharr informs: "When once during the night prayer, the Prophet (peace be upon him) reached the verse 'If You chastise them, they are Your servants; and if You forgive them, You are the All-Mighty, the All-Wise' (5: 118), he kept repeating it until it became dawn." *Musnad* of Imām Aḥmad (5, 156 and 170), and Ibn Mājah, (*K. Iqāmah al-Ṣalāt*).

5. The Prophet (peace be upon him) was asked to offer prayers at night because God was about to cast upon him a weighty message. He should better develop the capacity for shouldering this onerous duty. He can reinforce himself by abandoning sleep during the night and instead

(6) Surely getting up at night[6] is the best means of subduing the self[7] and is more suitable for uprightness ▶	إِنَّ نَاشِئَةَ ٱلَّيْلِ هِىَ أَشَدُّ وَطْـًٔا وَأَقْوَمُ

engage in prayer until midnight or a little earlier or later than it. The Qur'ān is designated here as "a weighty word" for abiding by its commands, exemplifying what it preaches, conveying its message amid all-round opposition, and bringing a revolution in the entire system of their belief and thought, morals and manners, culture and civilisation. Indeed, they are the most difficult tasks any human being has ever been charged with. It is referred to as a "weighty word" also in view of the fact that bearing the heavy weight when it was revealed to the Prophet (peace be upon him) was not an easy task. Zayd ibn Thābit states: "Once the Prophet (peace be upon him) received revelation while his knee was resting on my knee. I felt the heavy pressure of the weight and apprehended my leg may break." Bukhārī (*K. al-Tafsīr, Sūrah al-Nisā'*). 'Ā'ishah relates: "I saw the Prophet (peace be upon him) receiving revelation on an intensely cold day. Yet he sweated profusely on his brow." Bukhārī (*Bāb Kayfa kāna Bad' al-Waḥī*), Muslim (*K. al-Īmān Bāb Bad' al-Waḥī*, Mālik (*Muwaṭṭa', K. al-Qur'ān*), Tirmidhī (*K. al-Manāqib*) and Nasā'ī. In another report 'Ā'ishah informs that as he received revelation while riding a she camel, the she camel was forced to rest her chest on the ground until the revelation was over. *Musnad* of Imām Aḥmad (5, 118) Ḥākim (*al-Mustadarak, Tafsīr Sūrah al-Muzzammil*) and Ibn Jarīr al-Ṭabarī (*Tafsīr*, 23, 360).

6. The expression *nāshi'ah* is explained by the Qur'ān commentators and lexicographers in the following four ways: (i) The person who gets up at night, (ii) hours of night, (iii) getting up at night, and (iv) getting up not only at night but rising after having some sleep. The last meaning is preferred by 'Ā'ishah and Mujāhid, Ibn Jarīr al-Ṭabarī (*Tafsīr*, 23, 366–369).

7. The expression *ashaddu waṭ'an* used in this verse is so vast in meaning that it cannot be translated in one sentence. At one level, the meaning is that since getting up at night for prayer and standing up for long hours is against human nature, and the body then demands rest. It is the most effective exercise to control and subdue the soul. One who gains such control over his mind and body and becomes able to use this

in speech.[8] (7) You are indeed much occupied during the day with the affairs of the world. (8) So remember the name of your Lord[9] and devote yourself to Him with exclusive devotion. (9) He is the Lord of the East and the ▶

قِيلًا ۝٦ إِنَّ لَكَ فِي ٱلنَّهَارِ سَبۡحٗا طَوِيلٗا ۝٧ وَٱذۡكُرِ ٱسۡمَ رَبِّكَ وَتَبَتَّلۡ إِلَيۡهِ تَبۡتِيلٗا ۝٨ رَّبُّ ٱلۡمَشۡرِقِ

power in the way of God, he can most effectively strive to make the message of the true faith prevail in the world. Another meaning could be that it is the effective strategy for achieving harmony between one's heart and tongue, for man has uninterrupted access to Allah in the small hours of the night. Whatever he utters with his tongue, it resonates the inner-most voice of his heart. Yet another meaning could be that this exercise is a very effective means for bringing one's public and private selves in close conformity, for one who sacrifices his comfort and gets up at night for prayer will do surely only out of utmost sincerity, without any tinge of hypocrisy or showing off. The fourth meaning could be that since worshipping at night is more difficult than doing it in the daytime, it invests one with a high degree of steadfastness, facilitating his quest in the way of God with fortitude. Such a person is more likely to bear with all kinds of hardships with greater constancy and determination.

8. Although the literal meaning of *aqwamu qīlā* is: "more suitable for uprightness in speech", the underlying message is that in the tranquillity of the small hours of the night, one can better concentrate and grasp the meaning and message of the Qur'ān. According to Ibn 'Abbās, the verse instructs that this is the most suitable time for one to reflect on the message and contents of the Qur'ān. Abū Dāwūd (*K. al-Taṭawwu', Bāb Naskh Qiyām al-Layl*).

9. The reference to the Prophet's preoccupations during the daytime is followed by the directive: "Remember the name of your Lord", which implies that one should not neglect the remembrance of Allah even when he is engaged in mundane pursuits. He should commemorate His name in one form or the other at all times. (For details see *Towards Understanding the Qur'ān*, vol. IX, *Sūrah al-Aḥzāb* 33: n. 63, pp. 59–60.)

West; there is no god but He. So take Him alone for your Guardian,[10] (10) And bear patiently the vain things they utter, and gracefully forsake them.[11] ▶	وَٱلْمَغْرِبِ لَآ إِلَـٰهَ إِلَّا هُوَ فَٱتَّخِذْهُ وَكِيلًا ۝٩ وَٱصْبِرْ عَلَىٰ مَا يَقُولُونَ وَٱهْجُرْهُمْ هَجْرًا جَمِيلًا ۝١٠

10. The word *wakīl* is used for someone to whom one entrusts all affairs on account of complete trust in him. It is used to denote a legal expert to whom a person entrusts his judicial case, which one does because of his confidence that the advocate will present the case on his behalf in the best possible manner, dispensing with the need that one plead it for oneself. Thus, the verse means that the Prophet (peace be upon him) should not feel worried on account of the storm of opposition and the problems faced by him in view of the call to truth presented by him. His Lord is He Who is the Master of the east and the west, and the entire universe. No one besides Him has any right to divinity. He should therefore entrust his case to Allah and be assured that He will fight the Prophet's case, deal with his enemies, and take care of his interests fully.

11. The directive to "gracefully forsake them" does not mean to break off all relations with such people and to give up conveying God's message to them. It simply means that the Prophet (peace be upon him) should graciously disregard his opponents' depraved behaviour. He should not stoop to their level, and should abstain from responding to their vile acts. It is essential that this "forsaking" should not be accompanied by expressions of injury, anger, or irritation. The "forsaking" instead should be of the kind to which a decent person resorts when a disreputable person hurls an obscene abuse: one should ignore it so that it does not leave a bad taste in one's mouth. This should not, however, cause any misunderstanding that the Prophet (peace be upon him) did not behave properly, so God gave him the above advice. As a matter of fact, he was already following in this honourable way. The reason the Qur'ān issued this directive was to tell the disbelievers that the lack of any response to their misconduct should not be misconstrued by them as a sign of the Prophet's weakness. Indeed, it is God Who has instructed him to behave in a gracious manner in all such circumstances.

(11) Leave it to Me to deal with the affluent ones[12] who give the lie (to the Truth), and bear with them for a while. (12) We have heavy fetters[13] and a blazing Fire in store for them; (13) and a food that chokes, and a grievous chastisement. (14) (They will come across all this) on the Day when the earth and the mountains shall tremble violently and the mountains shall crumble into heaps of scattered sand.[14]

وَذَرۡنِي وَٱلۡمُكَذِّبِينَ أُوْلِي ٱلنَّعۡمَةِ وَمَهِّلۡهُمۡ
قَلِيلًا ﴿١١﴾ إِنَّ لَدَيۡنَآ أَنكَالٗا وَجَحِيمٗا ﴿١٢﴾
وَطَعَامٗا ذَا غُصَّةٖ وَعَذَابًا أَلِيمٗا ﴿١٣﴾
يَوۡمَ تَرۡجُفُ ٱلۡأَرۡضُ وَٱلۡجِبَالُ وَكَانَتِ
ٱلۡجِبَالُ كَثِيبٗا مَّهِيلًا ﴿١٤﴾

12. It is fairly evident from the above verse that those Makkans who were at the forefront in rejecting the Prophet (peace be upon him) and in misleading people by resorting to all sorts of cheating, fraud, and instigation, were the well-to-do, prosperous, and affluent ones, for their interests were hit hard by the Islamic scheme of reform. The Qur'ān clarifies that it was not something peculiar to the Prophet Muḥammad (peace be upon him). Earlier Messengers also faced similar stiff opposition from such class of people. Instances in point are verses 60, 66, 75 and 88 of *Sūrah al-A'rāf*; 33 of *Sūrah al-Mu'minūn*; 34–35 of *Sūrah Saba'* and 23 of *Sūrah al-Zukhruf*.

13. The culprits will be heavily fettered in Hell. Not for preventing their escape, rather this will immobilise them, rendering them unable to rise. These fetters are for tormenting them further.

14. Since the law binding the mountains together will then cease to work, these will be reduced to heaps of loose sand. Furthermore, the quake shaking the earth will scatter their sand, rendering the earth as a level plain. The Qur'ān portrays the same scene in *Sūrah Ṭā Hā* thus: "They ask you concerning the mountains: 'Where will they go?' Say: 'My Lord will scatter them like dust, and leave the earth a levelled plain in which you shall find no crookedness or curvature.'" (*Sūrah Ṭā Hā* 20: 105–107).

(15) Surely We have sent to you[15] a Messenger as a witness[16] over you, just as We had sent a Messenger to Pharaoh. (16) But Pharaoh disobeyed Our Messenger, so We seized him with a terrible seizing. (17) If you persist in disbelieving, how will you guard yourself against the (woe of the) Day that will turn children grey-haired,[17] (18) the Day whose severity shall cause the heaven to split asunder? Allah's promise is ever bound to be fulfilled. (19) Indeed this is nothing but a Good Counsel; so let him who will take a way leading to his Lord.

إِنَّآ أَرْسَلْنَآ إِلَيْكُمْ رَسُولًا شَٰهِدًا عَلَيْكُمْ
كَمَآ أَرْسَلْنَآ إِلَىٰ فِرْعَوْنَ رَسُولًا ﴿١٥﴾ فَعَصَىٰ
فِرْعَوْنُ ٱلرَّسُولَ فَأَخَذْنَٰهُ أَخْذًا وَبِيلًا
﴿١٦﴾ فَكَيْفَ تَتَّقُونَ إِن كَفَرْتُمْ يَوْمًا يَجْعَلُ
ٱلْوِلْدَٰنَ شِيبًا ﴿١٧﴾ ٱلسَّمَآءُ مُنفَطِرٌۢ بِهِۦ ۚ كَانَ
وَعْدُهُۥ مَفْعُولًا ﴿١٨﴾ إِنَّ هَٰذِهِۦ تَذْكِرَةٌ ۖ
فَمَن شَآءَ ٱتَّخَذَ إِلَىٰ رَبِّهِۦ سَبِيلًا ﴿١٩﴾

15. The discourse now turns to the Makkan disbelievers who were vehemently decrying the Prophet (peace be upon him) as a liar.

16. The Prophet (peace be upon him) has been sent as a witness in the sense that his words and deeds in this world might serve as a testament to truth for mankind. Furthermore, on the Day of Judgement in God's court the Prophet (peace be upon him) will testify that he had presented before mankind the message of truth. (For details see *Towards Understanding the Qur'ān*, vol. I, *Sūrah al-Baqarah* 2: n. 144, pp. 120–121; vol. II, *Sūrah al-Nisā'* 4: n. 64, p. 40; vol. IX, *Sūrah al-Aḥzāb* 33: n. 82, pp. 70–73 and *Sūrah al-Fatḥ* 48: n. 14.)

17. The disbelievers are told that if they do not accept the call of the Messenger of God, they will meet the same horrible end which had engulfed the Pharaoh earlier. But even if they do not face any punishment in this life, how can they escape God's chastisement on the Day of Judgement?

(20) (O Prophet),[18] your Lord knows that you sometimes stand up in Prayer nearly two-thirds of the night, and sometimes half or one-third of it,[19] and so does a party of those with you;[20] Allah measures ▶

۞ إِنَّ رَبَّكَ يَعْلَمُ أَنَّكَ تَقُومُ أَدْنَىٰ
مِن ثُلُثَيِ ٱلَّيْلِ وَنِصْفَهُۥ وَثُلُثَهُۥ
وَطَآئِفَةٌ مِّنَ ٱلَّذِينَ مَعَكَ ۚ وَٱللَّهُ يُقَدِّرُ

18. There are divergent reports about the date of this verse which contains the revised command about the *Tahajjud* prayer. The following report is cited by Aḥmad, Muslim, and Abū Dāwūd on 'Ā'ishah's authority that the revised command was laid down only one year after the original command, changing the status of this prayer from obligatory (*farḍ*) to voluntary (*nafl*). Another report by Ibn Jarīr and Ibn Abī Ḥātim (*Tafsīr*, 10, 3379), however, credits 'Ā'ishah with the view that there was an interval of eight months between the two commands. Ibn Jarīr al-Ṭabarī, (*Tafsīr*, 23, 359). Yet another report attributed to her by Ibn Abī Ḥātim, however, speaks of the difference of sixteen months between the two. Abū Dāwūd (*K. al-Taṭawwu', 'Bāb Naskh Qiyām al-Layl*), Ibn Jarīr (23, 359) and Ibn Abī Ḥātim, state, on the authority of 'Abdullāh ibn 'Abbās, the period of one year. However, Sa'īd ibn Jubayr insists that these verses were revealed ten years later (Ibn Jarīr al-Ṭabarī, 23, 361 and Ibn Abī Ḥātim). In our opinion, this last view seems most credible, for the first section of the *Sūrah* is patently Makkan in origin, and was sent down in the very early days of Islam, at most four years after the Prophet (peace be upon him) assumed his office. In contrast, on the basis of its internal evidence, the second section appears to have been revealed in Madīnah when the fighting had commenced with the disbelievers and the command for paying *Zakāh* had also come into force. So, there must be a gap of at least ten years between the revelation of the two sections.

19. Although the command for standing in prayer was up to midnight or a bit more or less than it, one engaged in prayer could not keep an exact count of time, especially when there were no clocks around. So, at times, the prayer went up to two-thirds or was reduced to one-third of the night.

20. The command was initially directed at the Prophet (peace be upon him), advising him to stand up in prayer at night. However, since the

the night and the day. He knows that you cannot keep an accurate count of it, so He has shown mercy to you. So now recite as much of the Qur'ān as you can.[21] He knows that there are among you those who are sick and others who are journeying in the land in quest of Allah's ▶

ٱلَّيۡلَ وَٱلنَّهَارَۚ عَلِمَ أَن لَّن تُحۡصُوهُ فَتَابَ
عَلَيۡكُمۡۖ فَٱقۡرَءُواْ مَا تَيَسَّرَ مِنَ ٱلۡقُرۡءَانِۚ عَلِمَ
أَن سَيَكُونُ مِنكُم مَّرۡضَىٰ وَءَاخَرُونَ
يَضۡرِبُونَ فِي ٱلۡأَرۡضِ يَبۡتَغُونَ مِن فَضۡلِ ٱللَّهِ

---

early Muslims were very keen on emulating the Prophet (peace be upon him) and earning reward, most of the Companions too made it a point to offer the *Tahajjud* prayer regularly.

21. Since the length of a prayer depends on the amount of the Qur'ān recitation in it, the directive was to recite as much of the Qur'ān as the Prophet (peace be upon him) could do. By shortening the recitations, the length of the prayer would also be automatically reduced. Although the command appears to be imperative, the consensus view is that the *Tahajjud* prayer is not a *farḍ* but a *nafl* prayer. This is further clarified in a *ḥadīth* that when someone enquired of the Prophet (peace be upon him) about the obligatory prayer, he replied: "The five daily prayers are obligatory on you." When he further queried whether he was obliged to offer anything else, he replied: "No, unless you desire to offer something else besides it." Bukhārī (*K. al-Īmān, Bāb al-Zakāh*), and Muslim (*K. al-Īmān, Bāb Bayān al-Ṣalawāt*).

Another point emerging from the above verse is that like *rukū'* (bowing) and *sujūd* (prostration), the Qur'ān recitation is also an essential component of the prayer. As at other places, God has used the words *rukū'* and *sujūd* to mean the prayer, here He mentions the recitation of the Qur'ān as a synonym for the prayer. Were one to raise the question that since the *Tahajjud* prayer itself is *nafl*, how can the Qur'ān recitation as part of it be obligatory? The answer is that all the requisites of a prayer are to be fulfilled, even if it is a *nafl* prayer. No one can say that in the *nafl* prayer, purity of the clothes and body, ablution, and covering the body are not obligatory, and the recitation of the Qur'ān, making *rukū'* and prostration are just voluntary.

bounty,[22] and still others who are fighting in the cause of Allah.[23] So recite as much of the Qur'ān as you easily can, and establish Prayer, and pay *Zakāh*,[24] and give Allah a goodly loan.[25] Whatever good you send forth for yourselves, ▶

وَءَاخَرُونَ يُقَـٰتِلُونَ فِى سَبِيلِ ٱللَّهِ ۖ
فَٱقْرَءُوا۟ مَا تَيَسَّرَ مِنْهُ ۚ وَأَقِيمُوا۟ ٱلصَّلَوٰةَ
وَءَاتُوا۟ ٱلزَّكَوٰةَ وَأَقْرِضُوا۟ ٱللَّهَ قَرْضًا حَسَنًا ۚ
وَمَا تُقَدِّمُوا۟ لِأَنفُسِكُم مِّنْ خَيْرٍ

22. "Travelling in the land in quest of God's bounty" is the Qur'ānic phrase for seeking lawful means of livelihood.

23. Seeking lawful sustenance and fighting in the cause of God are mentioned together in the above. Those engaged in these as well as those disabled by sickness are offered a concession for *Tahajjud* prayer. This underscores the importance of earning lawful sustenance in Islam. 'Abdullāh ibn Mas'ūd relates that the Prophet (peace be upon him) said: "One who brings grain in a town of Muslims and sells it at the price of the day will attain proximity with Allah". After making this observation, he recited the Qur'ānic verse under discussion. (Ibn Marduwayh in *al-Kashshāf*, 6, 249) 'Umar remarked: "Next to the fighting in the cause of God, I would love to die while journeying through a mountain valley in search of my livelihood." Then he recited the above verse. (Bayhaqī, *Fī Shu'ab al-Īmān* as well as in *al-Kashshāf*, 6, 249)

24. Commentators on the Qur'ān agree that "prayer" here denotes the five daily prayers which are obligatory. Likewise, *Zakāh* denotes the obligatory alms.

25. According to Ibn Zayd, reference here is to spend one's wealth in the way of God, apart from paying *Zakāh*, whether it is in the cause of fighting in the path of God, helping the servants of God, or acts of public welfare or any philanthropic work. Ibn Jarīr al-Ṭabarī, (*Tafsīr*, 23, 398). We have already explained the meaning of "giving God a goodly loan" at several places. (See for example *Towards Understanding the Qur'ān*, vol. I, *Sūrah al-Baqarah* 2: n. 267, p. 187; vol. II, *Sūrah al-Mā'idah* 5: n. 33, p. 142 and *Sūrah al-Ḥadīd* 57: n. 16.)

you shall find it with Allah. That is better and its reward is greater.[26] And ask for Allah's forgiveness; surely He is Most Forgiving, Most Compassionate.

تَجِدُوهُ عِندَ ٱللَّهِ هُوَ خَيْرًا وَأَعْظَمَ أَجْرًا ۚ وَٱسْتَغْفِرُوا۟ ٱللَّهَ ۖ إِنَّ ٱللَّهَ غَفُورٌ رَّحِيمٌۢ ﴿٢٠﴾

26. Whatever good things man sends forth for the Hereafter is much better than his wealth which he hoards in this life, refusing to spend it for winning God's pleasure. 'Abdullāh ibn Mas'ūd reports that once the Prophet (peace be upon him) asked: "Who among you holds his heir's belongings dearer than his own?" Those present replied: "No one among us holds his heir's belongings dearer than his own". He remarked: "Weigh carefully what you are saying: Your real belongings are those good acts of yours which you send forth for the Hereafter. Whatever you hold back actually belongs to your heir." Bukhārī (*K. al-Riqāq*), Nasā'ī (*K. al-Waṣāyā, Bāb al-Karāhiyah fī Ta'khīr al-Waṣīyah*) and *Musnad* of Abū Ya'lā.

Sūrah 74

Al-Muddaththir

(The Cloaked One)

(Makkan Period)

Title

The word *al-muddaththir* featuring in the opening verse of the *Sūrah* forms its title.

Period of Revelation

The first seven verses of this *Sūrah* were sent down in the earliest Makkan phase. Some reports, on the authority of Jābir ibn 'Abdullāh, cited by Bukhārī (*K. Tafsīr al- Qur'ān, Sūrah al-Muddaththir*), Muslim (*K. al-Īmān, Bāb Bad' al-Waḥī*), Tirmidhī (*K. Tafsīr al-Qur'ān, Sūrah al-Muddaththir*) and Aḥmad etc. (3, 306 and 392), even suggest that these are the very earliest verses of the Qur'ān revealed to the Prophet (peace be upon him). However, it is almost the consensus of the Muslim Ummah that verses 1–5 of *Sūrah al-'Alaq* are the earliest Qur'ānic revelation sent down to the Prophet (peace be upon him). However, what is established from authentic reports is that after the revelation of this passage from *Sūrah al-'Alaq*, no further revelation was received by the Prophet (peace be upon him) for quite some time. Then, when the revelation was resumed after this gap, it started with the verses of *Sūrah al-Muddaththir*. Imām Zuhrī recounts the details as follows:

> For a long time, revelation to the Prophet (peace be upon him) remained suspended, and it was such a period of deep grief that at times he would climb up to the top of the mountain in order to throw himself down, but whenever he came to the edge of the peak, the angel Gabriel appeared, reassuring him that he was God's Messenger, which would set his mind at rest and allowed him to regain his composure. (Ibn Jarīr al-Ṭabarī).

After this, Imām Zuhrī offers the following narration, on the authority of Jābir ibn 'Abdullāh: the Messenger of God describing the period of break in revelation (*Fatrat al-Waḥī*) said: "One day as I was walking, I suddenly heard a call from the heavens. As I raised my head, I saw the same angel who had visited me in the cave of Ḥirā', sitting on a chair hanging between the heavens and the earth. This struck such a terror in my heart that on reaching home quickly, I said: 'Cover me up! cover me up!'. My family members covered me with a quilt or a blanket. It was then that Allah revealed to me the opening verses of *Sūrah al-Muddaththir*. From then onwards, revelation became intense and regular." (Bukhārī, Muslim, Aḥmad and Ibn Jarīr al-Ṭabarī, 23, 401)

The remainder of the *Sūrah* (verses 8–56) was sent down on the first *Ḥajj* season after public preaching of Islam commenced in Makkah. Ibn Hishām in his book on *Sīrah* has described the story at length, which we will cite later.

Subject Matter and Theme

As already indicated, the following five verses of *Sūrah al-'Alaq* were the first to be revealed to the Prophet (peace be upon him) which ordained:

> *Recite in the name of your Lord Who created man from a clot of congealed blood. Recite and your Lord is Most Generous, Who taught by the pen, taught man what he did not know.*
>
> (*Sūrah al-'Alaq*, 96: 1–5)

It was the first experience for the Prophet (peace be upon him) to receive divine revelation all of a sudden. It did not spell out clearly the nature of his great mission and the future course of his action. He was given only a brief initiation and was left alone for some time. This allowed him to weather the heavy strain caused by the first experience and mentally prepare himself for receiving revelation and for shouldering the Prophetic mission in the future. When revelation resumed after the intermission, verses 1–7 of *Sūrah al-Muddaththir* were sent down to him. He was commanded now for the first time to arise and warn mankind about the consequences of following the wrong path which they had chosen and to proclaim God's glory in the world where others were being magnified without any right. Along with that, he was instructed that in keeping with his lofty mission, he was obliged to lead a pure and exemplary life in every respect, and to guide fellow human beings sincerely, without any worldly or selfish gain. Then in the last sentence, he was exhorted to bear with all the hardships he had to endure in carrying out this mission for the sake of his Lord.

As the Prophet (peace be upon him) commenced preaching Islam in response to the above divine command and started reciting the Qur'ānic *Sūrahs* revealed to him in quick succession, the people felt alarmed and it provoked a great storm of opposition and hostility in Makkah. A few months passed in this state until the *Ḥajj* season approached. This caused consternation among the Makkan disbelievers, for they apprehended that if the Prophet (peace be upon him) started visiting the caravans of the pilgrims arriving in Makkah from all parts of Arabia and recited the highly effective and spellbinding Qur'ānic passages before them in their camps, his mission will spread far and wide very quickly and will influence countless people. Therefore, the Quraysh chiefs held a consultative meeting, resolving that a propaganda campaign against the Prophet (peace be upon him) be launched among the pilgrims soon after their arrival in Makkah. After they agreed on this, Walīd ibn Mughīrah pointed out to the assembled people that if they said contradictory things against the Prophet (peace be upon him) they would all lose their credibility among the people. They should better reach consensus upon one opinion and follow it without any disagreement. Some proposed that he be branded a soothsayer, but Walīd rejected this proposal, saying: "By God, he is not a soothsayer. We know the soothsayers: what they rant and what they utter has no resemblance whatsoever with the Qur'ān". Others suggested that he be dubbed a mad person. Walīd disagreed, saying: "He is not possessed either. We have seen mad persons and lunatics. The way one talks and behaves irrationally and foolishly in this condition is known to all. Who will then believe that the message presented by Muḥammad is the ranting of a mad person or delirium of the one in a fit of lunacy?" Some others advised that he be projected as a poet. Walīd stressed: "No he is not a poet for we know poetry in all its forms. The Qur'ān does not fall into any category of poetry". Another suggestion was that he be discredited as a magician. Walīd refuted this too, affirming that the label of a magician also did not apply to the Prophet (peace be upon him), for he and others are aware of the ways and tricks of magicians. He further remarked: "Whatever accusation you make; it will not be accepted by the pilgrims. By Lord, his speech is immensely delightful, its roots are very deep and its branches are laden with fruit." Abū Jahl then urged Walīd that people will never be pleased until he suggests a way out. He asked for some time to think over it, and after prolonged thought and reflection, he told them that the nearest thing they can tell the Arabs is that he is a magician. The message presented by him was causing great dissensions within families, resulting in the separation between father and mother, between parents and children. They all agreed on Walīd's plan. As part of this organised strategy, Quraysh delegations called on pilgrims and warned them against the Prophet (peace be upon him), saying that a great magician has emerged. They portrayed him as a consummate magician whose magic is causing great distress and divisions within families. However, it proved to be counterproductive, as in doing so the Quraysh themselves made the name and mission of the Prophet (peace be upon him) known throughout Arabia. (*Sīrah* of Ibn Hishām, vol. I, pp. 306, 308) That Walīd had drawn this strategy at Abū Jahl's insistence is reported by Ibn Jarīr al-Ṭabarī in his *Tafsīr*, on the authority of 'Ikrimah (23, 429).

The second section of this *Sūrah* carries a critique on the above incident. The outline of the contents of the *Sūrah* is as follows:

Verses 8–10 warn those opposing the truth that they will face the terrible consequences of their rejection on the Day of Judgement.

Verses 11–26, without naming Walīd ibn Mughīrah, spell out how God bestowed numerous bounties on him yet he had the audacity to oppose the truth so blatantly. Attention is drawn also to the conflict in his mind, for, on the one hand, he was fully convinced of the truth of the Prophet (peace be upon him) and the Qur'ān, but on the other, he did not want to lose the privileged position he enjoyed within the Makkan society. The latter prevented him from embracing faith, and after a hard and prolonged struggle with his own conscience he finally resolved that he should seek to discredit the Prophet (peace be upon him), declaring him to be a magician with a view to dissuading people from accepting his message. His blatant falsehood is openly exposed and it is said that, notwithstanding such temerity, he expects to receive more divine blessings. However, he has made himself fully deserving of the Hellfire.

Verses 27–48 relate the horrors of Hell and specify what type of people will be consigned to it.

Verses 49–53 diagnose the root cause of the disbelievers' malaise. Since they have no fear regarding the Hereafter and look upon this life as an end in itself, they flee from the Qur'ān as frightened wild asses flee from a lion. Prompted by the same, they lay down unacceptable preconditions for their acceptance of Islam. Even if all their conditions are met, they will still be not inclined at all towards faith because of their denial of the Hereafter.

It is finally declared that God does not stand in need of anyone's faith and will therefore not meet anyone's preconditions. The Qur'ān stands out as divine guidance and admonition for everyone; they are free to accept or reject it. God has a right that the people should feel terrified at the thought of disobeying him. It befits His glory to pardon those who adopt piety and God-consciousness though they had committed various acts of disobedience in the past.

In the name of Allah, the Most Merciful, the Most Compassionate.

بِسۡمِ ٱللَّهِ ٱلرَّحۡمَٰنِ ٱلرَّحِيمِ

(1) O you enveloped in your cloak![1] (2) Arise, and warn,[2] (3) and magnify the glory of your Lord,[3] ▶

يَٰٓأَيُّهَا ٱلۡمُدَّثِّرُ ١ قُمۡ فَأَنذِرۡ ٢
وَرَبَّكَ فَكَبِّرۡ ٣

1. In light of the points highlighted in the Introduction to this *Sūrah* regarding the circumstantial setting of the opening verse, one may easily grasp why the Prophet (peace be upon him) is not addressed here as the Messenger or the Prophet, and why he is instead referred to as "O you enwrapped in your cloak". As he had become terrified on suddenly seeing Gabriel sitting on a chair, hanging between the heavens and the earth, on rushing home he asked his family members to cover him up. On the basis of that, God addresses him here as the enwrapped one. Another point implicit in this subtle address to His beloved servant is that as he is now charged with an onerous duty, he should get ready with a firm resolve to undertake this mission and arise from his solitude.

2. An identical command was given to the Prophet Noah (peace be upon him) when he was endowed with the office of Messengership: "Warn your people before a grievous chastisement comes upon them." (*Sūrah Nūḥ* 71: 1). Here the Prophet Muḥammad (peace be upon him) is directed to arise and to awaken his community lost in disbelief and heedlessness. He should warn them against the inevitable punishment if they persist in their disbelief. They should be clearly told that they are not living in a lawless kingdom and are free to lead their lives as they choose. They should not entertain false perceptions that they will never be called to account for their deeds.

3. This is the first and foremost duty that a Messenger has to perform in this world. His mission consists in rejecting the greatness of all man-made idols erected by the ignorant people. He should loudly proclaim that all glory belongs exclusively to God in the entire universe. This explains why the formula *Allāhu Akbar* (God is great) occupies such a pivotal place in the Islamic scheme of things. *Adhān* commences with the proclamation

(4) and purify your robes,[4] ▶	وَثِيَابَكَ فَطَهِّرْ ۝٤

of the same formula. So, does a Muslim when he begins his prayer, reciting the same, and repeating it throughout the postures of prayer. Even when he slaughters an animal, he pronounces the same: "In the name of God; God is Great". This phrase of glorification is the most distinguishing mark of Muslims throughout the world because God's Messenger himself had embarked on his noble mission while reciting the same.

Another subtle point worth considering that emerges from the circumstantial setting of these verses, is that this marks the first occasion when the Prophet (peace be upon him) was directed to arise for discharging his honourable duty as the Messenger of God. It is perhaps needless to add that the city and society in which he was asked to proclaim the call of monotheism was the hotbed of polytheism. Not only were the Makkans, like all other Arabs, polytheists, but more importantly, the city of Makkah housed the shrine of polytheism, of which the Quraysh were the custodians. It was therefore a highly risky venture for an individual to strive single-handedly for upholding monotheism and obliterating polytheism. The Qur'ānic directive for arising and warning is therefore immediately followed by the exhortation: "Magnify the glory of your Lord" (verse 3). He was thus advised to disregard the great dreadful powers of the day bent on opposing him. He should clearly proclaim that his Lord is far superior to all those determined to obstruct and impede his call. This was a great morale booster and encouragement with which God inspired the Prophet (peace be upon him) to undertake his mission, for one who has firm conviction in God's might and glory will feel no hesitation at all to challenge even the entire world for the sake of God.

4. These words of directive have a very comprehensive meaning: "Purify your robes" carries several meanings: At one level, it is the directive for keeping the clothes free from all impurity; for the cleanliness of the body and clothes goes hand in hand with the purity of the soul. A pure soul cannot co-exist with a dirty body and unclean clothes. The Prophet (peace be upon him) was to present his message in a society steeped not only in the evils of disbelief and immorality but also it was ignorant of the basic norms of purity and cleanliness. He was to instruct them about purity of all kinds. Accordingly, he is directed here to set up a high standard of cleanliness in his outward life as well. Thanks to this directive, he presented such comprehensive instructions about the

cleanliness of the body and clothes, that is unknown even to the most civilised nations of our day, what to say of the Arabs of the *Jāhiliyyah* period. Most of the languages of the world hardly even have a word which is synonymous with the Islamic term *ṭahārah.* In contrast, the works on *ḥadīth* and *fiqh* begin with a chapter on cleanliness, dealing at length with the distinction between purity and impurity and offering detailed instruction of how to attain purity and cleanliness in life.

The second meaning of this directive is to keep one's dress clean and tidy. Under the influence of monastic notions, it was assumed that the more unkempt and dirty a person is, the holier he is. One who was dressed decently was regarded as materialistic. These notions prevailed in the face of the fact that revulsion to impurity and dirt is innate in human nature. One who has even a little sense of decency feels at home in the company of a decently dressed person. It is therefore imperative that the one calling people to the way of God should outwardly appear so neat and clean that people receive him with great esteem. His personality and appearance should not be marred by any stain which may repel people from him.

The third meaning of this directive is that the clothes should not have any stain of moral degradation. The clothes should not only be clean and decent, but it should not betray any arrogance and vanity, ostentation, and grandeur on his part. A person's attire is often a first and lasting impression, enabling others to assess what type of person he is. Needless to add, the dresses of the chiefs and rulers, the clergy and religious functionaries, the arrogant, morally shallow and conceited people, the depraved persons, the people given to a life of pleasure and the characterless, all represent the tastes and tempers of the wearers. The temper of the person calling people to the way of God is naturally different and poles apart from all such people. His dress, therefore, should necessarily be distinct from all of them and should leave the impression that he is a decent and refined person, not suffering from any corruption of the heart.

The fourth meaning of the directive is: leading a pious life, keeping away from all moral evils. This interpretation is endorsed by Ibn 'Abbās, Ibrāhīm al-Nakha'ī, 'Aṭā', Mujāhid, Qatādah, Sa'īd ibn Jubayr, Ḥasan al-Baṣrī and other leading Qur'ān commentators. For them, the verses instruct that excellent morals and manners be observed while shunning all that is blameworthy. In the Arabic idiom, when it is said: "so and so is clean in his clothes", it figuratively means that he is morally sound and pure; on the other hand, when it is said "he is filthy in his garments", it implies that he is dishonest and unreliable in his words and dealings.

(5) and shun uncleanness,[5] (6) and bestow not favour in order to seek from others a greater return,[6] (7) and persevere for your Lord's sake.[7]	وَٱلرُّجْزَ فَٱهْجُرْ ۝٥ وَلَا تَمْنُن تَسْتَكْثِرُ ۝٦ وَلِرَبِّكَ فَٱصْبِرْ ۝٧

5. Uncleanliness includes every type of impurity, whether it is related to articles of faith and thought, morals and deeds, body and clothes, or lifestyle. The Prophet (peace be upon him) is directed to shun all types of vices prevalent in his society. This will not allow anyone to accuse him of indulging even in the minor vices which he is asking others to refrain from.

6. Verse 6 is quite comprehensive in its meaning. Its range of meanings cannot be translated into a single sentence. Some of the meanings conveyed by this verse are: (i) The Prophet (peace be upon him) should do favours to others without any selfish motive. His philanthropy and giving, his generosity and good treatment, should be for the sake of God alone. He should not have the slightest inclination to seek any return on the favours he did. In other words, it should be exclusively in God's way, without expecting or winning any favour in return. (ii) The Prophet's mission in itself constitutes a great favour to those deriving guidance from it. Yet he should not mention it as a favour to anyone. Nor should he ever use it for deriving any personal gain. (iii) Although the Prophet (peace be upon him) has been performing a very noble task, he should not regard it as his personal achievement, nor should he ever think that by risking his life and discharging his duty as the Messenger, he is doing a favour to his Lord.

7. The responsibility of Messengership is no doubt an arduous job. The Prophet (peace be upon him) is bound to face numerous hardships and sufferings in this cause. His own community will turn extremely hostile towards him. All of Arabia will be pitted against him, yet he should persevere for his Lord's sake amid all the hardships. He should keep discharging his duty with utmost constancy and resolve. Fear, greed, temptation, ties of friendship, and love will try to obstruct him, yet he should withstand all the temptations and pressures and acquit himself with consistency and determination.

These were some of the early directives which God gave to His Messenger when He asked him to arise and start the work of his prophetic

(8) When the Trumpet shall be sounded, (9) that will surely be a hard day,[8] (10) not an easy day for the unbelievers.[9] ▶	فَإِذَا نُقِرَ فِي ٱلنَّاقُورِ ٨ فَذَٰلِكَ يَوۡمَئِذٖ يَوۡمٌ عَسِيرٌ ٩ عَلَى ٱلۡكَٰفِرِينَ غَيۡرُ يَسِيرٖ ١٠

mission. On reflecting over these brief directives, one's heart testifies that there cannot be any better directives that could be given at the beginning of his prophetic mission, for these clearly lay down the features of his mission and instruct him in the morals and manners with which he should adorn his life and conduct. He is instructed also about the intention, mind-set, and approach with which he should be performing his duty. He is also warned about the difficulties with which he will be faced. At the same time, he is advised how to encounter the problems faced by him. As to the allegation levelled by those blinded by their prejudices that the Prophet (peace be upon him), God forbid, uttered these sentences during epileptic fits they should honestly and carefully study the above verses, and judge for themselves whether these are the utterances of one suffering from an epileptic fit or are divine directives from God to the one who is about to commence his mission as the Messenger of God.

8. As already stated in the Introduction to the *Sūrah*, these verses were revealed a few months after the revelation of the initial verses of the present *Sūrah* when the public preaching of Islam commenced and the time of the first *Ḥajj* approached. This was the occasion when the chiefs of the Quraysh held a conference wherein they decided to launch a vigorous propaganda campaign designed to poison the minds of the pilgrims, who came from outside Makkah, against the Qur'ān and the Prophet (peace be upon him). The above verses constitute the criticism on this strategy of the disbelievers. They are told that they are free to follow whatever they want. Even if they get some success in this life, how can they avert their terrible end in the Hereafter when the trumpet will be blown and the Resurrection held? (For details see *Towards Understanding the Qur'ān*, vol. II, *Sūrah al-An'ām* 6: n. 48, p. 244; vol. IV, *Sūrah Ibrāhīm* 14: n. 57, pp. 276–277; vol. V, *Sūrah Ṭā Hā* 20: n. 78, pp. 223–224, vol. VI, *Sūrah al-Ḥajj* 22:n.1, pp. 5–6; vol. IX, *Sūrah Yā Sīn* 36: nn. 46–47, pp. 265–266; *Sūrah al-Zumar* 39: n. 79 and *Sūrah Qāf* 50: n. 52.)

9. It is evident from the verse that it will be an easy day for the believers. Only the disbelievers who had rejected the truth will be subjected to

(11) Leave Me with him[10] whom I alone have created,[11] (12) whom I have endowed with abundant riches, (13) and sons ever present with him,[12] (14) and for whom I have smoothed the way (to power and riches), (15) and who still greedily desires that I should bestow upon him more.[13] ▶

ذَرۡنِي وَمَنۡ خَلَقۡتُ وَحِيدٗا ١١ وَجَعَلۡتُ لَهُۥ مَالٗا مَّمۡدُودٗا ١٢ وَبَنِينَ شُهُودٗا ١٣ وَمَهَّدتُّ لَهُۥ تَمۡهِيدٗا ١٤ ثُمَّ يَطۡمَعُ أَنۡ أَزِيدَ ١٥

all hardships on the Day of Judgement. Furthermore, it is clarified that the disbelievers are destined for eternal punishment; their ordeal will not be lessened. No laxity is expected to replace their severe punishment.

10. The address is directed to the Prophet (peace be upon him), informing him: "You should leave the case of Walīd ibn Mughīrah to Me for suggesting at the disbelievers' conference that you be discredited as a magician among the pilgrims coming from different parts of Arabia. I will deal with Walīd; you need not bother about this matter at all".

11. This statement is open to two meanings which are equally valid: (i) When Allah created Walīd, he was not born with any wealth, children, or a high social position. (ii) It is God alone Who created Walīd. As to the false gods for whose sake he so vigorously opposed the Prophet's mission, they were not Allah's associates and had no role whatsoever in his birth.

12. Walīd had a dozen sons. Of them, Khālid ibn al-Walīd became the most prominent in history. His sons are designated as *shahūd* in the above verse, which may have the following meaning: (i) That they do not have to struggle and go afar for seeking their livelihood. They are so wealthy that they are always present in their father's company, ready to assist him. (ii) That all of his sons are prominent and influential, and accompany him in all social gatherings and meetings. (iii) That they are reckoned as reliable witnesses in all kinds of dealings in view of their high social standing.

13. His greed is insatiable. Although he is endowed with everything, he still greedily desires more. According to Ḥasan al-Baṣrī and other

(16) By no means; he is stubbornly opposed to Our Signs. (17) I shall soon constrain him to a hard ascent. (18) He reflected and then hatched a scheme. (19) Ruin seize him, how did he hatch a scheme? (20) Again, ruin seize him, how did he hatch a scheme? (21) He looked (at others); (22) then frowned and scowled; (23) then he retreated and waxed proud, (24) and said: "This (Qur'ān) is merely a sorcery of yore; (25) this is nothing but the word of a mere mortal!"[14] (26) Him shall I soon roast in Hell. (27) And what do you know what Hell is? ▶

كَلَّآ إِنَّهُۥ كَانَ لِأَيَـٰتِنَا عَنِيدًا ﴿١٦﴾
سَأُرْهِقُهُۥ صَعُودًا ﴿١٧﴾ إِنَّهُۥ فَكَّرَ وَقَدَّرَ ﴿١٨﴾
فَقُتِلَ كَيْفَ قَدَّرَ ﴿١٩﴾ ثُمَّ قُتِلَ كَيْفَ قَدَّرَ
﴿٢٠﴾ ثُمَّ نَظَرَ ﴿٢١﴾ ثُمَّ عَبَسَ وَبَسَرَ ﴿٢٢﴾ ثُمَّ أَدْبَرَ
وَٱسْتَكْبَرَ ﴿٢٣﴾ فَقَالَ إِنْ هَـٰذَآ إِلَّا سِحْرٌ
يُؤْثَرُ ﴿٢٤﴾ إِنْ هَـٰذَآ إِلَّا قَوْلُ ٱلْبَشَرِ ﴿٢٥﴾
سَأُصْلِيهِ سَقَرَ ﴿٢٦﴾ وَمَآ أَدْرَىٰكَ مَا سَقَرُ ﴿٢٧﴾

---

scholars, this means that Walīd used to claim that if the Prophet Muḥammad's version about life after death and Paradise is true, then that Paradise is prepared for him.

14. Reference is to the conference held by the disbelievers, which is referred to in the introduction to this *Sūrah*. It emerges from its proceedings that Walīd realised in his heart and was convinced that the Qur'ān was indeed the Word of God. However, for maintaining and protecting his privileged position among his people, he was not ready to accept Islam. When he turned down the charges levelled against the Prophet (peace be upon him) by the chiefs of the Quraysh, he was obliged to frame an alternative charge which would poison the minds of Arabs against the Prophet (peace be upon him). In doing so, he tried hard to stifle the voice of his own conscience and experienced a mental ordeal, which is vividly projected in the above verse.

(28) It spares nothing; it leaves nothing intact;[15] (29) it scorches (even) the skin.[16] (30) Over it are nineteen keepers. (31) We[17] have ▶

لَا تُبْقِي وَلَا تَذَرُ ﴿٢٨﴾ لَوَّاحَةٌ لِّلْبَشَرِ ﴿٢٩﴾ عَلَيْهَا
تِسْعَةَ عَشَرَ ﴿٣٠﴾ وَمَا جَعَلْنَآ

15. It admits the following two meanings: (i) One who is hurled into Hell is reduced to ashes yet he will not die, as he will be revived and scorched repeatedly. The same truth is stated at another place thus: "He (a sinner) will neither die nor live in the Hellfire." (*Sūrah al-A'lā* 87: 13) (ii) Hell will not spare anyone who deserves to be chastised, and once it seizes anyone, it will not let him escape the punishment.

16. That the Hellfire will completely burn a sinner is followed by the statement: "It will scorch the skin as well," which seems somewhat unnecessary. However, this is mentioned to emphasise the tormenting and severe nature of its punishment, particularly of the face and skin. One dislikes it most that his face be disfigured, though he may reconcile to the disfiguring of some internal part of the body. Likewise, any ugly marks on one's skin also appear quite repulsive. Accordingly, it is said that those exulting presently in their beautiful faces, immaculate bodies, and unblemished skin will be severely disfigured and scorched, if they, like Walīd ibn Mughīrah, take to the path of mocking and opposing God's Word.

17. The whole passage commencing from the present verse until "And none knows the hosts of your Lord but He" (verse 31) is a parenthetical statement which has been inserted here to respond to the disbelievers' mockery when they heard from the Prophet that God had appointed only 19 angels as Hell's keepers. They instantly began to ridicule this statement. They considered it quite bizarre that on the one hand it was said that all people from the time of Ādam until the end of time who had rejected the true faith and had committed mortal sins would be cast into Hell. On the other, it was also claimed that Hell would have no more than 19 keepers to chastise such enormous hordes of people. The chiefs of the Quraysh are on record to have burst into laughter on hearing the above. Abū Jahl quipped: "Brothers, are you so powerless that ten of you together will not be able to overpower each of those 19 keepers?" A wrestler hailing from the Banī Jumaḥ tribe boasted: "I alone will overwhelm 17 of them; all of you together should take care

appointed none but angels as the keepers of the Fire,[18] and We have not made their number but as a trial for the unbelievers[19] so that those who have been endowed with the Book will be convinced[20] and the ▶	أَصۡحَٰبَ ٱلنَّارِ إِلَّا مَلَٰٓئِكَةٗۙ وَمَا جَعَلۡنَا عِدَّتَهُمۡ إِلَّا فِتۡنَةٗ لِّلَّذِينَ كَفَرُواْ لِيَسۡتَيۡقِنَ ٱلَّذِينَ أُوتُواْ ٱلۡكِتَٰبَ

of the other two." The parenthetical statement stands out as a rejoinder to these remarks by the disbelievers.

18. The strength of angels should not be foolishly likened to that of human beings. Man has no idea what tremendous power has been granted to the angels created by God.

19. Apparently, there was hardly any need for specifying the number of Hell's keepers. God however clarifies that their number is stated as a trial for the disbelievers, especially for the hypocrites who are concealing their inner doubt about God's divinity, His boundless power, or revelation and Messengership. For a hypocrite, notwithstanding his show of faith, is liable to betray his lack of faith on hearing the Qur'ānic statement that only 19 keepers of Hell will suffice to deal with countless number of sinners from amongst the *jinn* and human beings, and that they will inflict punishment on each sinner individually.

20. Some Qur'ān commentators interpret this in the sense that since the Scriptures of the people of the Book specify the same number of keepers of Hell, they were likely to be convinced that this statement is truly from God. However, in our opinion this view is unsound on the following two counts: (i) Despite our best efforts we could not locate this specific number of the keepers of Hell in their Scriptures. Moreover, they dismiss those statements which are common to the Qur'ān and their Scriptures, alleging that the Prophet (peace be upon him) had plagiarised these from their sources. So, the correct interpretation of the verse in our view is that the Prophet (peace be upon him) knew it well that his reference to the 19 keepers of Hell will be taken as a butt of mockery. Yet this, being divine revelation, was presented by him publicly without any

believers' faith will increase,[21] and neither those who have been endowed with the Book nor the believers will fall into any doubt.[22] As for those in whose hearts there is a sickness as well as the unbelievers, they will say: ▶

وَيَزْدَادَ ٱلَّذِينَ ءَامَنُوٓا۟ إِيمَـٰنًا ۙ وَلَا يَرْتَابَ ٱلَّذِينَ أُوتُوا۟ ٱلْكِتَـٰبَ وَٱلْمُؤْمِنُونَ ۙ وَلِيَقُولَ ٱلَّذِينَ فِى قُلُوبِهِم مَّرَضٌ وَٱلْكَـٰفِرُونَ

hesitation, disregarding the consequences of mockery to which he will be subjected. The pagans of Arabia were not familiar with the exalted status of the Messengers of God. However, the People of the Book knew it well that Messengers in every age faithfully convey the divine message, no matter how much it might be disliked by people. Given this, it was expected that at least, the People of the Book without hesitation would appreciate the Prophet's truthfulness in having honestly conveyed God's Word. It is worth stressing that the Prophet (peace be upon him) had acted in a similar fashion on several earlier occasions as well. The most instructive example is the event of the *mi'rāj* (the Night Journey) which he recounted without any reservation in the disbelievers' gathering. He was not perturbed at all that his detractors will criticise him vehemently on listening to this amazing account of his overnight ascent to the heavens.

21. It is stated at several places in the Qur'ān that on the occasion of every trial and tribulation, a believer displays his utmost commitment to faith and abandons the path of doubt and denial, disobedience and disloyalty to his belief. Since he adheres to the path of faith with loyalty and constancy, his faith increases tremendously. (For details see *Towards Understanding the Qur'ān,* vol. I, *Sūrah Āl 'Imrān* 3: 173 p. 299; *Sūrah al-Anfāl* 8: n. 2, pp. 137–138; *Sūrah al-Tawbah* 9: n. 125, p. 276; vol. IX, *Sūrah al-Aḥzāb* 33: n. 38, pp. 40–41 and *Sūrah al-Fatḥ* 48: n. 7.)

22. The Qur'ān generally speaks of "the sickness in the heart" figuratively for hypocrisy. In view of this word, some Qur'ān commentators are inclined to the view that this verse must have been revealed in Madīnah, as the hypocrites had only come into the limelight there. However, it is not correct for a number of reasons. First, it is an invalid assertion that there was no hypocrite in Makkah. We have pointed out this fallacy earlier (See *Towards Understanding the Qur'ān*, vol. VIII,

"What did Allah aim at by this strange parable?"[23] Thus does Allah let whomsoever He pleases to go astray, and directs whomsoever He pleases to the Right Way.[24] ▶

مَاذَآ أَرَادَ ٱللَّهُ بِهَـٰذَا مَثَلًا ۚ كَذَٰلِكَ يُضِلُّ ٱللَّهُ مَن يَشَآءُ وَيَهْدِى مَن يَشَآءُ ۚ

Sūrah al-'Ankabūt 29: Introduction and nn. 12–16, pp. 2–3 and 13–16). Secondly, in our opinion it is not a sound practice in the tradition of *tafsīr* writing to claim, all of a sudden, that a certain sentence which is part of a continuous discourse and was revealed on a particular occasion and circumstance was revealed on a different occasion and was inserted there without any relevance or rationale. From authentic sources that we know, this passage of the *Sūrah* was revealed in the context of a particular incident in the early phase of Makkah. The whole passage is coherent and has full relevance to the event. How could something, if revealed years later in Madīnah, be appended to it? As for the meaning of "the sickness in the heart", the reference is to the disease of scepticism and mental reservation. Not only in Makkah, but in the entire world, very few people reject outright the existence of God, the Hereafter, revelation, Prophethood, Paradise and Hell, etc. What is more common is the streak of doubt about their existence. Generally, people feel unsure whether God, the Hereafter, Paradise and Hell, and angels exist or not. Likewise, they remain doubtful about the credentials of the Messengers, and whether they did receive divine revelation or not. This scepticism in many people often culminates into disbelief. As already stated, total rejection of the articles of faith has never been a common phenomenon, for anyone with common sense realises that the matters related to faith may be true and that these are not to be rejected out of hand, for there is no rational grounds for their outright denial and rejection.

23. This does not mean that they believed in the Qur'ān as God's Word and still expressed their astonishment over this statement. Rather, they contended that a book containing such irrational and improbable matters could not be a revelation from God.

24. God tests man from time to time by such statements. One endowed with a sound mind and heart might readily gain guidance

And none knows the hosts of your Lord but He.[25] (And Hell has only been mentioned here) that people may take heed.[26] (32) Nay,[27] by the moon, (33) and by the night when it recedes, (34) and by the day when it dawns (with its radiance), ▶

وَمَا يَعْلَمُ جُنُودَ رَبِّكَ إِلَّا هُوَ ۚ وَمَا هِيَ إِلَّا ذِكْرَىٰ لِلْبَشَرِ ﴿٣١﴾ كَلَّا وَالْقَمَرِ ﴿٣٢﴾ وَاللَّيْلِ إِذْ أَدْبَرَ ﴿٣٣﴾ وَالصُّبْحِ إِذَا أَسْفَرَ ﴿٣٤﴾

---

from such a statement and follow the straight way. However, the same is used as a pretext by an obstinate and foolish person who wants to evade the truth. God guides and blesses the former for He does not misguide a seeker of truth. However, as the latter opts for error, God lets him pursue this course. Again, it is not God's way to compel man to follow the straight way if he is averse to the truth. (On the issue of God's guidance to man and His leading man astray see *Towards Understanding the Qur'ān* vol. I, *Sūrah al-Baqarah* 2: nn. 10, 16, 19 and 20, pp. 48–49, 51, and 52–53; vol. II, *Sūrah al-Nisā'* 4: n. 173, pp. 99–100; *Sūrah al-An'ām* 6: nn. 17, 28 and 90, pp. 223–224, 231 and 271; vol. IV, *Sūrah Yūnus* 10: n. 13, pp. 13–14; vol. V, *Sūrah al-Kahf* 18: n. 54, pp. 115–116 and vol. VII, *Sūrah al-Qaṣaṣ* 28: n. 71, p. 288.)

25. God alone knows what kinds of creatures He has created in the universe, what powers have been granted to them, and how they should serve Him. If man inhabiting this small planet, and on the basis of the limited knowledge accessible to him through his sense of perception, passes some judgment on the universe or God's working, it would betray his own foolishness, for it is beyond man to grasp even partially the working of the vast and limitless universe by his limited sight or instruments. He cannot fathom its vastness and greatness with his very finite knowledge.

26. Man had better take heed and protect himself from the overwhelming divine punishment before it overtakes him.

27. What is being said here is not baseless prattle or irresponsible gossip. There was no occasion, therefore, to subject it to ridicule.

(35) surely (Hell) is one of the greatest Signs,[28] (36) a warning to humankind, (37) a warning to everyone of you whether he would like to come forward or lag behind.[29]

(38) Each one is a hostage to one's deeds,[30] (39) save the People of the Right Hand[31] (40) who shall be in the Gardens, and shall ask ▶

إِنَّهَا لَإِحْدَى ٱلْكُبَرِ ﴿٣٥﴾ نَذِيرًا لِّلْبَشَرِ ﴿٣٦﴾
لِمَن شَآءَ مِنكُمْ أَن يَتَقَدَّمَ أَوْ
يَتَأَخَّرَ ﴿٣٧﴾ كُلُّ نَفْسٍۭ بِمَا كَسَبَتْ
رَهِينَةٌ ﴿٣٨﴾ إِلَّآ أَصْحَـٰبَ ٱلْيَمِينِ ﴿٣٩﴾ فِى
جَنَّـٰتٍ يَتَسَآءَلُونَ ﴿٤٠﴾

---

28. In the same way that the moon and the night and the day are all among the great signs of God's power, so too is Hell. The existence of the moon and the constant alternation of night and day are not something improbable, then why, in your view, has the existence of Hell become impossible? Man is not struck with wonder on observing something so amazing as the moon and the alternation of day and night. These things in themselves are miracles of the great marvels of God's creative power. Had man not observed first-hand the sun and the moon and been informed of the existence of the moon in the universe, or that there is a sun, when it sets, it leaves the world in complete darkness, and when it rises, it illuminates the world with a bright light, then he would have subjected this report to the same ridicule, with which they dismiss the existence of Hell.

29. Man is eloquently warned against Hell. It is now up to him to heed and come forward onto the correct path or to lag behind in error and disbelief.

30. For details see *Towards Understanding the Qur'ān, Sūrah al-Ṭūr* 52: n. 16.

31. The people of the left hand will be seized for their misdeeds whereas those of the right hand will salvage themselves by dint of their faith and good deeds. (For the explanation of the people of the left and the right hand see *Towards Understanding the Qur'ān, Sūrah al-Wāqi'ah* 56: nn. 5–6.)

(41) about the guilty ones:[32] (42) "What drove you to Hell?" (43) They will answer: "We were not among those who observed Prayer,[33] (44) and we did not feed the poor,[34] (45) and we indulged in vain talk with those who indulged in vain talk, (46) and we gave the lie to the Day of Judgement (47) until the inevitable event overtook us."[35] ▶

عَنِ ٱلْمُجْرِمِينَ ﴿٤١﴾ مَا سَلَكَكُمْ فِى سَقَرَ
﴿٤٢﴾ قَالُوا۟ لَمْ نَكُ مِنَ ٱلْمُصَلِّينَ ﴿٤٣﴾ وَلَمْ نَكُ
نُطْعِمُ ٱلْمِسْكِينَ ﴿٤٤﴾ وَكُنَّا نَخُوضُ مَعَ
ٱلْخَآئِضِينَ ﴿٤٥﴾ وَكُنَّا نُكَذِّبُ بِيَوْمِ
ٱلدِّينِ ﴿٤٦﴾ حَتَّىٰٓ أَتَىٰنَا ٱلْيَقِينُ ﴿٤٧﴾

---

32. As mentioned at several places in the Qur'ān, the dwellers of Paradise will be able, even while remaining there, to see and communicate with the inmates of Hell, notwithstanding the very long distance between them and the lack of any device for communication. (For examples see *Towards Understanding the Qur'ān*, vol. III, *Sūrah al-A'rāf* 7: n. 35, pp. 30–31 and vol. IX, *Sūrah al-Ṣāffāt* 37: n. 32, p. 292.)

33. They were not regular in offering daily prayers as the foremost duty imposed by God, and they were not firm believers in God, His Messenger, and His Book. It is worth stating that one who does not truly believe cannot offer prayer at all. It is an essential trait of a believer that he offers prayer regularly. If one abandons prayer, even though he may be a believer, it is clarified that he cannot escape the Hellfire.

34. This underscores the enormity of the crime in Islam of a person who finds a hungry person and does not feed him, despite having the means. It is mentioned in particular as one of the sins which will drag one to Hell.

35. They clung to the wrong path until their death, of which they were oblivious. "The inevitable event" stands for both death and the Hereafter.

(48) The intercession of the intercessors shall then be of no avail to them.[36]

(49) What is the matter with people that they are turning away from this Exhortation, (50) as though they were frightened wild asses, (51) fleeing from a lion?[37] (52) No indeed; each one of them desires that open letters be sent to each of them.[38] ▶

فَمَا تَنفَعُهُمْ شَفَـٰعَةُ ٱلشَّـٰفِعِينَ ﴿٤٨﴾ فَمَا لَهُمْ
عَنِ ٱلتَّذْكِرَةِ مُعْرِضِينَ ﴿٤٩﴾ كَأَنَّهُمْ حُمُرٌ
مُّسْتَنفِرَةٌ ﴿٥٠﴾ فَرَّتْ مِن قَسْوَرَةٍ ﴿٥١﴾ بَلْ يُرِيدُ
كُلُّ ٱمْرِئٍ مِّنْهُمْ أَن يُؤْتَىٰ صُحُفًا مُّنَشَّرَةً ﴿٥٢﴾

---

36. No intercessor's plea can avail those culprits who clung to the wrong faith until their last breath. The Qur'ān has clearly spelled out the doctrine of intercession at several places. In its light, one can easily find out who can intercede and who cannot, when one can intercede and when he cannot, for whom he can intercede and for whom he cannot, for whom it is beneficial and for whom it is not. Since this doctrine has misled many into error, the Qur'ān has clarified all that is required to know, leaving no room for any doubt. It will be in order to study the following Qur'ānic passages on intercession: Verses 255 of *Sūrah al-Baqarah*, 94 of *Sūrah al-An'ām*, 53 of *Sūrah al-A'rāf*, 3 and 18 of *Sūrah Yūnus*, 87 of *Sūrah Maryam*, 109 of *Sūrah Ṭā Hā*, 28 of *Sūrah al-Anbiyā'*, 23 of *Sūrah Saba'*, 43–44 of *Sūrah al-Zumar*, 18 of *Sūrah al-Mu'min*, 41–42 of *Sūrah al-Dukhān*, 26 of *Sūrah al-Najm* and 37–38 of *Sūrah al-Naba'*, and the explanatory notes on these.

37. This is an idiomatic Arabic expression. No sooner do wild asses sense danger then they are totally stupefied and flee in fright in a manner that no other animals do. The Arabs therefore liken panic-stricken persons to wild asses fleeing from the smell of a lion, or the sound of a hunter.

38. The Makkan chiefs were of the opinion that if God had indeed designated Muḥammad (peace be upon him) as a Prophet, He should have sent a letter to each of the chiefs and elders of Makkah informing them of this. The letter should be such that it convinces them that it is written by God Himself. Only then would they accept him as a Prophet. At another

(53) No indeed; the truth is that they have no fear of the Hereafter.[39] (54) Nay;[40] this is an Exhortation. (55) So, whoever wills may benefit from it. ▸	كَلَّا ۖ بَل لَّا يَخَافُونَ ٱلْـَٔاخِرَةَ ﴿٥٣﴾ كَلَّآ إِنَّهُۥ تَذْكِرَةٌ ﴿٥٤﴾ فَمَن شَآءَ ذَكَرَهُۥ ﴿٥٥﴾

place the Qur'ān reproduces this demand of the Makkan disbelievers in this way: "We will not believe until we are given what was given to the Messengers of God." (*Sūrah al-An'ām* 6: 124) Their other demand was: "We will not believe until you (the Prophet) ascend to the sky and bring down a book for them that they can read." (*Sūrah Banī Isrā'īl* 17: 93)

39. The main reason for their refusal to believe was not because of the non-fulfillment of their demands. Rather, they had no fear of the Hereafter. For them this world was all that there is. They were totally heedless of the Afterlife and that they have to face full accountability for their deeds. This lay at the core of their carelessness and irresponsibility in the world. For them the issue of truth and falsehood was meaningless for they were unaware of any truth which definitely brought them some gains in this world, or any falsehood which necessarily brought any evil in the world. They were simply not interested in the issue of truth and falsehood. Only one who regards this life as ephemeral and the Afterlife as eternal feels concerned about real truth and falsehood, for he believes in the recompense of reward for good and punishment for bad. Accordingly, such a person is likely to embrace faith on studying the cogent arguments and noble teachings presented in the Qur'ān. He will use his common sense and reflect on what is actually wrong in the beliefs and deeds which the Qur'ān brands as false. In contrast, one who disbelieves in the Hereafter and is not serious in the quest of truth will lay down preconditions for accepting faith and will not feel convinced, even if all of his demands are met. He will still find some other pretext for not embracing faith. The same truth is highlighted in the Qur'ān thus: "O Messenger, had We sent down to you a book inscribed on parchment, and had they touched it with their own hands, the disbelievers would still have said: This is nothing but plain magic.' (*Sūrah al-An'ām* 6: 7)

40. "No indeed" is said here to stress that God will never accede to any such requests.

(56) But they will not benefit from it unless Allah Himself so wills.[41] He is worthy to be feared;[42] and He is worthy to forgive (those that fear Him).[43]	وَمَا يَذْكُرُونَ إِلَّآ أَن يَشَآءَ ٱللَّهُ هُوَ أَهْلُ ٱلتَّقْوَىٰ وَأَهْلُ ٱلْمَغْفِرَةِ ﴿٥٦﴾

41. One's taking heed and following guidance does not depend solely on his own inclination. When Allah wills so, he follows the guidance for it is He Who, through His grace, enables him to derive guidance. In other words, it is stressed that man cannot do anything solely on his own volition. It is God's will that helps one accomplish what he sets out to do. It is a very delicate issue. Those unable to appreciate this are liable to falter. Had everyone been absolutely free to do what he desires, it would have disturbed the working of the world. The present order is in place owing to God's supreme will. Man may achieve something only when God wills so. The same holds true for man's guidance and error. Man's own inclination to be guided is not sufficient. Only when God decides to confer guidance upon him, he is blessed with it. Likewise, when God decides to let him wander into error in view of his proclivity for error, he takes to the wrong path. It is God Who enables man to do as much as He wills according to His supreme wisdom and expedience.

42. Allah does not stand in need of man deriving guidance. Therefore, man's refusal to be guided does not harm Him at all. Man is admonished because God wills that man should seek His pleasure and shun all that displeases Him.

43. It befits God to shower His mercy on a sinner when he mends his way, irrespective of the quantum of his disobedience. God is merciful and not vindictive towards His servants; He is not eager to punish them.

Sūrah 75

Al-Qiyāmah

(The Resurrection)

(Makkan Period)

Title

The title *al-Qiyāmah* is taken from the opening verse of this *Sūrah* and also happens to be its subject matter, for the entire *Sūrah* deals with the Resurrection.

Period of Revelation

There is no report to indicate its period of revelation. However, regrding the subject matter of this *Sūrah*, internal evidence indicates that it is one of the earliest *Sūrahs* revealed in Makkah, for, after verse 15, the discourse is suddenly interrupted and the Prophet (peace be upon him) is told: "Do not move your tongue hastily (to commit the revelation to your memory). Surely it is for Us to have you commit it to memory and to recite it. And so, when We recite it, follow its recitation attentively, then it will be for Us to explain its meaning." (Verses 16–19).

Then from verse 20 onwards the same theme which was interrupted at verse 15 is resumed. The background to this parenthetical statement in the *Sūrah* is that as Gabriel recited the *Sūrah*, the Prophet (peace be upon him) kept repeating it lest he might forget any word of it. It is thus fairly clear that it was revealed at a time when the experience of revelation was new for him and he was not accustomed to receiving it. There are two other instances of this in the Qur'ān; (a): "Hasten not with reciting the Qur'ān before its recitation to you is finished." (Verse 114 of *Sūrah Ṭā Hā*) and (b): "We shall make you recite (the Qur'ān) and then you will not forget it" (Verse 6 of *Sūrah al-A'lā*). Later, no such directive was issued to him as he had become accustomed to receiving revelation. That is why this advice is given to him only at three places in the Qur'ān.

Subject Matter and Themes

This and later *Sūrahs* up to the end of the Qur'ān were revealed after the sending down of verses 1–7 of *Sūrah al-Muddaththir*. In terms of their subject matter and style, these *Sūrahs* are almost identical and they were sent down in quick succession, one after another. They forcefully and effectively present the teachings of Islam, articles of Islamic faith and moral teachings in comprehensive but brief sentences. The Makkans are vehemently warned against their errors and deviations. This unnerved the Quraysh chiefs to the extent that they devised plans for discrediting the Prophet (peace be upon him) before the next *Ḥajj* season approached. They hurriedly organised the conference to devise the scheme which we have referred to in the introduction to *Sūrah al-Muddaththir*.

This *Sūrah* answers all the doubts and objections of the deniers of the Hereafter, one by one. Weighty arguments are adduced in support of the possibility, occurrence, and necessity of the Resurrection and the Hereafter. It is emphasised that the rejection of the Hereafter is not based on any rational logic. Driven by their selfish motives, the disbelievers are not ready to accept this reality. They are alerted to the occurrence of the inevitable Last Day when they will be presented with their record of deeds. Even before anyone sees his record, he will be fully aware of what he has done during his past life. He knows himself best, notwithstanding his pretexts and pleas for concealing his misdeeds from others and for assuaging his own conscience.

In the name of Allah, the Most Merciful, the Most Compassionate.	بِسْمِ ٱللَّهِ ٱلرَّحْمَٰنِ ٱلرَّحِيمِ
(1) Nay,[1] I swear by the Day of Resurrection;[2] ▶	لَآ أُقْسِمُ بِيَوْمِ ٱلْقِيَٰمَةِ ①

1. To open a discourse with "nay" itself indicates that this *Sūrah* was revealed in order to refute something. "Nay" in the present context signifies that the disbelievers' notions about the Resurrection and Life-After-Death are false. They not only rejected the belief of the Resurrection, but mocked it too. This is followed by a sworn statement enunciating what the truth really is. The stylistic feature is the refutation of a false view and the affirmation of the true one.

2. The Qur'ān speaks of the three types of the human self: (i) His base self prompts him to evil. It is designated as *nafs al-ammārah*. (ii) The self that regrets a bad deed or a false thought and reproaches man. This is called *nafs al-lawwāmah*, a synonym for conscience. (iii) *Nafs al-muṭma'innah* takes delight in following the correct path and in abandoning the wrong path.

The thing for which Allah has sworn an oath by the Day of Resurrection and the self-reproaching self has not been specified because the following sentence itself points it out. The oath has been sworn to stress that God will certainly resurrect man after his death and that He is fully capable to do so. Now the question arises as on what ground the oath of the two things has been taken.

As for the Day of Resurrection, the reason for swearing by it is that it is bound to happen. The order of the universe testifies that it is not eternal. It has not been there from the beginning, nor will it last forever. Man did not have the notion that this ever-changing world is eternal or immortal. The more knowledge man gains, the more convinced he gets that the universe came into existence at a point of time, prior to which it did not exist. Moreover, it has its end which is bound to come. For this reason, God affirms the occurrence of the Resurrection by taking recourse to swearing by the Day of Resurrection itself.

The above oath underscores that the present order will disintegrate one day. The self-reproaching soul is invoked as a second oath to assert the Resurrection, man's accountability about his deeds, and the recompense

(2) and nay, I swear by the self-reproaching soul! (3) Does man imagine that We will not be able to bring his bones together again?[3] ▶	وَلَآ أُقۡسِمُ بِٱلنَّفۡسِ ٱللَّوَّامَةِ ۝٢ أَيَحۡسَبُ ٱلۡإِنسَـٰنُ أَلَّن نَّجۡمَعَ عِظَامَهُۥ ۝٣

for his good and bad activities. Every human being is gifted with conscience, with a strong sense of good and evil. Even a headstrong sinner's conscience pricks him for his evil deeds and for his failure to do good, notwithstanding his own criteria of vice and virtue. This in itself vindicates that man is not a mere animal. Rather, he is a moral being. Instinctively he discerns good and evil. He considers himself responsible for both his good and bad deeds. Even if he silences his conscience over the wrong he inflicts upon someone else, he naturally demands punishment, if he is subjected to the same wrong which he had committed. The self-reproaching soul is an ineluctable part of human nature. Equally undeniable is the truth of the Hereafter, which is eloquently endorsed by the self-reproaching soul. The argument for Resurrection is innate in human nature. Man instinctively demands that good and bad be rewarded and punished respectively. This recompense is possible only in the Hereafter, for no sane person can deny that were man to disappear altogether after his death, he will be deprived of reward for many of his good deeds. Likewise, he will escape just and lawful punishment for his many evil deeds. Only such fools can deny the Hereafter who think that man has been placed in a haphazard universe, which has nothing to do with morality. The notion of the transmigration of souls is not natural either, for were man to be reborn regularly for facing the recompense, he would continue committing certain actions in each of his life cycles. He will have to be rewarded or punished for these. It would be an unending business, of which the account will never be settled. Nature demands that man should have only one life and be resurrected at the end of this world so that he is recompensed in full for his good and evil actions. (See also *Towards Understanding the Qur'ān*, vol. III, *Sūrah al-A'rāf* 7: n. 30, pp. 23–26.)

3. The two arguments given in the form of the oaths prove two truths: (i) The Last Day (i.e. the first stage of resurrection) is a certainty. (ii) Life-after-Death is essential, for this alone can meet the logical and

(4) Yes indeed; We have the power to remould even his finger-tips.[4] (5) But man desires to persist in his evil ways.[5] ▶	بَلَىٰ قَـٰدِرِينَ عَلَىٰٓ أَن نُّسَوِّيَ بَنَانَهُۥ ﴿٤﴾ بَلْ يُرِيدُ ٱلْإِنسَـٰنُ لِيَفْجُرَ أَمَامَهُۥ ﴿٥﴾

natural dictates of man's moral being. Man's conscience too, bears out the same. A third argument is advanced here to ascertain that Life-after-Death is possible. The Makkan disbelievers who denied the Resurrection repeatedly said that those who had died centuries before cannot be brought back to life for their bodies have been completely disintegrated, with their bones decomposed as well. Moreover, some were burnt to ashes, some were devoured by beasts, still others were drowned or eaten away by fish. Their body parts could not be put back together. It was beyond them that someone who had been dead for thousands of years could be brought back to life. God retorts, putting before them this succinct question: "Does man imagine that We will not be able to bring his bones again together?" (verse 3) Had the Qur'ān stated that your disintegrated bodies will be revived on its own and you will come back to life by yourself, then you have every reason to justify it as impossible. However, the Qur'ān specifically states that it will be accomplished by God the Almighty. Can they imagine that God being the Creator (whom they too regarded as the Creator of the universe) is unable to do so? One who believes in God as the Creator of the universe cannot take the position that God cannot resurrect what He created in the first place. A fool who persists in this error should be asked that since God created him out of numerous elements and substances, why now can He not easily re-constitute the same once again?

4. What to say of re-constituting man's body by bringing his big bones together, God has the power to remould the most delicate parts of his body, even his fingertips.

5. This brief sentence diagnoses the root cause of the malaise afflicting the disbelievers. They do not reject the Hereafter, deeming it as something improbable. They deny and disbelieve in it because its affirmation imposes certain moral restrictions on them. They are not ready to observe any restriction. Rather, they want to lead an unbridled way of life, free

(6) He asks: "When will the Day of Resurrection be?"[6] (7) When the sight is dazed,[7] (8) and the moon is eclipsed, (9) and the sun and the moon are joined together,[8] (10) on that Day will man say: "Whither the refuge?" (11) No, there is no refuge. (12) With your Lord alone will be the retreat that Day. ▶

يَسْـَٔلُ أَيَّانَ يَوْمُ ٱلْقِيَـٰمَةِ ﴿٦﴾ فَإِذَا بَرِقَ
ٱلْبَصَرُ ﴿٧﴾ وَخَسَفَ ٱلْقَمَرُ ﴿٨﴾ وَجُمِعَ ٱلشَّمْسُ
وَٱلْقَمَرُ ﴿٩﴾ يَقُولُ ٱلْإِنسَـٰنُ يَوْمَئِذٍ أَيْنَ
ٱلْمَفَرُّ ﴿١٠﴾ كَلَّا لَا وَزَرَ ﴿١١﴾ إِلَىٰ رَبِّكَ
يَوْمَئِذٍ ٱلْمُسْتَقَرُّ ﴿١٢﴾

to indulge in their sin and wickedness, error, injustice, and cheating. The doctrine of the Hereafter binds them to accountability. Thus their pervasive desires, rather than intellect, prevents them from believing in the Hereafter.

6. They asked this question not as a genuine query. Rather, they raised it out of denial and mockery. They derisively asked the Prophet, "Tell us when the Last Day with which you threaten us is coming?"

7. *Bariqa al-baṣar* signifies the dazzling of one's sight. However, in Arabic usage it also connotes one's amazement, awe, or shock over something bewildering or stunning. Another instance of its occurrence in the Qur'ān is verse 42 of *Sūrah Ibrāhīm*, which reads: "He is merely granting them respite until a Day when their eyes shall continue to stare in horror".

8. This is a brief account of the collapse of the present order as the first stage of the Last Day. Both the sun and the moon will lose their lustre; they will look alike, devoid of their light. Or it might mean that the earth will abruptly rotate in the opposite direction and both the sun and the moon will rise simultaneously in the West. Or it could mean that the moon will suddenly come out from the earth's sphere of influence and will merge with the sun on the Last Day. There could be some other meanings of this which man cannot fathom at this stage.

(13) On that Day will man be apprised of his deeds, both the earlier and the later.[9] (14) But lo, man is well aware of himself, (15) even though he might make up excuses.[10] ▶

يُنَبَّؤُا۟ ٱلْإِنسَـٰنُ يَوْمَئِذٍۭ بِمَا قَدَّمَ وَأَخَّرَ ﴿١٣﴾ بَلِ ٱلْإِنسَـٰنُ عَلَىٰ نَفْسِهِۦ بَصِيرَةٌ ﴿١٤﴾ وَلَوْ أَلْقَىٰ مَعَاذِيرَهُۥ ﴿١٥﴾

9. It is a comprehensive sentence, open to several meanings, all of which may be equally valid: "That on the Last Day man will be apprised of his deeds, both earlier and the later ones", conveys multiple meanings. On that Day, man will be informed of his record of deeds and their impact on subsequent generations. Or it might mean that he will be told about what he failed to do and what he did which he should not have done. Or a chronological record of his deeds will be presented before him. He will be told about both his good and bad deeds in the sense of his acts of commission and omission.

10. Man's record will be placed before him on the Day of Judgement. This will be done not to acquaint the evil-doers with their evil deeds, for each person is already aware of the evil deeds he has committed. The record will nevertheless be brought forward so as to fulfil the requirements of justice, which demand that proof of a culprit's offence be placed before the court. Otherwise, everyone knows well what type of a person he is. He does not need someone to apprise him of his misconduct. A liar may deceive the whole world, yet in his heart of hearts he knows he is lying. The same holds true for a thief – he may use hundreds of tricks to conceal his theft, but in his own heart he knows he is stealing. By the same token, an atheist or a disbeliever may advance an array of arguments, but his conscience tells him the real reason of his clinging to falsehood. He himself recognises what prevents him from acknowledging the truth. A wrongdoer, a cheat, a wicked person, or a sinner may try his best to silence his conscience in order to overcome his self-reproach. He may invent numerous pretexts for justifying his misconduct. Still, he is fully aware of each of his wrong doing, his usurping someone's due, his attack on another's honour, his cheating, and his unlawful earnings. So, in the court of the Hereafter every culprit, every sinner, every disbeliever, every hypocrite, and every wicked person will already be aware of the evil deeds he has committed in the world and in what capacity he stands before God.

(16) (O Prophet),[11] do not stir your tongue hastily (to commit the Revelation to memory). (17) Surely it is for Us to have you commit it to memory and to recite it. ▸

لَا تُحَرِّكۡ بِهِۦ لِسَانَكَ لِتَعۡجَلَ بِهِۦٓ ﴿١٦﴾ إِنَّ عَلَيۡنَا جَمۡعَهُۥ وَقُرۡءَانَهُۥ ﴿١٧﴾

---

11. The whole passage from here to "then it will be for Us to explain it" (Verses 16–19) is a parenthetical statement which interrupts the discourse to bring an important matter to the Prophet's attention as already explained in the introduction to this *Sūrah*. The need to do so arose because, when Gabriel was communicating this *Sūrah* to the Prophet (peace be upon him), the latter kept repeating it so that he could firmly commit it to his memory. Accordingly, he was instructed that he should not try to memorise while the revelation is being received by him. Rather, he should listen to it attentively. God will ensure that he fully commits it to his memory and can recite it accurately. He is also assured that he will neither forget a word of it, nor will he make any mistake in reciting it. This directive is followed by "nay" in verse 2, which those not familiar with the background take as something incoherent. However, the above account of the background explains why these directives were needed. It is akin to a note of warning by a teacher during his lecture on noting an inattentive student, which is followed by the resumption of his lecture. One not aware of this interruption might find the note of warning as incoherent. However, its circumstantial setting will set his mind at rest.

Our above explanation of the parenthetical statement is not based on any speculation. Authentic reports endorse the same. 'Abdullāh ibn 'Abbās's following report is cited by Aḥmad (*Musnad*, 1, 220 and 343), Bukhārī (*K. Tafsīr Sūrah al-Qiyāmah*), Muslim (*K. al Ṣalāt, Bāb Istimā' lil Qirā'ah*), Tirmidhī (*K. Tafsīr Sūrah al-Qiyāmah*), Nasā'ī (*K. al-Iftitāḥ, Bāb Jāmi' mā jā'a fī al-Qur'ān*), Ibn Jarīr al-Ṭabarī (23, 496–500), Al-Ṭabarānī, Bayhaqī and other *Ḥadīth* scholars: "When the Prophet (peace be upon him) received the revelation from Gabriel, he repeated the words with his tongue lest he forget any of it later. It was against this backdrop that he was advised: 'Do not move your tongue hastily.'" The above stance is supported also by Sha'bī, Ibn Zayd, Ḍaḥḥāk, Ḥasan al-Baṣrī, Qatādah, Mujāhid and other leading scholars of the Qur'ān (Ibn Jarīr al-Ṭabarī, *Tafsīr*, 23, 496–500).

(18) And so when We recite it,[12] follow its recitation attentively; (19) then it will be for Us to explain it.[13] ▶

فَإِذَا قَرَأْنَٰهُ فَٱتَّبِعْ قُرْءَانَهُۥ ﴿١٨﴾ ثُمَّ إِنَّ عَلَيْنَا بَيَانَهُۥ ﴿١٩﴾

---

12. Although Gabriel recited the revelation to the Prophet (peace be upon him), since he did so on God's behalf, the Qur'ān attributes this act to God Himself: "So when We recite it" (Verse 18).

13. It emerges from the above, and the same is expressed by some of the leading scholars of the Qur'ān, that in the early days, during receiving revelation, the Prophet (peace be upon him) sought clarification from Gabriel about a Qur'ānic verse or the meaning of its words or the thrust of its commands. The Prophet (peace be upon him) is therefore instructed to follow the recitation attentively. He is not only assured that its each and every word will be preserved in his memory and he will be enabled to recite the Qur'ān exactly as it was revealed originally, but at the same time he is also promised by God that the meaning and intent of each command and instruction will be explained to him fully.

It is indeed a very significant verse for it spells out certain principles and norms, which if properly understood, may help one to protect himself from the misconceptions spread by some people in the past and which are spread by some even today.

First, it clearly establishes that the Prophet (peace be upon him) used to receive not only that revelation which is recorded in the Qur'ān, but he was also given specific knowledge through means of revelation which does not feature in the Qur'ān. Had the Qur'ān itself contained the explanation of the Qur'ānic concepts, terms and commands, there was no need for this divine statement: "It is for Us to explain it" (verse 19). God explained to the Prophet (peace be upon him) the meaning and message of the Qur'ān by some other means as well. This constitutes the evidence for the existence of some implicit revelation (*Waḥī Khafī*), which is borne out by the Qur'ān itself. (This point is discussed at length in our Urdu book, *Sunnat kī Ā'inī Ḥaythīyat*, pp. 94–95 and 118–125.)

Secondly, the Prophet (peace be upon him) was given the explanation of the meaning, message, and commands of the Qur'ān for the purpose of communicating it to the people through his words and actions, and also to teach them how to act upon the message it entails. Had it not been so, and the explanation was given to him only for his personal understanding, it would then appear a futile exercise as it would not have helped him in any way to discharge his duty as God's Messenger. Therefore, only a fool can take the position that the explanatory knowledge which the Prophet (peace be upon him) acquired from God is not legal and is not something sanctioned by *Sharī'ah*. God Himself declares elsewhere in the Qur'ān: "We have now sent down this Reminder upon you [O Prophet] that you may elucidate to people the teaching that has been sent down for them." (For details see *Towards Understanding the Qur'ān*, vol. IV, *Sūrah al-Naḥl* 16: n. 40, pp. 332–334.) At four places in the Qur'ān, God has specified that the Prophet's responsibility was not only to recite the Qur'ānic verses but teaching the Book was also a part of the Prophet's assignment. (See verses 129 and 151 of *Sūrah al-Baqarah*, 164 of *Sūrah Āl 'Imrān* and 2 of *Sūrah al-Jumu'ah* and their elucidation in our Urdu book *Sunnat kī Ā'inī Ḥaythīyat*, pp. 74–77.) Given this, how can a believer in the Qur'ān dare deny that the Qur'ān's explanation, which the Prophet (peace be upon him) has conveyed through his words and actions, is not his personal explanation, but is based on the authentic and authoritative version taught by God. Therefore, one who disregards the Prophet's elucidation of the Qur'ān and offers his own whimsical interpretation commits an outrageous act which no believer can ever contemplate.

Thirdly, even a cursory study of the Qur'ān convinces that even a person well-versed in the Arabic language cannot really grasp the true meaning and intent of a number of verses simply through reading the Qur'ān. Nor can he ascertain how to act on a command prescribed by it. Take the Qur'ānic term *Ṣalāt* as illustrative. *Ṣalāt* is frequently emphasised in the Qur'ān, next only to belief. However, Arabic lexicon cannot guide us to its true meaning and form. From the frequent use of this word in the Qur'ān, one can at best assume that it relates to some special term and probably implies a particular act required to be performed by the believers. Yet even one having mastery over the Arabic language cannot ascertain what sort of act it is and how it is to be performed. If God had not appointed a teacher of His choice and explained to him its precise meaning and taught him the full detail of how to perform *ṣalāt*, there could never be any agreement even between two Muslims about its exact meaning and form. However, it is common knowledge that for the last almost 1,500 years, millions of Muslims, generations upon generations, have been performing *ṣalāt* in an identical manner. This is mainly because God has not only revealed the wording of the Qur'ān to the Prophet Muḥammad (peace be upon him), but explained to him fully the meaning and intent of the words which he then transmitted to all those who accepted the Qur'ān as the Word of God and him as the Messenger.

Fourthly, the only source for us to ascertain that the explanation of the Qur'ān was given by God to the Prophet (peace be upon him) and in turn he taught it to his *Ummah* through his own words and example of his actions, is nothing but the *ḥadīth* and the *sunnah*. *Ḥadīth* refers to all the reports about the Prophet's sayings and actions which reached from one generation to another through narrations with authentic chains. As to the *sunnah,* it represents the Prophet's teachings through his words and deeds, which were introduced in the individual and collective lives of Muslims. Their authentic details were transmitted from one generation to another and they witnessed these in practice in the former generation as well. Given this, one who refuses to accept the *ḥadīth* and the *sunnah* as sources of knowledge in fact asserts that God, who took the responsibility of explaining the meaning and message of the Qur'ān to the Prophet, somehow failed to fulfil His promise that "it is for Us to explain it". This responsibility was not undertaken to teach the Prophet in his personal capacity only, but the purpose was that through the medium of the Prophet it will be communicated to the entire *ummah*. The moment the *ḥadīth* and the *sunnah* are rejected as its sources of law, it is tantamount to indicating that God did not fulfil this responsibility. May God protect us against such outrageous notions. If somebody argues "then what about so many *aḥādīth* that have been fabricated by people?", we would say in response that the fabrication of *aḥādīth* in itself is strong proof that from the beginning of Islam, the sayings and actions of the Prophet were acclaimed as Islamic law by the entire Muslim community. Otherwise, why should the people who engage in spreading falsehood take the trouble of fabricating these? Only a valid currency is subject to counterfeiting. Which fool will venture to counterfeit currency which has no value in the market at all? Then those who raise the bogey of fabricated *aḥādīth* conveniently forget that Muslims have taken special effort from the very beginning to preserve the record of the Prophet's sayings and deeds and repel any attempt of ascribing any falsehood to him, as these constitute an integral part of Islamic law. As the danger of foisting false things on him started to increase, the well-wishers and the *ummah* took more and more stringent measures to ensure the accuracy and authenticity of *ḥadīth* and the *sunnah,* and prominently distinguished the genuine from falsehood. The science of distinguishing between genuine and falsehood is a major and elaborate branch of knowledge which until recently, none other than Muslims have been able to invent and develop. Unfortunate are those who, instead of acquiring the knowledge, fall victim to Western Orientalists and tend to discredit the authenticity of *ḥadīth* and the *sunnah*. In doing so, they fail to realise the immense damage they cause to Islam through their reckless ignorance.

(20) Nay;[14] the truth is that you love ardently (the good of this world) that can be obtained hastily, (21) and are oblivious of the Hereafter.[15] (22) Some faces on that Day will be fresh and resplendent,[16] ▶

كَلَّا بَلْ تُحِبُّونَ ٱلْعَاجِلَةَ ۝٢٠ وَتَذَرُونَ ٱلْآخِرَةَ ۝٢١ وُجُوهٌ يَوْمَئِذٍ نَّاضِرَةٌ ۝٢٢

14. It resumes the earlier discourse, interrupted by the parenthetical statement. The word "nay" here emphasises that the true reason for denying the Hereafter was not that they were truly convinced that it was beyond God's power to raise the dead to life. The true reason, instead, was that they ardently loved this world and wanted to pursue their worldly interests with full impunity.

15. This is another reason for the disbelievers' dismissal of the reality of the Hereafter. Verse 5 of this *Sūrah* spells out one of the first reasons for their denial: "Man desires to persist in his evil ways." Their base self prevents them from believing in the Hereafter, then they resort to some quasi-logical points to defend their rejection. In the verse under discussion, the Qur'ān states that since the disbelievers are myopic, their eyes are set only on worldly gains, and they disregard the long-term gains which could accrue in the Hereafter. They think they should exert their fullest efforts and energy only in seeking the pleasures and benefits of this world which is the be-all and end-all for them, no matter whether severe loss is waiting for them in the Hereafter. This accounts for their striving only for worldly concerns. They are not ready to forego their immediate gains, so their arguments do not have any real substance or logic. They are stubbornly bent upon denying the Hereafter. In doing so, they suppress the voice of their conscience and ignore altogether the weighty arguments of the Qur'ān, which vindicate the existence and necessity of the Hereafter. It does not occur to them that their counter-arguments are superfluous and baseless.

16. The faces of the believers will be resplendent with joy, for the Hereafter in which they had believed will be in front of their eyes, perfectly in accordance with their definite belief. They had kept themselves away

(23) and will be looking towards their Lord;[17] ▶	إِلَىٰ رَبِّهَا نَاظِرَةٌ ﴿٢٣﴾

from unlawful gains in the world for the sake of the Hereafter and had suffered some genuine losses. After the Day of Judgment, it will be so gratifying for them that they had taken absolutely the right decision about their way of life. The time has come when they will enjoy the best of the rewards in the Hereafter.

17. "That they will be looking towards their Lord" is interpreted metaphorically by some commentators of the Qur'ān. For them, it refers to their expectation of God's merciful and favourable decisions. However, many *aḥādīth* related to the commentary given by the Prophet on this subject confirms that they will have the ultimate privilege of seeing God in the Hereafter. Bukhārī (*K. al-Tawḥīd*), cites this *ḥadīth*: "You will publicly see your Lord." Muslim (*K. al-Īmān, Bāb Ithbāt Ru'yah al-Mu'minīn*) and Tirmidhī (*K. Tafsīr al-Qur'ān, Sūrah Yūnus*) quote Ṣuhaib to the effect: "The Prophet (peace be upon him) stated that after the believers' admission to Paradise, God will ask them whether they want Him to give them something more. They will submit: 'Have You not already made our faces resplendent? Have You not already admitted us to Paradise and saved us from Hell?' At that point, God will remove the barrier and for them it will be the highest reward imaginable in that they will physically see God". The Qur'ān alludes to the same reward thus: "For those who do good there is good reward and more besides." (Verse 26 of *Sūrah Yūnus*) Bukhārī (*K. al-Tawḥīd*) and Muslim (*K. al-Īmān, Bāb Ma'rifah Ṭarīq al-Ru'yah*) relate the following *ḥadīth* on the authority of Abū Sa'īd al-Khudrī and Abū Hurayrah: "People asked: 'O Messenger of God! Will we be able to see our Lord on the Day of Judgement?' He replied: 'Do you have any difficulty in seeing the sun and the moon when there is no cloud?' When they replied in the negative, he remarked: 'You will see your Lord in the same way.'" An identical *ḥadīth* narrated by Jarīr ibn 'Abdullāh is cited by Bukhārī (*K. al-Tawḥīd*) and Muslim (*K. al-Masājid, Bāb Faḍl Ṣalāt al-Ṣubḥ*). Aḥmad (*Musnad* of Imām Aḥmad, 2, 64), Tirmidhī (*K. al-Tafsīr, Sūrah al- Qiyāmah*), Dāraquṭnī, Ibn Jarīr al-Ṭabarī (*Tafsīr*, 23, 509), Ibn al-Mundhir, Al-Ṭabarānī, Bayhaqī, Ibn Abī Shaybah and some other scholars of *ḥadīth* have cited 'Abdullāh ibn 'Umar's report, with slight variations, which recounts that even dwellers of Paradise of the lowest rank will see the vastness of the Kingdom extending over two

thousand years of journey space, whereas the most exalted ones will see their Lord at least twice a day.

At that point, the Prophet (peace be upon him) recited this verse: "Some faces on that Day will be fresh and resplendent and will be looking towards their Lord." (Verses 22–23 of *Sūrah al-Qiyāmah*) Ibn Mājah quotes Jābir ibn 'Abdullāh's report: "God will look towards them and they towards Him. Until He places a barrier, they will not look at any other bounty of Paradise and will keep looking towards Him." In light of several other such reports, the consensus view is that the dwellers of Paradise will be blessed with the sight of God in the Hereafter. This is borne out by the Qur'ān thus: "No indeed! On that Day, they (the wicked) will be screened off from seeing their Lord." (Verse 15 of *Sūrah al-Muṭaffifīn*) One may easily infer from the above that only the sinners, not the pious, will be screened off from seeing their Lord.

It raises the question as to how man will be able to see God, for something must be at a particular place or direction and have a definite form and colour so that it could be seen. Its reflection should reach the human eye through the rays of light and its image should be conveyed to the human brain. Will God be seen in the above manner by man? However, this question is marred by a big fallacy. It fails to take into account the distinction between the essence of seeing and the particular act of seeing with which we are familiar in this world. As to the former, it calls for the following – the faculty of vision, and exposure to what is to be seen. However, in this world we see things in a particular manner and this act of seeing is routinely performed by human beings and animals, for this the eye is essential, together with its faculty of vision. Moreover, the eye should come into contact with something tangible, having a form and colour and its image should be conveyed to the eye through the rays of light. It is only then that the eye sees it. One's insistence on only this particular act of seeing betrays his own narrow outlook, for there could be numerous other ways of seeing according to divine dispensation, which we cannot even imagine. Those perturbed by this question should first answer this question – whether God has the faculty of sight or not. If He has and watches all that is in the universe, whether He sees all this with the body part known as the eye, in the same manner as human beings and animals do. Does He see in the same way as we do? Obviously, the answer to these questions is simply "no". Since this is so, there should not be any confusion or difficulty about appreciating that in the Hereafter the dwellers of Paradise will not see God in the way which we are accustomed to seeing here. The nature of seeing there will be completely different, which we cannot comprehend here. It is even more difficult for us to

(24) and some faces on that Day will be gloomy, (25) believing that a crushing calamity is about to strike them. (26) Nay;[18] when a man's soul reaches up to the throat, (27) and it is said: "Is there any enchanter[19] who can step forward and help (by his chanting)?" (28) and he realises that the hour of parting is come, (29) and calf is intertwined with calf.[20] (30) On that Day you will be driven to your Lord.

وَوُجُوهٌ يَوْمَئِذٍ بَاسِرَةٌ ﴿٢٤﴾ تَظُنُّ أَن يُفْعَلَ
بِهَا فَاقِرَةٌ ﴿٢٥﴾ كَلَّآ إِذَا بَلَغَتِ ٱلتَّرَاقِىَ ﴿٢٦﴾
وَقِيلَ مَنْ ۜ رَاقٍ ﴿٢٧﴾ وَظَنَّ أَنَّهُ ٱلْفِرَاقُ ﴿٢٨﴾
وَٱلْتَفَّتِ ٱلسَّاقُ بِٱلسَّاقِ ﴿٢٩﴾ إِلَىٰ رَبِّكَ
يَوْمَئِذٍ ٱلْمَسَاقُ ﴿٣٠﴾

perceive how this act will be performed than it is for a two-year-old child to understand the intricacies of matrimonial affairs, though at a later stage, when he grows up he will experience these in full.

18. This "nay" relates to the main subject under discussion. It underlines that they were mistaken in fancying that death would bring about their final extinction and that they would not return to their Lord for His reckoning.

19. *Rāq* may refer to amulets or may mean ascent. Taken in the former sense, it would mean that as carers despair of a patient's chance of recovery, they resort to sorcerers who may be able to cure him. According to its latter sense, the reference is to the taking possession of his soul by the angels, whether it is to be transported by the angels of punishment or mercy. At the time of his death it will be decided. If he is pious, angels of mercy will carry his soul. In the opposite case, they will not approach him at all. Rather, he will be seized by the angels of punishment.

20. *Sāq* is construed literally as a body part known as the calf by some commentators of the Qur'ān. They consider it as a reference to the time of his death when one calf will be intertwined with another. Some interpret

(31) But he did not verify the Truth, nor did he observe Prayer; (32) on the contrary, he gave the lie to the Truth and turned his back upon it, (33) then he went back to his kinsfolk, elated with pride.[21] (34) This (attitude) is worthy of you, altogether worthy; (35) again, it is worthy of you, altogether worthy.[22]

فَلَا صَدَّقَ وَلَا صَلَّىٰ ۝٣١ وَلَـٰكِن كَذَّبَ
وَتَوَلَّىٰ ۝٣٢ ثُمَّ ذَهَبَ إِلَىٰٓ أَهْلِهِۦ يَتَمَطَّىٰٓ ۝٣٣
أَوْلَىٰ لَكَ فَأَوْلَىٰ ۝٣٤ ثُمَّ أَوْلَىٰ لَكَ فَأَوْلَىٰٓ ۝٣٥

---

it figuratively in accordance with the Arabic idiom, signifying hardship and crisis. At his death, a sinner will be gripped with these two problems: agony over leaving this world and all that is in it, and the torment of being seized as a culprit. Every disbeliever, hypocrite, and wicked person will have this agonising experience at the time of his death.

21. Reference is to the disbeliever who listened to these Qur'ānic verses yet persisted in his disbelief. Even after listening to these, he went back to his folk, elated with pride. According to Mujāhid, Qatādah, and Ibn Zayd, the verse alludes to Abū Jahl. It appears from the wording of the verse that it is an allusion to a particular person who had behaved thus after listening to these verses of *Sūrah al-Qiyāmah*.

That he did not verify the truth nor did he observe prayer deserves attention. It is evident that the first and foremost prerequisite of believing in God, His Messenger, and His Book is that one should offer prayers. Other *Sharī'ah* duties may be fulfilled later at their appointed time. However, soon after embracing faith it is time for performing one of the five daily obligatory prayers. This tests one's commitment to his faith, proving his sincerity or otherwise.

22. The commentators of the Qur'ān have offered several interpretations of the Qur'ānic expression *awlā laka*: "Shame on you, you may perish. Woe and misery persist with you". However, in our opinion, Ibn Kathīr's version is the most appropriate: "Since you have the audacity of disobeying your Creator, it befits you to walk in this manner." (*Tafsīr*, 8, 282)

(36) Does man[23] think that he will be left alone,[24] unquestioned? (37) Was he not a drop of ejaculated semen, (38) then he became a clot, and then Allah made it into a living body and proportioned its parts, ▶

أَيَحْسَبُ ٱلْإِنسَـٰنُ أَن يُتْرَكَ سُدًى ﴿٣٦﴾ أَلَمْ يَكُ نُطْفَةً مِّن مَّنِىٍّ يُمْنَىٰ ﴿٣٧﴾ ثُمَّ كَانَ عَلَقَةً فَخَلَقَ فَسَوَّىٰ ﴿٣٨﴾

A similar sarcastic remark features at another place in the Qur'ān: "Taste this (the Hellfire), you are a person mighty and noble." (Verse 49 of *Sūrah al-Dukhān*)

23. The theme of Life after Death is resumed here as a conclusion as it was stated at the beginning that life after death is both essential and possible.

24. *Ibilun suda* is used in the Arabic idiom for a camel that wanders about, aimlessly, grazing at will, one whom there is nobody to keep an eye over. The Qur'ān asks man whether he thinks that he will be left alone, irresponsible, and unquestioned by His Creator. Is he not obliged to fulfil his duties? Is there nothing that is forbidden for him? Will he not be called to account for his deeds some day? The same theme is enunciated in the Qur'ān elsewhere, thus: "Did you imagine that We created you without any purpose, and that you will not be brought back to Us?" (Verse 115 of *Sūrah al-Mu'minūn*) In both the instances, the argument for the necessity of the Hereafter has been presented in the form of a question. Man is asked if he considers himself to be some animal. Does he not realise the manifest difference between him and an animal, that whereas he enjoys free will, the latter does not? The latter's actions are not subject to any moral code while man is surely answerable for all his actions. Given this, how could a man think that, like an animal, he is also an irresponsible and unanswerable being? It is readily understandable as to why animals will not be resurrected, for they led their lives dictated by their instincts. They were not guided by any philosophy fabricated by them. Nor did they invent any religion. Likewise, they did not defy anyone, nor did they lay any claim to divinity. Their actions were amoral, neither good nor bad. They did not initiate something good or bad which

(39) and then He made of him a pair, male and female? (40) Does He, then, not have the power to bring back the dead to life?[25]	فَجَعَلَ مِنْهُ ٱلزَّوْجَيْنِ ٱلذَّكَرَ وَٱلْأُنثَىٰٓ ﴿٣٩﴾ أَلَيْسَ ذَٰلِكَ بِقَٰدِرٍ عَلَىٰٓ أَن يُحْـِۧىَ ٱلْمَوْتَىٰ ﴿٤٠﴾

influenced subsequent generations. Therefore, they do not deserve any reward or punishment. Their extinction after death is plausible for they did not realise the consequences of their actions and hence they will not be resurrected for any recompense. However, man cannot be exempted from the Hereafter. His own mind told him until his last breath about the goodness or evil of his actions. If someone kills an innocent person and he himself immediately dies in an accident, how can he go unpunished? Should he not face the consequence for the wrong committed by him? Does man reconcile to the proposition that someone who sowed the seeds of mischief in the world which afflicted generations upon generations, should have his final extinction with his death? Should he not be brought back to life and undergo punishment for his misdeeds which destroyed the lives of hundreds of thousands of human beings? By the same token, does he who strove throughout his life for the sake of truth, justice, goodness, peace, and suffered tremendous hardship in this cause have no right to be rewarded for all that he did?

25. This constitutes a strong argument for life after death. As to those who believe in God's creative power behind the creation of man, from a sperm drop into an adult human being, they cannot refute this weighty argument, no matter how diffident they might be in their rejection. They readily recognise that God Who creates man in such a wonderful fashion, is quite capable of bringing him back to life after his death. Those who dismiss it as an accident have no answer whatsoever to the fact that since the beginning of this world the ratio between the birth of girls and boys has always been consistent in every part of the world and among all communities. Never has this ratio suffered any steep change, resulting in the birth of baby boys or baby girls only, which could jeopardise the continuation of the human race. Those denying this fact can unabashedly claim that even the major towns of the world such as London, New York, Moscow, and Beijing came into existence all of a sudden accidentally.

(For details see *Towards Understanding the Qur'ān*, vol. VIII, *Sūrah al-Rūm* 30: nn. 27–30, pp. 89–92 and *Sūrah al-Shūrā* 42: n. 77.)

It is clear from several reports that on reciting this verse, particularly in response to the question put forward by God, the Prophet (peace be upon him) used to say *balā* (why not!) or *subḥānaka Allāhumma fa balā* (Glory be to You, O Lord, why not?) or *subḥānaka fabalā* or *subḥānaka wa balā*. Ibn Jarīr al-Ṭabarī (*Tafsīr*, 23, 528), Ibn Abī Ḥātim (10, 3389) and Abū Dāwūd, and *Tafsīr* of Ibn Kathīr (8, 284). On the authority of Abū Hurayrah, Abū Dāwūd (*K. al-Ṣalāt, Bāb Miqdār al-Rukū' wa al-Sujūd*) narrates this report: The Prophet instructed: "When you recite verse 8 of *Sūrah al-Ṭīn*, you should say: *balā wa anā 'alā dhālika min al-shāhidīn* (Yes! I am one of those who testify to it). When you recite verse 40 of *Sūrah al-Qiyāmah*, you should say: *balā* (why not!). Likewise, on reciting verse 50 of *Sūrah al-Mursalāt* you should say: *āmannā bi Allāh* (we believe in Allah). Reports with a similar tenor are cited by Aḥmad (*Musnad*, 1, 377 and 2, 249), Tirmidhī (*K. Tafsīr al-Qur'ān, Sūrah al-Ṭīn*), Ibn al-Mundhir, Ibn Marduwayh, Bayhaqī and Ḥākim.

Sūrah 76

Al-Dahr

(Time)

(Madīnan Period)

Title

This *Sūrah* has two titles – *al-Dahr* and *al-Insān* – and both these words occur in the opening verse of the *Sūrah*.

Period of Revelation

Most of the Qur'ānic scholars including 'Allāmah al-Zamakhsharī, Imām al-Rāzī, Qāḍī al-Bayḍāwī, 'Allāmah al-Nīshāpūrī, Ḥāfiẓ Ibn Kathīr and many others regard it a Makkan *Sūrah*. 'Allāmah al-Ālūsī refers to this as the consensus view. However, some Qur'ānic commentators are of the opinion that the entire *Sūrah* was revealed in Madīnah. Some others think that it is indeed a Makkan *Sūrah*, but verses 8–10 were sent down in Madīnah.

As to its contents and stylistic features, it very much differs from Madīnan *Sūrahs*. On reflection, it appears that it is not only a Makkan *Sūrah*, but it was revealed during the early phase of the Makkan period, which began just after the revelation of the first seven verses of *Sūrah al-Muddaththir*. Verses 8–10 of this *Sūrah* clearly appear to be its essential part. If they are read in their proper context, there is nothing to suggest that the verses preceding and following these had come down some 15–16 years earlier and the three verses (8–10) were revealed several years later and inserted into the *Sūrah*.

What has lent credence to taking it as a Madīnan *Sūrah* is the report by 'Aṭā' on Ibn 'Abbās's authority. According to this report, Ḥasan and Ḥusain once fell ill and the Prophet (peace be upon him) and a number of Companions called on their father, 'Alī. Some Companions suggested that 'Alī make a vow to Allah for their recovery. Accordingly, 'Alī, Fāṭimah, and their maid, Fiḍḍah vowed that if Allah cured Ḥasan and Ḥusain, they will fast for three days to show their gratitude. By God's grace they recovered and all three persons started observing fasts. 'Alī did not have any food in his house, so he borrowed three *ṣā'* of barley from somebody (one report says that he had earned this grain through manual labour). On the first day as they sat to break their fast, a needy person begged for food. They gave him all the food they had and went to bed after consuming only water. The next day exactly the same happened, when an orphan appeared and they gave all the food to him, keeping only water for themselves. On the third day, while they were about to break their fast, a prisoner asked for food and they gave him everything. On the fourth day, 'Alī called on the Prophet (peace be upon him) along with both of his sons. He noted their miserable condition on account of hunger. He accompanied them on their return home and saw Fāṭimah suffering from the pangs of hunger. Tears welled in his eyes. It was then that Gabriel visited him and gave him the glad tiding that Allah had felicitated him regarding his blessed family. Gabriel then recited the whole *Sūrah* to him. According to Ibn Mihrān, he recited only verses 5–31. However, Ibn 'Abbās's report, narrated by Ibn Marduwayh, specifies that only verse 8 was sent down in the context of 'Alī and Fāṭimah. It makes no reference to the above incident. This story appears in 'Alī ibn Aḥmad al-Wāḥidī's *Tafsīr al-Basīṭ* (4, 104), which was most probably used as the source by al-Zamakhsharī (*al-Kashshāf*, 6, 278–279), al-Rāzī (*al-Tafsīr al-Kabīr*, 30, 244) and al-Nīshāpūrī.

The above story is extremely unreliable in terms of the chain of its narrators. Moreover, on scrutiny, it appears equally incredible. Had a single person begged for food, it was beyond reason that he was given the food of all five members of the family. Even after giving him food, the five family members could have shared the food of four. Equally unbelievable is the version that 'Alī and Fāṭimah, who possessed insights into matters of faith, preferred to starve their weak children who had just recovered from their illness, taking it as an act of virtue. Furthermore, to ask the prisoners to beg for food was never practised in Islamic history. Had the state imprisoned them, it provided for both their food and clothing. Had a prisoner been placed under someone's custody, that person was responsible for looking after his needs. It was unthinkable in Madīnah that a prisoner would have begged for food.

Even if one overlooks all these flaws in the report and accepts it as it is, it tells, at most, that when the Prophet's family members did this good act, Gabriel congratulated the Prophet (peace be upon him), informing him that Allah had approved their good deed, for they had done what is approvingly mentioned in this *Sūrah*. However, it does not necessarily mean that this *Sūrah* was revealed on that occasion. When it is said in a report that a particular verse was sent down with reference to a particular incident, it does not mean that the dates of both tally exactly. What the report signifies is that the verse applies exactly to the particular incident. Imām al-Sūyuṭī has cited Ibn Taymiyyah's opinion in his *al-Itqān*: "When the reporters say that a particular verse was occasioned by a certain incident, it may mean that the same incident occasioned its revelation, or it may mean that while the verse applies to the matter, it did not occasion its revelation." He has quoted (1, 90) also Badr al-Dīn al-Zarkashī's following stance which features in his *al-Burhān fī 'Ulūm al-Qur'ān*: "It was customary on the part of the Companions and Successors to speak of a verse in connection with a particular matter, signifying that a particular command is related to that. This does not mean that a particular matter caused the revelation of that verse, only that a command is inferred from it." (*al-Itqān fī 'Ulūm al-Qur'ān* I, p. 31. [1929 edition])

Subject Matter and Themes

The theme of this *Sūrah* is to apprise man of his true position in this world. It further instructs man that if he realises his position well and behaves with gratitude towards God, he will have an undisclosed happy end. If he takes to the path of disbelief, his end will be in an undisclosed terrible manner. This theme features in the larger *Sūrahs* of the Qur'ān too, in greater detail. However, in the early Makkan *Sūrahs*, the same truth is presented in a manner which is very short and brief but highly effective. Such brief and elegant sentences are easy to memorise and recite.

First, man is reminded that in his earliest stage he was not even worthy of mention. He was created out of a drop of an intermingled sperm. Even his mother was unaware at that stage of conception. No one then could say that this microscopic entity would grow one day into a human being, the supreme creature of God on earth. Next, man is warned that he has been created in the form and shape that he is, so that God might try and test him in this world. Accordingly, in contrast with other creatures, he is invested with certain faculties, and both the paths of gratitude and ingratitude have been kept open for him. He is therefore free to be grateful or ungrateful to God. He is granted a specific time on earth in order to test whether he emerges as a thankful or unthankful servant of his Lord.

Then, just in one sentence, it is categorically asked of those who will emerge as disbelievers from the test, what sort of outcome will they have to face in the Hereafter?

After this, verses 5–22 spell out, one after another, details of the bounties which will be conferred on the believers who have been thankful to their Lord. Not only is their reward mentioned in these verses, it is also clarified in brief which of their actions will entitle them to divine reward. One of the striking features of the early Makkan *Sūrahs* is that, along with briefly introducing the basic articles of Islamic faith and concepts, at some places it also highlights the moral values and virtuous deeds on which Islam places a premium. Moreover, at some other places, the vices which Islam wants man to shun have been identified. The consequences of these virtues and vices in this life are not discussed. Rather, the focus of attention is on their impact in the eternal and everlasting life of the Hereafter, irrespective of whether a bad action is proven to be rewarding in this world or a good action is proven to be harmful.

Three important points are brought to the Prophet's attention in the next section of the *Sūrah*. The first one is that God has revealed the Qur'ān to him in brief instalments. The disbelievers are thus told that the Qur'ān is not the product of the Prophet's mind. Out of His infinite wisdom, God has decided to send down the Qur'ān in stages. The second message imparted to the Prophet (peace be upon him) is that he should continue discharging his duty, no matter how long it takes to enforce God's decree. He should carry out his mission with perseverance. Never should he yield to the pressure of the wicked and disbelieving people. The third point highlighted is that the Prophet (peace be upon him) should glorify God morning and evening, offer prayers, and worship Him during the long watches of the night. This will bless him with steadfastness in confronting the mischievous atrocities of the disbelievers.

Then, in one sentence, the true reason of the disbelievers' dereliction is exposed. They are guilty of having disregarded the Hereafter and are only after the enjoyments of this world. In the second sentence, they are reminded that it is God Who has created them; they are not there on their own. They owe their physical attributes and strength to Him rather than to themselves. He is able to do to them whatever He wishes. He may disfigure them or replace them with another community after destroying them. Equally powerful is He to create them again in any other form.

The concluding verses state that the Qur'ān stands out as an exhortation. Whoever wills may accept it and follow the path to his Lord. However, man's desire and willingness is not everything in this world; it will be of no avail until God Himself so wills. He decides things out of His knowledge and wisdom. He admits to His mercy whoever He pleases and He has prepared a grievous chastisement for those whom He finds among the wrongdoers and wicked.

In the name of Allah, the Most Merciful, the Most Compassionate.	بِسۡمِ ٱللَّهِ ٱلرَّحۡمَٰنِ ٱلرَّحِيمِ
(1) Was there a period of time when man was not even worthy of a mention?[1] ▶	هَلۡ أَتَىٰ عَلَى ٱلۡإِنسَٰنِ حِينٞ مِّنَ ٱلدَّهۡرِ لَمۡ يَكُن شَيۡـٔٗا مَّذۡكُورًا ١

1. Most of the Qur'ānic commentators and translators take the opening statement to mean that man has no doubt passed through such a period. However, the word *hal* is interrogative in Arabic usage. It does not necessarily mean that a question is always posed whenever this word is used. For example, sometimes, when we want to know whether a certain incident has occurred or not, we ask: "Is it true that this has happened?" At times, the purpose is not to ask a question but an expression of denial when we say: "Can anybody else also do this?" Sometimes we want somebody to admit something and we say: "Have I paid you back your money?" Sometimes, in asking one whether I had done him any wrong, he is asked not only to confirm this but also to think about the rationale behind his doing a wrong to one despite one not doing any wrong to him. While the statement in the verse under discussion is couched in the form of a query, its purpose is to make man confirm that there indeed was a time when he was not "even worthy of mention". This should also make him realise that if he was brought into existence from non-existence, why then can he not be restored to life after death?

The second part of the sentence means that there was a long, endless period about the beginning and end (*al-Dahr*), of which man has no knowledge, and at that time the human race did not exist. At some point of time, the human species was created. Then every human being passed through a period when he was brought in to existence from non-existence.

The third sentence: "When he was not even worthy of mention" implies that his origin came from his father's microscopic drop of sperm and his mother's ovum. It was only in recent human history that man came to know of this composition of his. Now, with the help of the microscope, the above truth has been established, yet it is still hard to identify the exact ratio of sperm and ovum in it. The earliest cells formed by this intermingling can be seen only by using a very powerful

(2) Verily We created man out of a drop of intermingled sperm[2] so that We might try him,[3] and We therefore endowed him with hearing ▶	إِنَّا خَلَقْنَا ٱلْإِنسَـٰنَ مِن نُّطْفَةٍ أَمْشَاجٍ نَّبْتَلِيهِ فَجَعَلْنَـٰهُ سَمِيعًا

microscope. While viewing this cell no one can claim that it will grow one day into a human being. Nor can anyone determine the appearance, height, weight, personality, and all other faculties of that person. The verse covers all these meanings in asserting that in the earliest stage man was not yet a thing worthy of mention, even though the process of beginning his being as a man had been initiated.

2. "The intermingled sperm" signifies that man's birth is not caused by male sperm or female ovum alone. It is the intermingling of both that leads to his birth.

3. Testing man is the real purpose behind his creation. He should live his life keeping this reality in mind, for it establishes his role and status in the world. Unlike trees and animals, there is a specific objective behind his creation. He does not come to his final death when his natural life span ends. This world is not meant as a place of torture for him, as is falsely assumed by those given to the monastic way of life. Nor is man fully recompensed here, as is mistakenly held by those believing in the transmigration of souls theory. Equally wrong are the materialists in regarding the world as a place of entertainment and enjoyment alone, nor is it a battleground between the classes, as is conceived by the devotees of Marx and Darwin. It is essentially a testing ground for him. That duration which man regards as his age is in fact the period of his trial in this world. Likewise, the faculties with which man is endowed, his various roles in life, and his interpersonal relationships in this world, are his test papers. This test goes on until his last breath. The result of this test will not be declared in this world, but in the Hereafter, after the thorough evaluation of his exam papers. His success or failure depends mainly on the position he takes in appearing at this test and exhibiting his performance. If he led life as a polytheist or atheist without any belief in his answerability in the Hereafter, he will miserably fail the test. However, if he acted all along as the servant of the One True God and in accordance with His will, with his eyes set on his accountability in the Hereafter, he will pass the test.

and sight.[4] (3) Surely We showed him the Right Path, regardless of whether he chooses to be thankful or unthankful (to his Lord).[5]	بَصِيرًا ۝٢ إِنَّا هَدَيْنَٰهُ ٱلسَّبِيلَ إِمَّا شَاكِرًا وَإِمَّا كَفُورًا ۝٣

This truth is stated at numerous places in the Qur'ān. The Qur'ān is the only Scripture which has explained this truth so extensively.

4. Reference is to granting man the faculties of hearing and sight. That is, God endowed man with certain abilities which made him a significant species. Obviously, it is the figurative account of man's ability to discern. Otherwise animals too have the faculties of hearing and sight. It is a pointed reference to man's ability to acquire knowledge and to infer. These are mentioned, in particular, since they are the most important means of gathering knowledge. Moreover, these human faculties differ from those given to animals; the human brain analyses the information obtained through the senses of hearing and sight, arrives at some conclusion, and forms some opinion which has its bearing on his way of life. Significantly, man's faculties of hearing and sight and discernment are stated in the context of his test. God has endowed man with these so that he may appear at this test. Unless one is totally devoid of reason and knowledge, he cannot be exempted from this test.

5. Not only has God endowed man with mental faculties and knowledge, He has showed him the right way so that he realises which path takes him to thankfulness and which to ungratefulness. He will thus himself be responsible for whichever path he chooses. The same truth is pointed out in the Qur'ān at other places thus: "We showed him the two high roads (of good and evil)." (verse 10 of *Sūrah al-Balad*); "We perfectly proportioned and imbued the human soul with the consciousness of its evil and its piety." (verse 7–8 of *Sūrah al-Shams*) In light of the above and other Qur'ānic passages, one learns that God has arranged for man's guidance in an endless variety of ways. Some of these are:

i. Apart from knowledge and reason, man has also been granted a moral sense, which instinctively enables him to distinguish between good and evil. Though he indulges in some sins, he recognises that these are evil acts. Likewise, he fails to do something good, though he knows these are among the good and noble quality of works. Even those who have fabricated elaborate theories under the influence of their base self for justifying their evil deeds, they condemn these evil acts if these are done against them. This explains that they too, regard these as evil. Likewise, some may dismiss some pious and righteous acts as something outdated, foolish, and ignorant. However, on getting some benefit from somebody's noble behaviour, he feels compelled to admit it as something noble and valuable.

ii. God has invested every human being with the self-reproaching soul (*al-nafs al-lawwāmah*) that keeps alerting and dissuading him when he commits or is about to commit a sin. Man may try to silence or suppress this, yet he cannot altogether eliminate the voice of his conscience. He may publicly appear to be immune to the pangs of conscience and may deceive people with his false, flawed logic. He may invent innumerable pretexts for deceiving himself and justifying his wrongdoings. But despite all these, the active and very self-reproaching censor that God has placed in his being does not allow the sinner to conceal the true nature of their evil and awful personality he possesses. The same issue is clearly stated in the Qur'ān in *Sūrah al-Qiyāmah*: "Man is well aware of himself, even though he might make up excuses" (verses 14–15).

iii. There are numerous signs in and around the existence of the human being which eloquently prove the existence of God and there is nothing that can happen without His permission. These also affirm that this universe cannot be the creation of several gods. Rather, it is created and managed by the One True God. These inward and outward signs vindicate also the truth of the Resurrection and the Hereafter. If man turns blind to, or refuses to reflect on, or declines to believe in these signs, it is his fault. God has placed numerous signs for persuading him to the ultimate truth.

iv. Numerous incidents in man's own life, in the contemporary world, and in numerous experiences of the past, prove that this universe is governed by a superior power and that man is utterly helpless before Him. God's decision overrides everything whereas man constantly stands in need of His help. Man's essential nature, coupled with these events, is cognisant of the existence of this supreme authority. Even a staunch atheist turns to God, invoking His help as he faces a crisis. Likewise, even the worst polytheists abandon their false gods and seek help from only the One True God.

(4) For the unbelievers, We have kept ready chains and fetters and a Blazing Fire.

(5) The virtuous[6] shall drink from a cup tempered with camphor water. ▶

إِنَّآ أَعْتَدْنَا لِلْكَـٰفِرِينَ سَلَـٰسِلَا۟ وَأَغْلَـٰلًا وَسَعِيرًا ۝٤ إِنَّ ٱلْأَبْرَارَ يَشْرَبُونَ مِن كَأْسٍ كَانَ مِزَاجُهَا كَافُورًا ۝٥

v. Common sense and man's own nature demand that evil ought to be punished and good be rewarded. This explains the presence of courts and justice systems in every society in one form or another. Rewards are given in various forms to those who exhibit a commendable performance. This is clear proof that there is an essential nexus between morals and the law of recompense which man cannot deny. It is common knowledge that many crimes in this world go unpunished. Similarly, many who perform well do not get any reward, what to say of receiving their full and adequate share. Given this, there is no alternative for man but to believe in the Hereafter. Only a fool or a stubborn person or one who pays no attention to the concept of justice can deny the Hereafter. It is worth considering for these people as to why this concept of justice is innate in human nature.

vi. For guiding man further with clear evidence, God sent down His Messengers and revealed Books which explain what it means to give thanks to God and being ungrateful to Him. These categorically spell out the consequences of following any of the two paths of thankfulness or ungratefulness. The teachings brought by the Messengers and the Books have directly or indirectly spread throughout the world on a large scale. For this reason, no human society has ever been unaware of the concepts of God, the Hereafter, good and evil, and moral principles and legal commands. At times, man acquires this knowledge without realising that their sources are God's Messengers and Books. Even today, those who reject God's Messengers and Books or are unaware of these sources unconsciously follow the divine teachings which have somehow attracted them.

6. *Abrār* stands for such virtuous persons, who strictly abide by God's commands, fulfil the duties prescribed by Him, and shun all those acts which are forbidden by Him.

(6) This will be a gushing spring[7] wherefrom Allah's servants[8] shall drink wine, a spring from which they will take out channels wherever they wish.[9] (7) These will be the ones who fulfil their vows[10] and dread the Day whose woe shall be spread far and wide; ▶

عَيْنًا يَشْرَبُ بِهَا عِبَادُ ٱللَّهِ يُفَجِّرُونَهَا تَفْجِيرًا ۝٦ يُوفُونَ بِٱلنَّذْرِ وَيَخَافُونَ يَوْمًا كَانَ شَرُّهُۥ مُسْتَطِيرًا ۝٧

7. Reference is to a natural spring, of which the water will be so cool and fragrant as if it was tempered with camphor.

8. Although *'Ibād al-Raḥmān* (servants of the Most Compassionate One) literally stands for all the human beings, in the Qur'ānic parlance it refers specifically to the pious. Since the evil ones have excluded themselves from servitude to God, they do not deserve to be addressed with the honorific appellation of being God's servants.

9. This is not to say that they will literally dig channels with the use of spades and shovels. What is meant is that they will get the spring at any place they wish.

10. Fulfilling a vow signifies doing what one is obliged to do. At another level, it means that one must do what he has vowed to. He should fulfil his pledge. This is the generally understood meaning of fulfilling a vow. The Qur'ān, in this verse, praises those who fulfil the obligations prescribed for them by God. Or they are complimented for doing even such good acts which they are not obliged to perform. However, they pledge to do these for God's sake. Of course, they are not lax in fulfilling the normal duties laid down by God.

As to the norms applicable to a vow, we have discussed these at length in *Towards Understanding the Qur'ān*, vol. I, *Sūrah al-Baqarah* 2: n. 310, p. 211. A detailed account of a vow follows below with a view to correcting some misperceptions regarding it and instructing people about its norms:

i. Jurists speak of four types of vow: (i) One's pledge to God that he will do a certain virtuous act for seeking Allah's pleasure.

(ii) His vow to do a certain virtuous act if God meets his need. Both these types bear the technical name, *nadhr tabarrur* (a vow for a good cause). Jurists are unanimous in their ruling that such a vow should be fulfilled as an obligatory act. (iii) One may take a vow for doing something unlawful or for refusing to perform any of his obligatory duties. (iv) One may take a vow to do a desirable act obligatory on him or do an unworthy thing. Jurists brand these two types of vows as *nadhr lajāj* (a vow brimming with heedless ignorance and stubbornness). The consensus view is that the third type of vow is not tenable. There is some disagreement on its fourth type. Some jurists hold that it should be fulfilled while others insist that its breaking entails expiation. Some are of the view that one is free to either fulfil it or pay a penalty. For Shāfi'īs and Mālikīs this type of vow is untenable. Ḥanafīs maintain that expiation is to be paid for the last two types of vows.

ii. Several *aḥādīth* clarify that the Prophet (peace be upon him) discouraged making a vow that presupposes one's fate will change owing to his vow, or instead of seeking God's pleasure and expressing gratitude towards Him, he makes an offer to God to do a virtuous act if He fulfils his desire. 'Abdullāh ibn 'Umar relates: "Once the Prophet (peace be upon him) forbade people from making a vow, remarking that it cannot change what is destined to happen. However, it extracts something from the miserly person." (Muslim *K. al-Nadhr* and Abū Dāwūd *K. al-Aymān wa al-Nudhūr, Bāb Karāhiyah al-Nadhr*) The last part of the above *ḥadīth* means that a miserly person was not to spend anything in God's way. However, lured by a vow, he spends some money out of his belief that God may change his fate in lieu of his offer. Another report on the authority of 'Abdullāh ibn 'Umar is: "A vow can neither advance nor defer what is destined to happen. However, it may make a miserly person pay some money." (Bukhārī and Muslim) In yet another report he says: "The Prophet (peace be upon him) forbade taking a vow, remarking: 'It does not help in getting anything. However, it makes a miserly person pay some money.'" (Bukhārī and Muslim) Several reports of similar import are cited by Muslim on the authority of Abū Hurayrah. Both Bukhārī and Muslim quote this *ḥadīth*: "The Prophet (peace be upon him) observed: 'A vow cannot help the children of Ādam get something which He has not already ordained for them. A vow follows one's fate.

It makes a miserly person spend money which he was otherwise not going to pay.'" 'Abdullāh ibn 'Amr's report elaborates the above further: "A genuine vow is that which is made for seeking Allah's pleasure." (Ṭaḥāwī, *K. al-Aymān wa al-Nudhur, Bāb al-Rajul Yandhuru*) Abū Dāwūd (*K. al-Aymān wa al-Nudhur, Bab al-Yamīn*) *Musnad* of Imām Aḥmad (20, 185), Bayhaqī (*Sunan al-Kubrā, K. al-Nudhur*)

iii. The Prophet (peace be upon him) laid down another principle regarding vows: only that vow should be fulfilled which conforms to obedience to God. A vow which leads to any disobedience to God should never be fulfilled. There cannot be a vow regarding something which one does not own. Nor can it be for something which is beyond man's capacity. 'Ā'ishah relates that the Prophet (peace be upon him) said: "One who vows that he will obey God should fulfil his vow. One who vows that he will disobey God should not disobey Him." Bukhārī, (*K. al-Aymān wa al-Nudhur, Bāb al-Nadhr fī al-ṭā'ah*), Abū Dāwūd (*K. al-Aymān wa al-Nudhur*), Tirmidhī (*Abwāb al-Nudhur wa al-Aymān*), Nasā'ī (*K. al-Aymān wa al-Nudhur, Bāb al-Nadhr fī Ma'ṣīyah*), Ibn Mājah (*K. al-Kaffārah, Bāb al-Nadhr fī al-Ma'ṣiyah*) and Ṭaḥāwī (*K. al-Aymān wa al-Nudhur*). Thābit ibn Ḍaḥḥāk reports the Prophet's observation: "Fulfilling a vow which involves disobedience to God is out of the question. Nor is it tenable regarding something which one does not own." Abū Dāwūd, (*K. al-Aymān wa al-Nudhur*). Muslim cites an identical report narrated by 'Imrān ibn Ḥuṣayn. Abū Dāwūd (*K. al-Aymān wa al-Nudhūr*) quotes 'Abdullāh ibn 'Amr ibn al-'Āṣ' report to this effect: "There is no vow which entails something beyond man's capacity or disobedience to God or severing the ties of kinship."

iv. One should not fulfil a vow which is not related to a virtuous act or which involves something pointless or too arduous or self-torturing, regarding it as an act of virtue. The Prophet's directives regarding the above are quite categorical and emphatic. 'Abdullāh ibn 'Abbās informs that "once while the Prophet (peace be upon him) was delivering a sermon, he noticed someone standing in the sun. On enquiry, he was told that he is Abū Isrā'īl who has vowed that he will keep standing, not sit, nor be under any shade, nor talk to anyone, and will go on fasting. On hearing that, the Prophet said: 'Tell him to speak, to come in the shade and sit, but he should complete the fast.'" Bukhārī

(*K. al-Aymān wa al-Nudhur*), Abū Dāwūd (*K. al-Aymān wa al-Nudhur*), Ibn Mājah (*K. al-Kaffārah*) and Mālik (*K. al-Nudhur wa al- Aymān*). 'Uqbah ibn 'Āmir Juhanī reports: "My sister had vowed that she will proceed on the *Ḥajj* journey bare-footed and will not cover her head. Upon hearing this, the Prophet (peace be upon him) advised her to take a ride and cover her head." Abū Dāwūd and Muslim (*K. al-Aymān wa al-Nudhur*) have cited several similar reports, though with minor variants. 'Abdullāh ibn 'Abbās has quoted the Prophet's following remark regarding the vow made by 'Uqabah ibn 'Āmir Juhanī's sister: "Allah does not stand in need of such a vow. Tell her to take a ride." (Abū Dāwūd) Another report is as follows: "Abdullāh ibn 'Abbās informs that someone told the Prophet (peace be upon him) that his sister had vowed to go on foot for *Ḥajj*. To this he replied: 'Allah does not want your sister to undergo such hardship. She should take a ride for the *Ḥajj* journey.'" (Abū Dāwūd) Anas ibn Mālik states that probably during the *Ḥajj* journey, the Prophet (peace be upon him) saw an old man walking, supported by his two sons. The Prophet asked: "What is the matter with him?", to which he was told that the old man had vowed to go on *Ḥajj* on foot. Upon this he remarked: "Allah does not want that man should torment his body." He then directed him to ride. Bukhārī (*Abwāb al-'Umrah*) and Muslim (*K. al-Nudhur*). Muslim has also related a similar report, narrated by Abū Hurayrah.

v. If one is unable to fulfil his vow, he may opt for another form of its fulfillment. Jābir ibn 'Abdullāh informs: "On the day of the conquest of Makkah, someone stood up and said: 'O Messenger of God! I had vowed that if Allah enabled you to conquer Makkah, I will offer two *raka'ah* prayer at Bayt al-Maqdis.' To this he replied: 'You better perform it here.' He enquired again and the Prophet (peace be upon him) gave him the same reply. When he queried again, he told him 'do as you please'. Another report ascribes this remark to the Prophet (peace be upon him): 'By Him Who has sent Muḥammad with truth, if you pray here, it will suffice for your performing the prayer at Bayt al-Maqdis.'" Abū Dāwūd (*K. al-Aymān wa al-Nudhur*).

vi. Jurists have differences of opinion about the vow which involves giving away one's entire belongings in God's way. Imām Mālik opines that such a person is obliged to give only one-third of all that he has. Among Mālikīs, however, Saḥnūn is of the view that he should give only that much which does not cause him any hardship. Imām Shāfi'ī's ruling is that if this vow is for a virtuous act, he should give away all of his belongings. If his vow is not of this category, he has two options, either he fulfils his vow or pays expiation. Imām Abū Ḥanīfah's stance is that he should give away those belongings on which *Zakāh* is levied. However, such belongings which are exempt from *Zakāh*, such as one's house or other estate, do not fall within the purview of his vow. Among Ḥanafīs, Imām Zufar is of the view that he should give everything in charity, except the amount required for maintaining his dependents for two months. (*'Umdatul Qārī* 23, 214, and Shāh Walīullāh's *Sharḥ Muwaṭṭa'*) The *aḥādīth* that deal with the above issue are as follows: Ka'b ibn Mālik informs: "When I received pardon for the penalty I faced on account of staying behind in the Tabūk expedition, I submitted to the Prophet (peace be upon him): 'While repenting I had vowed that I will give in charity all of my belongings for the cause of Allah and His Messenger'. He asked me not to do so. When I offered to donate half of my belongings, he again refused. He however approved that I give one-third of it." (Abū Dāwūd) A variant report adds that the Prophet (peace be upon him) told him to retain some of his belongings for himself. Bukhārī (*K. al-Aymān wa al-Nudhur*). Imām Zuhrī says that he received this report that: "Abū Lubābah, who had incurred divine displeasure regarding the same Tabūk expedition, submitted to the Prophet (peace be upon him): 'I forego all of my belongings as charity for the cause of Allah and His Messenger.' To this he replied that it will suffice for him to give only one-third of it. (*Muwaṭṭa', K. al-Nudhur wa al-Aymān, Bāb Jāmi' al-Aymān*)."

vii. Should one fulfil his vow after accepting Islam if he had vowed in his pre-Islamic days to do a virtuous act? The Prophet's ruling is that such a person should fulfil his vow. Bukhārī (*K. al-Aymān wa al-Nudhur, Bāb Idhā Nadhara*). According to a tradition in Abū Dāwūd (*K. al-Aymān wa al-Nudhūr, Bāb Idhā Nadhara*) and Ṭaḥāwī (*K. al-Aymān wa al-Nudhur, Bāb al-Rajul Yandhur*) it is narrated about 'Umar that, prior to accepting Islam, he had vowed to spend a day or night in devotional retreat in the holy mosque. After having embraced Islam, he asked the Prophet (peace be upon him) whether he should fulfil his vow. The Prophet (peace be upon him) replied. "Fulfil your vow". Some jurists understand the Prophet's ruling to mean that it was obligatory on 'Umar to do so, whereas others think it was only a desirable act.

viii. Are the heirs obliged to fulfil a vow by the deceased which he could not execute? Jurists have different opinions on this issue. According to Aḥmad, Isḥāq ibn Rāhawayh, Abū Thawr, and the Ẓāhirīs, they are obliged to fulfil it, if the deceased's vow involved a fast or prayer. Ḥanafīs hold that they are not obliged to fulfil a vow related to physical acts of worship such as prayer or fasting. If it involves a monetary form of worship and if the deceased had not asked his heirs to fulfil it, they are not obliged to do so. However, if he has made a will, then it will be obligatory to fulfil it out of one-third of the inheritance he left behind. Mālikīs endorse the same stance. Shāfi'ī's, however, are of the view that if the deceased's vow relates to monetary or non-monetary forms of worship and if he did not leave any inheritance behind, his heirs are not obliged to fulfil his vow. If he left behind some inheritance, they should fulfil his vow related to the monetary form of worship, irrespective of whether the deceased person has left any will or not. Nawāwī's *sharḥ Muslim* (7, 261) and *Badhl al-Majhūd Sharḥ Abū Dāwūd* (11, 81–82). In the *ḥadīth* corpus, one comes across the following report related by 'Abdullāh ibn 'Abbās: "Sa'd ibn 'Ubādah sought the Prophet's ruling about the unfulfilled vow of his deceased mother. He directed Sa'd to fulfil it." Abū Dāwūd and Muslim (*K. al-Nadhr*). Ibn 'Abbās's other report reads as follows: "During a sea voyage a woman took the vow that if she returned home safely, she will fast for a month. On return, however, she died. Her sister or daughter sought the Prophet's advice, who directed her to fast on behalf of the deceased." Abū Dāwūd (*K. al- Aymān wa al-Nudhur, Bāb fī Qaḍā' al-Nadhr*). A similar report is cited by Abū Dāwūd on Buraydah's authority, that a woman made a similar query to the Prophet (peace be upon him) who gave her an identical reply. Since the above reports do not clarify whether the Prophet's ruling was obligatory or desirable, and since the form of worship is not clear in the report about Sa'd ibn 'Ubādah's mother, jurists have taken different positions on this issue.

ix. It is patently clear that a wrong and unlawful vow should not be fulfilled. However, there is a difference of opinion whether it necessitates an expiation or not. Owing to divergent reports on this issue, the opinion of jurists is divided. A set of reports indicate that the Prophet (peace be upon him) prescribed expiation in such a case. Take the following report by 'Ā'ishah as illustrative: "There is no vow for doing a wrong and its expiation is the same as for breaking an oath." Abū Dāwūd (*K. al-Aymān wa al-Nudhur, Bāb man ra'ā 'alayhi Kaffārah*). The case of 'Uqbah ibn Āmir Juhanī's sister, as discussed earlier, exemplifies that the Prophet (peace be upon him) directed her to break her vow and fast for three days. Muslim (*K. al- Aymān wa al-Nudhur*) and Abū Dāwūd (*K. al-Aymān wa al-Nudhur*). Likewise, in another case involving a woman who had vowed to go for *Ḥajj* on foot, he asked her to ride and to pay expiation for her vow. (Abū Dāwūd) Ibn 'Abbās reports the Prophet (peace be upon him) as saying: "Whoever makes a vow, without specifying the object of his vow, should pay the same expiation as is due for breaking an oath. Whoever vows to do something evil should also pay expiation. Whoever makes a vow to perform something that he does not have the power to do should expiate for that oath. However, one who makes a vow which he can fulfil, he should do so." Abū Dāwūd (*K. al-Aymān wa al-Nudhur*). At the other end of the scale, there are reports suggesting that there is no expiation in this case. After citing the case of the person who had vowed to keep standing in the sun and not talk to anyone, Imām Mālik observes in his *Muwaṭṭa'* (*K. al-Nudhūr wa al-Aymān*): "I could not find any source that indicates that apart from asking him to break his vow, the Prophet (peace be upon him) had asked him also to pay expiation." 'Abdullāh ibn 'Amr ibn al-'Āṣ asserts: "The Prophet (peace be upon him) remarked: "One who makes a vow and later notes something better, he should break the former and do the latter. Breaking the former itself constitutes its expiation.'" Abū Dāwūd (*K. al-Aymān wa al-Nudhur, Bāb al-Yamīn fī Qaṭ' al-Raḥim*). Bayhaqī, however, contests the authenticity of this and the other report by Abū Hurayrah which records: "One should do what is better and this itself constitutes its expiation." While analysing these reports in his *Sharḥ Muslim*, Imām Nawawī states: "In the opinion of Mālik, Shāfi'ī, Abū Ḥanīfah, Dāwūd Ẓāhirī, and leading 'Ulamā', it is invalid to make a vow to do something impermissible. There is no expiation for not fulfilling it. However, Imām Aḥmad maintains that there is expiation."

(8) those who, for the love of Him,[11] feed[12] the needy, and the orphan, and the captive,[13] (9) (saying): "We feed you only for Allah's sake; we do not seek of you any recompense or thanks,[14] (10) we fear from our Lord a Day that shall be long and distressful." ▶

وَيُطْعِمُونَ ٱلطَّعَامَ عَلَىٰ حُبِّهِۦ مِسْكِينًا
وَيَتِيمًا وَأَسِيرًا ﴿٨﴾ إِنَّمَا نُطْعِمُكُمْ لِوَجْهِ
ٱللَّهِ لَا نُرِيدُ مِنكُمْ جَزَآءً وَلَا شُكُورًا ﴿٩﴾
إِنَّا نَخَافُ مِن رَّبِّنَا يَوْمًا عَبُوسًا قَمْطَرِيرًا ﴿١٠﴾

---

11. Most of the Qur'ān commentators interpret that the pronoun in the phrase "*'Alā-ḥubbihī*" refers to food, therefore notwithstanding that it is their favourite food and they are in need of that food, they offer it to others. Ibn 'Abbās and Mujāhid are of the view that they do so out of their desire for feeding the needy. Fuḍayl ibn 'Ayāḍ and Abū Sulaimān al-Dārānī, however, opine that they do so out of love of God. In our opinion, the next verse ("we feed you for Allah's sake") clearly supports this interpretation.

12. It was customary in ancient times for prisoners, while being handcuffed and fettered, to be taken out daily and beg for food on streets. It was the Islamic rule that abolished this practice (Abū Yūsuf, *Kitāb al-Kharāj*, 1382H, p. 150). The verse refers to every type of prisoner, be he a disbeliever or Muslim, and a prisoner of war or a convict, and whether he is provided with food in prison or he is obliged to beg for it. Feeding such a helpless person, who cannot earn his bread, is an act of great virtue.

13. Although feeding the poor is in of itself an act of great virtue, meeting their other needs, for example clothing them, or giving them medical help, or repaying their debts when being harassed by their creditors are acts of equally great virtue. A particular form of help, i.e. feeding the needy, is presented here as an example. The overbearing message is that the needy should be helped.

14. It is not necessary that this should be verbally said while feeding the needy. One may keep this in his heart. In the sight of God, it is as good as saying it verbally. The reason this point is mentioned here in particular

(11) So Allah shall guard them against the woe of that Day, and will procure them freshness and joy,[15] (12) and will reward them for their steadfastness[16] with Paradise and robes of silk. (13) There they will recline on elevated couches and will be subjected neither to the burning heat of the sun nor to bitter cold. ▶

فَوَقَىٰهُمُ ٱللَّهُ شَرَّ ذَٰلِكَ ٱلْيَوْمِ وَلَقَّىٰهُمْ
نَضْرَةً وَسُرُورًا ﴿١١﴾ وَجَزَىٰهُم بِمَا صَبَرُوا۟ جَنَّةً
وَحَرِيرًا ﴿١٢﴾ مُّتَّكِـِٔينَ فِيهَا عَلَى ٱلْأَرَآئِكِ ۖ
لَا يَرَوْنَ فِيهَا شَمْسًا وَلَا زَمْهَرِيرًا ﴿١٣﴾

is that the needy person should be assured that the help is offered to him, not in expectation of any thanks or recompense from him. He should enjoy it without any apprehension.

15. Reference is to the freshness and joy radiating from their faces. In other words, only the disbelievers and culprits will undergo the ordeal of all sorts on the Day of Judgement. In contrast, the pious will be protected from all hardship. They will be joyful and well-pleased. The same truth is enunciated in the Qur'ān elsewhere thus: "The hour of the great terror shall not grieve them. The angels shall receive them saying: 'This is your Day which you had been promised.'" (*Sūrah al-Anbiyā'* 21: 103) The same features also in the following verse: "Whosoever comes with good will receive a reward better than his deed, and they will be made secure from the terror of that Day." (*Sūrah al-Naml* 27: 89)

16. *Ṣabr* has a wide range of meanings in the context of this verse. A pious person's whole life is characterised by steadfastness and perseverance. It consists in his controlling all unlawful desires from his coming of age until his last breath, his observance of the limits set by God, his discharging the duties prescribed by God, his sacrificing his time, money, effort, and talent, and even his life in God's cause, his spurning all temptations and gains which could lead him astray, his bearing with all the dangers and hardships confronted in pursuing the straight way, his forsaking all the unlawful gains, his perseverance over all the losses, sorrows, and torment to which he is subjected on account of his adherence

(14) The shades of Paradise will bend over them, and its fruits will be brought within their easy reach; (15) and there shall be passed around them vessels of silver[17] and goblets of crystal, (16) goblets bright as crystal but made of silver,[18] filled to exact measure.[19] ▶

وَدَانِيَةً عَلَيْهِمْ ظِلَـٰلُهَا وَذُلِّلَتْ قُطُوفُهَا
تَذْلِيلًا ﴿١٤﴾ وَيُطَافُ عَلَيْهِم بِـَٔانِيَةٍ مِّن
فِضَّةٍ وَأَكْوَابٍ كَانَتْ قَوَارِيرَا۠ ﴿١٥﴾
قَوَارِيرَا۠ مِن فِضَّةٍ قَدَّرُوهَا تَقْدِيرًا ﴿١٦﴾

---

to truth, and his trust in God's promise that he will be rewarded for all this in the Hereafter, not in this life. Such an outlook on life inspire a believer's conduct with steadfastness. This is all-embracing, life-long, and eternal perseverance. (For details see also *Towards Understanding the Qur'ān*, vol. I, *Sūrah al-Baqarah* 2: n. 60 and *Sūrah Āl 'Imrān* 3: nn. 13, 107 and 131, pp. 71, 240, 291 and 305–306; vol. II, *Sūrah al-An'ām* 6: n. 23, p. 228; vol. III, *Sūrah al-Anfāl* 8: nn. 37 and 47, pp. 156–157 and 166–167; vol. IV, *Sūrah Yūnus* 10: n. 9, pp. 8–9, *Sūrah Hūd* 11: n. 11, pp. 84–85, *Sūrah al-Ra'd* 13: n. 39, p. 236, *Sūrah al-Naḥl* 16: n. 98, p. 362; vol. V, *Sūrah Maryam* 19: n. 40, p. 167; vol. VII, *Sūrah al-Furqān* 25: n. 94, pp. 46–47 and *Sūrah al-Qaṣaṣ* 28: nn. 75 and 100, pp. 232–233 and 246; vol. VIII, *Sūrah Luqmān* 31: nn. 29 and 56, pp. 135 and 145–146, *Sūrah al-Sajdah* 32: n. 37, p. 176; vol. IX *Sūrah al-Aḥzāb* 33: n. 58, p. 58; *Sūrah al-Zumar* 39: n. 32; *Sūrah Ḥā Mīm al-Sajdah* 41: n. 38 and *Sūrah al-Shūrā* 42: n. 53.)

17. According to *Sūrah al-Zukhruf* 43: 71, "vessels of gold" shall be passed around the God-fearing. In this *Sūrah,* we find that "vessels of silver" will be passed around. All this shows is that on some occasions vessels of gold and on others, vessels of silver will be passed around to the people of Paradise.

18. Although these vessels will be of silver, they will be as transparent as crystal. This variety of silver does not exist in this world; it will be special to Paradise. Vessels of silver as transparent as crystal will be served at the tables of the dwellers of Paradise.

19. Everyone's goblet will be filled according to his desire, neither more nor less. In other words, those serving them will be intelligent and

(17) Therein they shall be served a cup flavoured with ginger, (18) drawn from a spring (in Paradise) called Salsabīl.[20] (19) There boys of everlasting youth shall go about attending them: when you see them, you would think that they are scattered pearls.[21] (20) Whitherto you look around, you will see an abundance of bliss and the glories of a great kingdom.[22] (21) They [i.e., the virtuous]▶

وَيُسْقَوْنَ فِيهَا كَأْسًا كَانَ مِزَاجُهَا زَنجَبِيلًا
﴿١٧﴾ عَيْنًا فِيهَا تُسَمَّىٰ سَلْسَبِيلًا ﴿١٨﴾ ۞ وَيَطُوفُ
عَلَيْهِمْ وِلْدَٰنٌ مُّخَلَّدُونَ إِذَا رَأَيْتَهُمْ
حَسِبْتَهُمْ لُؤْلُؤًا مَّنثُورًا ﴿١٩﴾ وَإِذَا رَأَيْتَ ثَمَّ
رَأَيْتَ نَعِيمًا وَمُلْكًا كَبِيرًا ﴿٢٠﴾ عَـٰلِيَهُمْ

careful enough to serve the drinks to the dwellers of Paradise exactly in accordance with their desire. (For the discussion on the characteristics of the drink of Paradise see *Towards Understanding the Qur'ān*, vol. IX, *Sūrah al-Ṣāffāt* 37: nn. 24–27, pp. 290–291; *Sūrah Muḥammad* 47: n. 22; *Sūrah al-Ṭūr* 52: n. 18 and *Sūrah al-Wāqi'ah* 56: n. 10.)

20. Since the Arabs were fond of drinks blended with a ginger-flavoured water, a pointed reference is made to the same in the above verse. This blending will not be like mixing ginger-water into the drinks, rather it will flow from a natural spring, with the flavour of ginger, though without its bitterness. For this reason it will be called *Salsabīl*, i.e. such water which is sweet, light, well-flavoured, and delicious to drink. For most commentators of the Qur'ān, *Salsabīl* is the adjective of the spring, not its name.

21. For further details see *Towards Understanding the Qur'ān*, vol. IX, *Sūrah al-Ṣāffāt* 37: n. 26, pp. 290–291; *Sūrah al-Ṭūr* 52: n. 19 and *Sūrah al-Wāqi'ah* 56: n. 9.

22. One may have been a pauper in this world, but as he will be admitted to Paradise in recognition of his good deeds, he will enjoy the glory of being the master of a great kingdom.

shall be attired in garments of fine green silk and rich brocade[23] and will be adorned with bracelets of silver.[24] Their Lord will give them a pure wine to drink.[25] (22) Behold, this is your recompense and ▶

ثِيَابُ سُندُسٍ خُضْرٌ وَإِسْتَبْرَقٌ وَحُلُّوٓاْ أَسَاوِرَ مِن فِضَّةٍ وَسَقَىٰهُمْ رَبُّهُمْ شَرَابًا طَهُورًا ﴿٢١﴾ إِنَّ هَٰذَا كَانَ لَكُمْ جَزَآءً

23. The same point features in verse 31 of *Sūrah al-Kahf*: "They will be arrayed in green garments of silk and rich brocade, and will recline on raised couches." Therefore, those Qur'ān commentators who interpret these as curtains hanging on their couches or bedsteads, or as the dress of the boys engaged in serving them, are incorrect.

24. It is stated in *Sūrah al-Ḥajj* 22: 23, *Sūrah al-Kahf* 18: 31 and *Sūrah Fāṭir* 35: 33. On reading those verses together, three variations would seem possible: (a) Sometimes, they will prefer to wear bracelets of gold and sometimes bracelets of silver. Both types of ornaments will be available to use according to their preference. (b) They will be free to wear both bracelets of gold and silver together in combination as it enhances the beauty. (c) They will be equally free to wear bracelets of gold or bracelets of silver according to their taste. As to the issue of men, rather than women, wearing bracelets, it was customary for the kings and the rich of the yore to adorn their hands, necks, and to crown of their heads with a variety of ornaments. The rajas and nawabs during the British Raj followed the same custom up to the middle of the twentieth century. The following Qur'ānic passage related to the appearance of the Prophet Moses (peace be upon him) in the Pharaoh's court is also instructive. Upon hearing from Moses that he was God's Messenger, the Pharaoh asked his courtiers in astonishment: "Why were bracelets of gold not bestowed upon him? Why did a retinue of angels not accompany him as attendants?" (*Sūrah al-Zukhruf* 43: 53). Moses was, of course, dressed in ordinary clothes, carrying his rod.

25. Reference was made earlier to two types of drinks tempered with camphor and *zanjabīl*. In this verse, a third one is mentioned as "a pure wine to drink". It means that it will be an exquisite drink, of the best quality, signifying God's special favour to the dwellers of Paradise.

your endeavour has been appreciated.[26]	وَكَانَ سَعْيُكُم مَّشْكُورًا ﴿٢٢﴾ إِنَّا نَحْنُ نَزَّلْنَا
(23) (O Prophet), indeed We have revealed the Qur'ān to you in portions.[27] (24) So persevere with the command of your Lord[28] ▶	عَلَيْكَ ٱلْقُرْءَانَ تَنزِيلًا ﴿٢٣﴾ فَٱصْبِرْ لِحُكْمِ رَبِّكَ

26. The original words are *"kāna sa'yukum mashkūrā"* (your endeavour has been appreciated). Endeavour (*sa'ī*) implies the lifelong accomplishment which a person performs in this world. The combination of energies and abilities that he spends in accomplishing his good work and noble causes is referred to as *sa'ī*. The word *"mashkūr"* (appreciated) means that man's entire effort has been approved and appreciated by God. *Shukr* (thankfulness) when it is expressed by man towards God means an expression of his profound gratitude for the divine bounties conferred upon him. Likewise, when it is expressed by God towards His servant, it means that He has accepted and appreciated his good deeds. It is indeed the height of a man's achievement when his Lord appreciates and accepts (*mashkūr*) all his work, carried out in accordance with His will.

27. Apparently, this is addressed to the Prophet (peace be upon him). However, the purpose of this statement is to refute the disbelievers' contention that the Qur'ān represents the Prophet's own thoughts. They used to argue that had it been from God, it would have come down in one piece rather than in fragments. At some places in the Qur'ān, this objection of the disbelievers has been cited and refuted (See *Towards Understanding the Qur'ān*, vol. IV, *Sūrah al-Naḥl* 16: nn. 102 and 104–106, pp. 364–366 and vol. V, *Sūrah Banī Isrā'īl* 17: n. 119, p. 80). In the above verse, however, without citing the disbelievers' charge, God emphatically declares that it is He Who has revealed it and that the Prophet (peace be upon him) is not its author. God sends it down in stages. It is out of His wisdom that He revealed it in portions, not as a whole, complete Book immediately.

28. The Prophet (peace be upon him) is advised to remain steadfast in discharging his mission, to endure patiently the hardships and difficulties that he might encounter in that regard, and not to allow anything to cause him to waver in his resolve.

and do not pay any heed to the wicked and the unbelieving,[29] (25) and remember the name of your Lord, morning and evening;[30] (26) and prostrate yourself before Him at night, and extol His Glory during the long watches of the night. ▶

وَلَا تُطِعْ مِنْهُمْ ءَاثِمًا أَوْ كَفُورًا ﴿٢٤﴾ وَٱذْكُرِ
ٱسْمَ رَبِّكَ بُكْرَةً وَأَصِيلًا ﴿٢٥﴾ وَمِنَ ٱلَّيْلِ
فَٱسْجُدْ لَهُۥ وَسَبِّحْهُ لَيْلًا طَوِيلًا ﴿٢٦﴾

---

29. The Prophet (peace be upon him) should not forsake his preaching of the truth under pressure from the disbelievers. Nor should he alter any of the moral teachings or articles of faith however small it may be, in deference to the wishes of the wicked and deniers of truth. He should publicly pronounce what is lawful and what is not. He should not show any laxity in divine commands, no matter how much the evildoers may try to persuade him. What is false should be proclaimed as false, and what is true as true by him even if the disbelievers exert any kind of pressure for silencing his voice or for trying to strike a deal with him.

30. Whenever there is an injunction to remember God alongside the mention of a specific time, such injunctions refer to the prescribed prayer. Moreover, this is stated immediately after the directive to Muslims to practise perseverance and steadfastness in their encounter against the disbelievers. Needless to say, believers derive the requisite energy from prayers in taking on the disbelievers in the cause of faith.

In the present verse two words are used: (i) *bukrah*, which denotes "morning" and (ii) "*aṣīl*", which denotes the period of time beginning with the sun's decline until the sunset. This covers the time for *Ẓuhr* and *'Aṣr* prayers. This is followed in the next verse by the injunction to "prostrate yourselves before Him at night". Since the "night" starts from sunset, the injunction to prostrate "at night" covers the *Maghrib* and *'Ishā'* Prayers. Next comes the injunction in the same verse to "extol His glory during the long watches of the night." This clearly refers to *Tahajjud* prayers (For details see *Towards Understanding the Qur'ān*, vol. V, *Sūrah Banī Isrā'īl* 17: nn. 92–97, pp. 63–66 and *Sūrah al-Muzzammil* 73: n. 2.) One thus learns that even in the very early days of Islam these

(27) Verily they love (the good of this world) that is hastily obtainable and are oblivious of the burdensome Day ahead of them.[31] (28) We created them and strengthened their joints; and whenever We wish, We can change their faces entirely.[32] (29) Verily this is an Exhortation; so let him who so will take a way to his Lord. (30) But your willing shall be of no avail until Allah Himself so wills.[33] Surely Allah is All-Knowing, Most Wise. ▶

إِنَّ هَٰٓؤُلَآءِ يُحِبُّونَ ٱلْعَاجِلَةَ وَيَذَرُونَ
وَرَآءَهُمْ يَوْمًا ثَقِيلًا ﴿٢٧﴾ نَّحْنُ خَلَقْنَٰهُمْ
وَشَدَدْنَآ أَسْرَهُمْ ۖ وَإِذَا شِئْنَا بَدَّلْنَآ أَمْثَٰلَهُمْ
تَبْدِيلًا ﴿٢٨﴾ إِنَّ هَٰذِهِۦ تَذْكِرَةٌ ۖ فَمَن شَآءَ
ٱتَّخَذَ إِلَىٰ رَبِّهِۦ سَبِيلًا ﴿٢٩﴾ وَمَا تَشَآءُونَ
إِلَّآ أَن يَشَآءَ ٱللَّهُ ۚ إِنَّ ٱللَّهَ كَانَ عَلِيمًا حَكِيمًا ﴿٣٠﴾

---

were the appointed hours of prayer. However, the five daily Prayers, with their respective number of *raka'ah* were prescribed on the occasion of the Prophet's Night Journey.

31. The reason the disbelieving Quraysh persisted in disbelief, immorality, and the show of extreme hostility to the Prophet's call was on account of their worldliness and their disregard of the Hereafter. Their path was markedly different from the one pursued by the believers, and hence there cannot be any scope of compromise between the two.

32. That "God may change their faces entirely" may be explained in a variety of ways. God may destroy them and replace them with members of the same species, whose conduct will be different. He may change their faces altogether, or afflict them with any serious disease or disability. Alternatively, God may re-create them after their death in a different form, as He pleases.

33. For details see *Sūrah al-Muddaththir* 74: n. 41 (See also Appendix 1).

(31) He admits to His Mercy whomsoever He pleases. As for the wrong-doers, He has prepared for them a grievous chastisement.[34]	يُدْخِلُ مَن يَشَآءُ فِى رَحْمَتِهِۦ ۚ وَٱلظَّـٰلِمِينَ أَعَدَّ لَهُمْ عَذَابًا أَلِيمًۢا ﴿٣١﴾

34. This point is explained in the Introduction to this *Sūrah* (See also Appendix 2).

Sūrah 77

Al-Mursalāt

(Those Sent Forth)

(Makkan Period)

Title

The expression *al-mursalāt* featuring in the opening verse of the *Sūrah* happens to be its title.

Period of Revelation

It emerges from its contents that it must have been revealed in the early Makkan period. On reading this *Sūrah,* along with the two *Sūrahs* preceding it – *Sūrah al-Qiyāmah* and *Sūrah al-Dahr*, and the two following it – *Sūrah al-Naba'* and *Sūrah al-Nāzi'āt*, they feature the same themes in multifaceted ways for the admonition of the Makkans. This suggest that all five were revealed in the same period.

Subject Matter and Themes

The *Sūrah* affirms the truth of the Resurrection and the Day of Judgement and informs people of the consequences for rejecting or affirming these truths.

Verses 1–7 adduce the arrangement of winds as a sign bearing out the veracity of the Qur'ān and the Prophet's tidings about the Resurrection. It is inevitable, for God the Absolutely Powerful, Who has put in place the amazing arrangement of the earth, can easily bring about the Resurrection. The wonderful wisdom underlying the above system underscores the need for the Hereafter. There is a purpose behind every act of God and nothing is vain and purposeless. Without the Afterlife, the present worldly order loses its meaning and purpose.

The Makkans repeatedly challenged the Prophet (peace be upon him) to bring upon them the forewarned Resurrection; only then would they believe in it. In verses 8–15, without citing their demand, a response is given, stating that the Resurrection is not something trivial, to be presented on the whims of any human being. It happens to be the Day of Judgement for all of humanity. God has already decreed its hour; it will occur at its affixed time. It will strike everyone so terribly that the disbelievers, who presently demand it mockingly, will be utterly panic-stricken. Then their fate will be decided by the testimony of their Messengers whose call they have rejected unabashedly. Only then will they realise how they have brought destruction upon themselves.

Verses 16–28 present arguments, one after another, for the need and occurrence of Resurrection and the Hereafter. Man's history, his creation, and the constitution of the earth which he inhabits all testify to the possibility and occurrence of Resurrection and the Hereafter. It is evident from the annals of history that all those nations who disbelieved in the Hereafter faced decline and destruction. This means that the occurrence of the Hereafter is such a reality that if a nation rejects and defies it, it invites its own destruction in the same way that a blind man rushes headlong into an approaching train and meets his miserable end. It also means that the universe is governed not only by physical laws, but also by moral laws, which are at work here. As a result, in this world the process of recompense is in operation. However, in the present life, this recompense cannot be dispensed in full. The moral laws of the universe therefore demand that, at a point of time, everyone should be recompensed in full for all good and evil deeds. It will thus compensate for the partial recompense in this world. The second life after death is therefore essential for this. Likewise, if one reflects on man's birth, he cannot dare deny that God, Who let him grow from an insignificant sperm drop into an adult human being, cannot bring him back to life. The components of one's body do not vanish from the earth after his death. Rather, these survive. Man is nourished on all the treasures that the earth produces, and after death, he returns to the same earth. God, Who created man from clay in the first place, is quite capable of retrieving him from the earth after his death. One who reflects on God's power cannot deny this possibility. If one studies the issue in the perspective of Allah's wisdom, he will realise that He is perfectly justified in holding man answerable for the powers that He granted him. His infinite wisdom dictates that man should not be let off, rather he should be called to render his account.

Verses 28–40 and 41–45 describe the fate of the disbelievers and the believers in the Hereafter, respectively. The former refused to accept the existence of the Hereafter, whereas the latter, during their worldly life, strove to brighten their prospects for the next life. They embraced faith and shunned the evils of disbelief, thought, morality, actions, conduct, and character, which may offer worldly gains but destroy one's prospects in the Hereafter.

Finally, the deniers of the Hereafter and those refusing to worship God are warned that they may enjoy the pleasures of this world for a while. However, they are destined for an extremely terrible end. The discourse concludes on the assertion that whoever fails to derive guidance from the Qur'ān cannot obtain it from any other source.

In the name of Allah, the Most Merciful, the Most Compassionate.

(1) By the (winds) sent forth in quick succession, (2) which then blow tempestuously (3) and raise (clouds) and scatter them around, (4) then winnow them thoroughly, (5) and then cast (Allah's) remembrance (in people's hearts), (6) to serve as an excuse or a warning.[1] (7) Surely what you are promised[2] shall come to pass.[3]

بِسۡمِ ٱللَّهِ ٱلرَّحۡمَٰنِ ٱلرَّحِيمِ

وَٱلۡمُرۡسَلَٰتِ عُرۡفٗا ١ فَٱلۡعَٰصِفَٰتِ
عَصۡفٗا ٢ وَٱلنَّٰشِرَٰتِ نَشۡرٗا ٣ فَٱلۡفَٰرِقَٰتِ
فَرۡقٗا ٤ فَٱلۡمُلۡقِيَٰتِ ذِكۡرًا ٥ عُذۡرًا
أَوۡ نُذۡرًا ٦ إِنَّمَا تُوعَدُونَ لَوَٰقِعٞ ٧

1. The winds serve several important purposes. Sometimes when they cease to blow, they give rise to the frightful prospect of a famine which tends to soften people's hearts. This at times leads people to turn sincerely to God and repent. On other occasions, winds bring generous rainfall, filling people's hearts with gratitude to God. On still other occasions, they blow tempestuously, inspiring fear in all hearts. As a result, many turn to God, dreading His chastisement that would wreak havoc on them (See also Appendix 3).

2. It could be a reference to the Day of Resurrection and the Hereafter against which they are warned.

3. The oath regarding the inevitability of the Day of Resurrection is taken here with reference to the following five features: (i) The (winds) sent forth in quick succession, (ii) which blow tempestuously, (iii) which raise (clouds) and scatter them around, (iv) which winnow them thoroughly and (v) which cast (God's) remembrance. In the above account,

the focus is only on the features, without specifying the object that is endowed with these attributes. As a result, the Qur'ān commentators differ as to whether all the above five features are of the same entity or of various entities. There is also disagreement among them in identifying these. A group of them is of the view that all these attributes are of the wind. This is contested by some, who think these are related to the angels. Some hold that the first three are the features of winds while the last two are of angels. Some ascribe only the first two to winds and the rest to angels. Some scholars hold the view that the first and the second are the features of the angels of mercy and punishment respectively, while the last three refer to the verses of the Qur'ān.

In our opinion, since these five features are described one after another, without any indication of a break in the discourse, it would be unsound to assume that the reference is to more than one object. The cohesion and coherence of the text rather suggests that the whole passage is about the features of one particular entity. The purpose of this is to stress that the things related to the oath are absolutely true and correct. It is therefore unlikely that an intangible thing will be adduced as an argument for an intangible thing. Rather, a tangible entity is more apt. In our opinion, the reference is to winds. We do not accept the view of those who interpret the five things to be angels, for they too, like the Day of Resurrection, belong to the realm of the Unseen.

Let us now focus on how the system of winds serves as an argument for affirming the truth of the Resurrection. Air is one of the most important factors essential for sustaining animal and plant life on earth. Its close link with the life cycle itself proves that it is devised by the All-Powerful, Most-Wise Creator of the Universes. He has put in place everything in the perfect proportion needed for supporting the life cycle. The winds do not merely encompass the earth. Rather, out of His power and Wisdom, God has ensured their various states and features which regulate, since the beginning of time, the alternation of seasons and various states of weather, such as the blowing of a breeze, scorching heat, chilling cold, thick clouds, and heavy rainfall. At times, winds lead to devastating storms or beneficial rain, or even famine. There are varieties of winds which blow at their appointed time and serve numerous functions. The very system testifies to a powerful divine scheme of things. It is not difficult for Him to bring life into existence or take it away, or recreate it after it was obliterated. Only a fool may take the excellent working of the Universe as a sport, lacking any underlying sublime purpose. Man is so helpless against this

(8) So when the stars are extinguished,[4] (9) and the sky is rent asunder,[5] (10) and the mountains are blown away, (11) and the appointed time to bring the Messengers together arrives,[6] (then shall the promised event come to pass). (12) To which Day has this task been deferred? (13) To the Day of Judgement. (14) What do you know what the Day of Judgement is? ▶

فَإِذَا ٱلنُّجُومُ طُمِسَتْ ۝٨ وَإِذَا ٱلسَّمَآءُ
فُرِجَتْ ۝٩ وَإِذَا ٱلْجِبَالُ نُسِفَتْ ۝١٠ وَإِذَا
ٱلرُّسُلُ أُقِّتَتْ ۝١١ لِأَىِّ يَوْمٍ أُجِّلَتْ ۝١٢ لِيَوْمِ
ٱلْفَصْلِ ۝١٣ وَمَآ أَدْرَىٰكَ مَا يَوْمُ ٱلْفَصْلِ ۝١٤

---

wonderful arrangement that he can neither blow any wind for himself, nor can he protect himself against devastating, gale-force winds. Despite his obstinate and stubborn disbelief, winds, at times, remind him of his servitude to his All Powerful Master and Lord Who may use this most important means of life to bring His mercy or His curse upon him. As it is, man is utterly helpless to defy His decree. (For details see also *Sūrah al-Jāthiyah* 45: n. 7 and *Sūrah al-Dhāriyāt* 51: nn. 1–4.)

4. The stars will lose their brightness.

5. The present system which binds all the celestial entities to their respective orbits will come to an end and all the barriers will be rent asunder.

6. It is mentioned quite often in the Qur'ān that when God examines mankind's record on the Day of Judgement, the Messenger of each nation will be summoned to testify that he had conveyed God's message to his people. This will be the first and clinching argument from God against the wicked and wrongdoers. It will conclusively establish that they themselves were responsible for their error and misconduct, for God had employed every conceivable measure for warning them. (For further details see *Towards Understanding the Qur'ān*, vol. III, *Sūrah al-A'rāf* 7: nn. 134–135, pp. 97–101; *Sūrah al-Zumar* 39: n. 80 and *Sūrah al-Mulk* 67: n. 14.)

(15) Woe on that Day to those that give the lie to the Truth![7]

(16) Did We not destroy many a nation of the earlier times?[8] (17) And We shall cause those of later times to follow them.[9] (18) Thus do We deal with the guilty. (19) Woe on that Day to those that give the lie to the Truth![10]

وَيْلٌ يَوْمَئِذٍ لِّلْمُكَذِّبِينَ ﴿١٥﴾ أَلَمْ نُهْلِكِ
الْأَوَّلِينَ ﴿١٦﴾ ثُمَّ نُتْبِعُهُمُ الْآخِرِينَ ﴿١٧﴾ كَذَٰلِكَ
نَفْعَلُ بِالْمُجْرِمِينَ ﴿١٨﴾ وَيْلٌ يَوْمَئِذٍ
لِّلْمُكَذِّبِينَ ﴿١٩﴾

---

7. Meaning the disbelievers who rejected the tidings of the Resurrection and led their lives in the world assuming that they will never have to stand before God, rendering their record of deeds and be accountable for the same.

8. This argument for the Hereafter is taken from the annals of history, which man should study. All those nations who denied the Hereafter considered this world as the entirety of their existence, and determined moral principles based on the outcome of good and evil in this life alone, were eventually destroyed without any exception. This proves that the Hereafter is a reality, the rejection of which ruins one's life in the same way as when one turns a blind eye to the realities of this life and severely harms himself. (For details see *Towards Understanding the Qur'ān*, vol. IV, *Sūrah Yūnus* 10: n. 12, pp. 11–13; vol. VII, *Sūrah al-Naml* 27: n. 86, pp. 180–181; vol. VIII, *Sūrah al-Rūm* 30: n. 8, pp. 78–79 and vol. IX, *Sūrah Saba'* 34: n. 25, pp. 173–174.)

9. This is God's permanent law. The rejection of the Hereafter, which proved fatal for the earlier nations, will prove the same for communities in the future as well. No nation has escaped this fate in the past and none will be an exception in the future.

10. This is said to emphasise that howsoever woeful a person's lot might be in this world, it does not represent the real chastisement that might lie in store for him. It is only on the Day of Judgement that each

(20) Did We not create you of a mean fluid, (21) which We then placed in a secure repository[11] (22) until an appointed time?[12] (23) See that We had the power to do so. Great indeed is Our power to do what We will.[13] ▶

أَلَمْ نَخْلُقكُّم مِّن مَّآءٍ مَّهِينٍ ۝٢٠ فَجَعَلْنَٰهُ فِى قَرَارٍ مَّكِينٍ ۝٢١ إِلَىٰ قَدَرٍ مَّعْلُومٍ ۝٢٢ فَقَدَرْنَا فَنِعْمَ ٱلْقَٰدِرُونَ ۝٢٣

person will come to know the full extent of the chastisement that awaits him. The punishment in this world represents, at most, the detention of a criminal who continues committing crimes, refusing to mend his ways. Not in this world but in the court of the Hereafter alone will his case be decided, and he will be duly punished for his crimes. That will indeed be the actual day of his doom. (For further details see *Towards Understanding the Qur'ān*, vol. III, *Sūrah al-A'rāf* 7: nn. 5–6, pp. 4–5 and vol. IV, *Sūrah Hūd* 11: n. 105, p. 133.)

11. This appointed time is known to God alone. It is beyond man to tell beforehand for how many months, days, hours, minutes, and seconds the baby will remain inside the mother's womb and exactly what will be the precise time of its birth. God has ordained an appointed time for each baby, of which only He has the knowledge.

12. After conception, the foetus is placed in the safe repository of the mother's womb. The baby is placed there with such arrangements of security and nourishment that it cannot be miscarried unless there is a serious accident. Notwithstanding all the latest advancements in medical science, its abortion is still a difficult and risky process in view of its secure placement in the womb.

13. This is another weighty argument for Life-after-Death. Since God is able to create man out of an insignificant drop of sperm, why can He not then easily re-create him in any form after his death? The process of man's creation itself testifies to God's excellent creative power. He is in no way helpless to cause man's rebirth after having created him in the first place.

(24) Woe on that Day to those that give the lie to the Truth![14]

(25) Did We not make the earth a receptacle, (26) for the living and the dead, (27) and did We not firmly fix towering mountains on it and give you sweet water to drink?[15] ▶

وَيۡلٞ يَوۡمَئِذٖ لِّلۡمُكَذِّبِينَ ٢٤ أَلَمۡ نَجۡعَلِ
ٱلۡأَرۡضَ كِفَاتًا ٢٥ أَحۡيَآءٗ وَأَمۡوَٰتٗا ٢٦ وَجَعَلۡنَا
فِيهَا رَوَٰسِيَ شَٰمِخَٰتٖ وَأَسۡقَيۡنَٰكُم
مَّآءٗ فُرَاتٗا ٢٧

14. Despite confronting the overwhelming argument for the possibility of Life-after-Death, those people who are denying it are free today to mock this belief as much as they like. They may even dismiss its believers as conservative, outdated, and superstitious in their outlook. But when the Day of Judgement, which they were denying and scoffing at, will appear, then they will realise this is the day of their complete ruin and disaster.

15. It constitutes another argument as to why the doctrine of the Hereafter is sound and tenable. Billions of creatures have inhabited the earth for millions of years, including human beings, and different animals and plant species. It has been sustaining them all along with its numerous resources and products. Furthermore, numerous creatures die every day on earth, yet there is an amazing system in place for disposing of their dead bodies in no time. The earth then gets itself ready for sustaining the new members of all species. The earth is not made-flat or level plain. Mountain ranges and high mountains are part of the landscape. These are instrumental in bringing about climatic changes, variations in seasons, rainfall, causing rivers to flow, creating fertile meadows, and in providing huge trees supplying timber, and a variety of minerals and stones. The earth is also a vast reservoir of water. Equally baffling is the arrangement of the rising of the vapours from the sea and their descent later to the earth as rainfall. All this points to the existence of the All-Powerful Creator, One Who is All-Hearing and All-Seeing. If this earth has been created with all its provisions and skilful management requirements, only by His power and wisdom, why then should an intelligent person have any difficulty in grasping

(28) Woe on that Day to those that give the lie to the Truth![16]

(29) Proceed[17] now towards that which you were wont to deny as false; (30) proceed towards the three-pronged shadow,[18] (31) which neither provides (cooling) shade nor protection against the flames; (32) it indeed throws up sparks like castles, (33) which seem as though ▶

وَيۡلٞ يَوۡمَئِذٖ لِّلۡمُكَذِّبِينَ ۝٢٨ ٱنطَلِقُوٓاْ إِلَىٰ مَا
كُنتُم بِهِۦ تُكَذِّبُونَ ۝٢٩ ٱنطَلِقُوٓاْ إِلَىٰ ظِلّٖ ذِي
ثَلَٰثِ شُعَبٖ ۝٣٠ لَّا ظَلِيلٖ وَلَا يُغۡنِي مِنَ
ٱللَّهَبِ ۝٣١ إِنَّهَا تَرۡمِي بِشَرَرٖ كَٱلۡقَصۡرِ ۝٣٢ كَأَنَّهُۥ

that the same all-Powerful God can put an end to the world and create a new one to His liking? His wisdom demands that He should build a different world after this, so that He may call man to account for the deeds he has done in this world.

16. People decry the coming of the Hereafter and accountability for their activities as false, calling it both impossible and irrational. They do so in spite of the stunning manifestations of God's power and wisdom. They may remain immersed in their puerile fancies if they so wish. But a day will certainly come when they will see that many a thing, quite contrary to their expectations, will come to pass. It is then that they will fully realise how foolish they were in precipitating such devastation upon themselves.

17. After proffering the evidence that the Hereafter is bound to occur, the disbelievers are told about the treatment that they will receive after the Hereafter becomes a reality.

18. "Shadow" here denotes the shadow caused by smoke. What is meant by its three-pronged form can be grasped by observing a thick pall of smoke splitting into several branches.

they are yellow-coloured camels.[19] (34) Woe on that Day to those that give the lie to the Truth!

(35) That will be the Day on which they will not (be able to) utter a word, (36) nor will they be allowed to proffer excuses.[20] (37) Woe on that Day to those that give the lie to the Truth!

(38) That is the Day of Judgement on which We have assembled you as well as all those who went before you. (39) So if you have ▶

جِمَٰلَتٌ صُفْرٌ ﴿٣٣﴾ وَيْلٌ يَوْمَئِذٍ لِّلْمُكَذِّبِينَ
﴿٣٤﴾ هَٰذَا يَوْمُ لَا يَنطِقُونَ ﴿٣٥﴾ وَلَا يُؤْذَنُ
لَهُمْ فَيَعْتَذِرُونَ ﴿٣٦﴾ وَيْلٌ يَوْمَئِذٍ
لِّلْمُكَذِّبِينَ ﴿٣٧﴾ هَٰذَا يَوْمُ ٱلْفَصْلِ
جَمَعْنَٰكُمْ وَٱلْأَوَّلِينَ ﴿٣٨﴾ فَإِن كَانَ

19. Each of its sparks will be as massive as a palace. As these sparks burst, it will seem as though they are yellow-coloured camels running about.

20. This will be their last condition when they will be consigned to Hell. In the grand assembly, they will resort to all sorts of pretexts and pleas in self-defence, blame others for their misdeeds in a bid to plead their innocence, and revile their chiefs for having misled them. Some will even have the temerity to deny their misdeeds, as the Qur'ān states at several places. However, the irrefutable and solid evidence will prove them to be offenders and moreover their own limbs will testify against them, leaving no room for any allowance to be made to them, they will be left utterly speechless because the punishment will be awarded to them after fulfilling the due process of law and justice. They will then be unable to put up any defence whatsoever, nor will they be allowed to proffer any excuse. This does not mean that they will be declared guilty without giving them a chance to defend their case. What is meant is that as their crimes will be conclusively proved, they will not be in a position to offer any further pretext or excuse. They will be silenced by the irrefutable evidence against them.

any ploy, try it against Me![21] (40) Woe on that Day to those that give the lie to the Truth!

(41) Behold, today the God-fearing[22] will be amidst shades and springs, (42) and the fruits that they desire (will be ready at hand). (43) Eat and drink and may every joy attend you as a reward for your deeds. (44) Thus do We reward those that do good. (45) Woe on that Day to those that give the lie to the Truth![23]

لَكُمْ كَيْدٌ فَكِيدُونِ ﴿٣٩﴾ وَيْلٌ يَوْمَئِذٍ
لِّلْمُكَذِّبِينَ ﴿٤٠﴾ إِنَّ ٱلْمُتَّقِينَ فِى ظِلَٰلٍ
وَعُيُونٍ ﴿٤١﴾ وَفَوَٰكِهَ مِمَّا يَشْتَهُونَ ﴿٤٢﴾ كُلُوا۟
وَٱشْرَبُوا۟ هَنِيٓـًٔا بِمَا كُنتُمْ تَعْمَلُونَ ﴿٤٣﴾
إِنَّا كَذَٰلِكَ نَجْزِى ٱلْمُحْسِنِينَ ﴿٤٤﴾ وَيْلٌ
يَوْمَئِذٍ لِّلْمُكَذِّبِينَ ﴿٤٥﴾

---

21. Since they indulged in all sorts of frauds and falsehood in the world, they are sarcastically asked to try any of their ploys against God to escape in the Hereafter.

22. The God-fearing are those who shunned the rejection of the Hereafter. They led their lives in the world firmly believing that they will have to render an account of their words, deeds, character, and conduct in the Hereafter.

23. Another affliction will be that they will be standing in the grand assembly as culprits, their crimes will be publicly announced, leaving them stunned and speechless. They will ultimately become the fuel for the Hellfire. What will torment them worse is that the believers, whom they fought all along, contemptuously dismissing them as imbecile, conservative, regressive, and worthless, will be there enjoying the bliss of Paradise.

(46) Eat[24] and enjoy yourselves for a while.[25] Surely you are evil-doers. (47) Woe on that Day to those that give the lie to the Truth! (48) When it is said to them: "Bow down (before Allah)," they do not bow down.[26] (49) Woe on that Day to those that give the lie to the Truth! (50) In what discourse after this (Qur'ān) will they, then, believe?[27]

كُلُوا۟ وَتَمَتَّعُوا۟ قَلِيلًا إِنَّكُم مُّجْرِمُونَ ﴿٤٦﴾
وَيْلٌ يَوْمَئِذٍ لِّلْمُكَذِّبِينَ ﴿٤٧﴾ وَإِذَا قِيلَ لَهُمُ
ٱرْكَعُوا۟ لَا يَرْكَعُونَ ﴿٤٨﴾ وَيْلٌ يَوْمَئِذٍ
لِّلْمُكَذِّبِينَ ﴿٤٩﴾ فَبِأَىِّ حَدِيثٍۭ بَعْدَهُۥ
يُؤْمِنُونَ ﴿٥٠﴾

---

24. The *Sūrah* concludes by addressing these words not only to the Makkan disbelievers, but to the disbelievers of all times, wherever they happen to be.

25. Meaning in the short-lived life of this world.

26. Bowing down includes not only serving God but also believing in His Messengers and His Book, and abiding by His commands.

27. The Qur'ān has been sent down as the best guide for illustrating before them the distinction between truth and falsehood, and directing them towards the path of guidance. If one does not embrace faith even after listening to or studying it, nothing else can guide him to the straight path.

Appendices

Appendix I

Note 33 of *Sūrah al-Dahr*

This verse highlights the following three points: (i) Man has the choice to follow the path leading to His Lord. (ii) One's wish alone does not bring about anything. It is only God's will that makes something happen. (iii) God is Most-Wise, All-Knowing. On reflecting upon the above truths thoroughly, one may fully grasp the nexus between God's will and man's freedom of choice. It helps allay the misperceptions about fate which often confuse the minds of men.

The Qur'ānic verse asserts that man's freedom is only to the extent of choosing any one of the numerous ways of leading his life. This is the freedom of choice that God has granted him. For example, for earning his living man has several options, some of which are lawful, such as manual labour, employment, business, industry, skills-based work or agriculture. As opposed to these, some are unlawful, such as stealing, robbery, pick-pocketing, prostitution, interest based transactions, gambling, bribery, and unlawful types of jobs and business. Man is free to choose any of these for obtaining his livelihood. The same holds true for morality; on the one hand, there are the values of honesty, integrity, nobility, decency, justice, mercy, sympathy, chastity, and modesty. On the other, there are the evil traits of wickedness, meanness, tyranny, dishonesty, indecency, and rudeness. Once again, man is free to practise the types of morals which he prefers. Almost the same is true of faith. One has many options – atheism, rejection of God, polytheism and idol worship, and a mixture of polytheism and monotheism, as well as pure monotheism, which is what the Qur'ān prescribes. Man has been given the freedom to choose any of these. God does not compel man into doing anything. If he seeks lawful means of income, God does not force him to engage in unlawful means. Likewise, if he wishes to abide by the Qur'ān, God does not compel him into professing and practising atheism or polytheism. If one chooses to be a good person, he is not compelled to be evil.

Nonetheless, after making his choice, whether man can practically do this depends on God's will, His decree, and His grace. In other words, if He wills that one may do what he wishes or decides, only then may he do so. Otherwise, without His leave and will one cannot do anything, no matter how hard he may try. This truth is stressed in the second verse under discussion. This could better be understood through an example. Had man been absolutely free to do whatever he wished, and had he enjoyed all powers in the world, it would have created chaos and confusion, resulting in the disruption of the entire world order. A single murderer would have been enough to murder everyone in the world if he had the power and freedom to do so. A pickpocket would have robbed everyone if he had enjoyed absolute power. A thief or a fornicator or a robber would not have spared anyone if each of them were free to do as they wished. That is why God controls the power and allows or disallows how far one should go in doing what he wishes to do. If one decides to give up error and follow guidance, it is God's will that lets him do so. It comes into effect, however, after man himself resolves to move away from evil to good. As God does not compel anyone to become a thief, murderer, atheist, or polytheist, in the same way He does not compel one to become a believer either.

After this, the third verse addresses another misconception and clarifies that God's will is not something arbitrary. While removing this misconception, it is asserted that He is All-Knowing and Most-Wise. He knows everything and all His actions are marked by perfect knowledge and wisdom. Therefore, He is infallible and there cannot be any possibility of error in His judgement. Out of His perfect knowledge and wisdom, He decides who and how much grace should be granted to a person, and who should not receive it; who should be allowed to do what type of work and who should not. He facilitates the path for man to do what He has decided for him to accomplish within a particular limit, be it good or bad. The issue of guidance is no exception. Again, on the basis of His perfect knowledge and wisdom, He decided who is eligible for guidance and who is not.

Appendix II

Note 34 of *Sūrah al-Dahr*

The verse speaks of those wrongdoers who deliberately and consciously decide not to accept God's Word and His Messenger's teachings after these are clearly conveyed to them. Included among them are those wicked people who reject God outright, or those who do not hesitate to say that they do not accept the Revelation as God's Revelation and the Messenger as God's Messenger at all; and also those who, notwithstanding the lack of their denial of God, the Messenger, and the Qur'ān, refuse to obey and follow them. As a matter of fact, both types of people are wrongdoers. The former's case is unmistakable. The latter, apart from being wrongdoers, are also hypocrites and treacherous, for they verbally pledge their belief in God, the Messenger, and the Qur'ān, yet in their hearts and minds they are bent upon not following them. Rather, they act contrary to all the teachings. God declares that He has prepared a grievous chastisement for both these types of wrongdoers. They may ardently love this world, pursue their enjoyment with full impunity, and boast of their greatness in this world. Ultimately, however, a terrible punishment will overwhelm them. In no way can they have any portion of God's mercy.

Appendix III

Note 1 of *Sūrah al-Mursalāt*

These verses describe the winds that bring rain in the following order: first the winds blow in quick succession, then these turn into a storm, then they raise the clouds and scatter them far and wide. Then they winnow them thoroughly. Then, instead of mentioning rainfall, the verse says that these winds infuse God's remembrance into people's hearts to serve as an excuse or a warning. To put it another way, when the tempestuous winds blow, man's heart is filled either with fear, which compels him to remember God, or one confesses his sins and invokes God to protect him from ruin. He also pleads that, out of His mercy, God should bless him with rain. If it has not rained for a long time, and there is an acute shortage of water, at that time even a staunch disbeliever, when he looks at the tempestuous wind blowing and clouds approaching, begins to remember God. Depending upon the degree of famine or draught, there is, however, a slight difference in the response of people. In the case of a mild famine, an ordinary person who has not forsaken God will turn to Him while others will cite some natural or scientific reasons for this calamity. They will try to reassure others, saying there is nothing to be worried about, and there are certain reasons for not having rain at the moment. They further assert that it is a sign of weak faith to invoke God for such a minor issue. However, in the event of a severe famine devastating the entire country, even the leading disbelievers begin to remember God. Though they may not publicly confess their wrongdoings, they privately repent over their sins and ingratitude. They earnestly beseech God that the tempestuous winds raising clouds should now bring rain to their country. This is the meaning of the verse that says the winds serve as an excuse for them for the remembrance of God. In regard to these winds causing fear, the reference is to the changing of the winds into a severe storm, which in turn causes a deluge, destroying all settlements in its path. In this eventuality, even the staunch disbelievers turn to God in repentance, sobbing profusely. At that time, they forget all about the scientific theories on storms or floods.

It is in the above sense that the Qur'ān speaks of the winds casting God's remembrance into people's hearts to serve as an excuse or a warning. The entire system working in the universe reminds man that the earth has not been placed under his control. On the contrary, there is a Supreme Being above Who controls his destiny. He is so powerful that if He wills, He can use the same elements to sustain and nourish mankind, and He can use them for their destruction if He so wills.

The system of winds is adduced as an argument for the veracity of the promise of the Resurrection which is certain to occur. Let us now examine how this system testifies to the above truth.

Generally speaking, there are two questions which agitate the human mind about the issue of Resurrection and the Hereafter: (i) Is this at all possible, (ii) What is the need for this? While grappling with these questions, man at times grows sceptical as to whether the Resurrection will ever occur or not. He tends to take it as a flight of fancy. For removing such doubts, the Qur'ān has, at several places, drawn attention to the working of the possibility of the Hereafter, its rationale, and its inevitability. At times, an oath is taken with reference to some of the numerous divine signs of His kingdom, stating that it is bound to happen. It thus vindicates arguments for its need, possibility, and occurrence.

In the verses under discussion, the focus is mainly on the blowing of winds and rainfall. With reference to these, it is asserted that there is a definite system governing these phenomena which have been devised by the All-Wise, All-Powerful Creator. All this is not because of some accident. The rising of vapours from the sea, their ascent facilitated by winds, their turning into clouds, and then scattering clouds over various parts of the earth, and the eventual rainfall are not some chance happenings. It is not something haphazard set in motion by blind laws of nature. On the contrary, all this represents a well thought out, deliberate, and precise system, which has been constantly in place. That is why the sun rays falling over the sea raise only vapours; these do not produce ice on the surface. The seasonal winds never blow in the reverse order and suppress these vapours; they always facilitate their ascent. The formation of clouds never ceases, nor do winds ever stop carrying clouds to dry parts of the earth. Rainfall is another consistent, regular phenomenon. All this has been going on for millions of years. Had this not been so, human life could not have come into existence and flourish on Earth.

We note a definite purposiveness and a regular law in the working of the universe. One can clearly see that there is a deep nexus between winds and rainfall, and the human, animal, and plant life on earth. It is absolutely clear that this water supply has been there for supporting the creation of life, and is perfectly in accordance with the requisite needs. The system is also subject to an elaborate law. The same purposiveness permeates each and every facet of the working of the universe. All man's advancements in science and technology are contingent upon the same, for in the presence of these constant laws of nature, man is able to discover what exists and how it works. The more man learns about their functions and the laws underlying these, the easier it becomes for him to utilise these in numerous ways. It contributes also to the development of technology. New inventions and discoveries result in the development of man's culture and civilisation. Had man not have this innate belief that the world has a definite purpose and all that exists in it is subject to certain laws, he could never think of entertaining its purpose and utilisation.

Since this world and all that it has are marked by purposiveness and governed by definite laws, and as all this has been in place for billions of years, only a stubborn person can deny that the world has been created by the All-Knowing, Most-Wise and All-Powerful Lord. Equally foolish is the notion that the One Who created and manages it cannot demolish and re-create it if He so wills. Ignorant atheists in the past placed much premium on their notion that matter is immortal. However, the latest studies have disproved this. It is now an acknowledged scientific fact that matter converts into energy and vice versa. It is therefore perfectly logical to assert that the Ever Living and Self Subsisting God may let this universe exist as long as He wishes. He can change it into energy with His single command. Likewise, He is able to recreate it in no time in any material form or shape that He wills.

The possibility of the Resurrection cannot be challenged by any scientific and rational argument. As to the issue that it must happen, it flows from the truth that it alone will help reward and punish everyone who deserves it. One who recognises man's moral duties and realises also that reward and punishment are an essential part of the moral code are bound to believe that there must be the Hereafter. No human society or state in this world can punish every crime and reward every good deed. As to the notion that self-reproach of the conscience is of sufficient punishment for the culprit and the satisfaction of the conscience is sufficient for the doer of good is nothing but a meaningless philosophical exercise. Hence, if one kills an innocent man and himself dies soon after this crime, he will not have any opportunity to suffer from the reproach of his conscience. Likewise, one who goes to the battlefield in the cause of defending truth and justice, and is instantly killed by a bomb blast will not have any time to derive the satisfaction that he laid down his life for a noble cause. The truth is that all the pretexts fabricated for negating the belief in the Hereafter are without any substance and are meaningless. Reason demands that there must be the Hereafter. The same is the dictate of human nature, that justice be dispensed. As it is, justice cannot be dispensed in this world in full measure and adequately. It is possible only in the Hereafter, and only at the command of the All-Knowing, All-Aware God. Denial of the Hereafter betrays the denial of justice and fair play.

Man's intellect can, at most, direct him to the conclusion that the Hereafter is possible and should occur. However, it is the revelation that has conclusively given the knowledge that there will definitely be the Hereafter which is being promised to mankind. Aided by reason alone, man cannot arrive at this truth. Revelation blesses us with the conviction that the Hereafter is both possible and inevitable.

Glossary of Terms

'Ahd (covenant) in 2: 27, for instance, refers to the command of God to His servants. This *'ahd* consists of God's eternal command that His creatures are obliged to render their service, obedience and worship to Him alone. In other usages in the Qur'ān, the word denotes commitment, contract or obligation of a person with respect to others (see, for instance, 2: 177, 8: 56, 9: 4, etc.)

Ahl al-Kitāb, literally 'People of the Book', refers to the followers of Divine Revelation before the advent of the Prophet Muḥammad (peace be upon him).

Ākhirah (Afterlife, Hereafter, Next World). The term embraces the following ideas:

1. That man is answerable to God.
2. That the present order of existence will some day come to an end.
3. That the real measure of success or failure of a person is not the extent of his prosperity in the present life, but his success in the Next.
4. That those who are reckoned good will be sent to Paradise, whereas the evil-doers will be consigned to Hell.
5. That when that happens, God will bring another order into being in which He will resurrect all human beings, gather them together and examine their conduct, and reward them with justice and mercy.

Amānah (trusts) encompass all types of trust which either God or society or an individual places in someone's charge.

Āyah, (pl. *āyāt*), means sign (or 'token'), that which directs one to something significant. In the Qur'ān this word has been used in five different meanings: (1) sign or indication; (2) the phenomena of the universe (called *āyāt* of God for the reality to which they point is hidden behind the veil of appearances); (3) miracles performed by the Prophets; (4) God's major acts of punishing the wicked, such as the Flood which inundated and destroyed the people of Noah; and (5) the individual units (i.e. verses) of the Qur'ān.

Dhikr means remembrance. In the Islamic context, it is used in the sense of the 'remembrance of God'. In verse 2: 199, *dhikr* refers to remembering God on a specific occasion, namely during the Pilgrimage at Minā. As used in 23: 71, *dhikr* has three possible meanings: (1) human nature; (2) admonition and good counsel; and (3) honour. Each of the above meanings seems to be correct in the context of the verses mentioned.

al-Dīn carries in the Qur'ānic parlance two meanings: (1) divine recompense in the Hereafter, and (2) the faith of Islam.

Firdaws, a word occurring with reference to Paradise in the Qur'ān literally denotes a large, enclosed garden adjoining one's residence, a garden that abounds in fruits, especially grapes.

Fisq transgression; disobeying God's command.

Futūr denotes crack, rift, fissure, cleaving, or breaking apart.

Ghayb literally means "hidden, covered, or concealed". As a term, it means all that is unknown and is not accessible to man by the means of acquiring knowledge available to him. *Ghayb* therefore refers to the realm that lies beyond the ken of sense perception.

Ḥadīth: the word *ḥadīth* literally means communication or narration. In the Islamic context it has come to denote the record of what the Prophet (peace be on him) said, did, or tacitly approved. According to some scholars, the word *ḥadīth* also covers reports about the saying and deeds, etc. of the Companions of the Prophet in addition to those of the Prophet himself. The whole body of Traditions is termed *ḥadīth* and its science as *'Ilm al-Ḥadīth*.

Ḥajj (Major Pilgrimage) is one of the five pillars of Islam, a duty one must perform during one's life-time if one has the financial resources for it. It resembles *'Umrah* (q.v.) in some respect, but differs from it insofar as it can be performed only during certain specified dates of the month of Dhū al-Ḥijjah. In addition to *ṭawāf* and *sa'ī* (which are also required for *'Umrah*), there are a few other requirements but especially one's 'standing' (i.e. stay) in 'Arafāt during the daytime on 9 Dhū al-Ḥijjah. For details of the rules of *Ḥajj*, see the books of *Fiqh*.

Ḥashr literally means "to gather", and signifies the doctrine that with the blowing of the Second Trumpet all those who had ever been created will be resurrected and brought forth to the Plain where all will be made to stand before God for His judgement.

Hijrah signifies migration from a land where a Muslim is unable to live according to the precepts of his faith to a land where it is possible to do so. The *Hijrah par excellence* for Muslims is the *Hijrah* of the Prophet (peace be upon him) which not only provided him and his followers with refuge from persecution, but also an opportunity to build a society and state according to the ideals of Islam.

'Ibādah is used in three meanings: (1) worship and adoration; (2) obedience and submission; and (3) service and subjection. The fundamental message of Islam is that man, as God's creature, should direct his *'ibādah* to God in all the above-mentioned meanings of the term, and associate none with God in rendering it.

Iblīs literally means "thoroughly disappointed; one in utter despair". In Islamic terminology it denotes the *jinn* (Iblīs), who refused the command of God to prostrate before Ādam out of vanity. He also asked God to allow him a term in which he might mislead and tempt mankind into error. This term was granted to him by God whereafter he became the chief promoter of evil and prompted Ādam and Eve to disobey God's order. He is also called *al-Shayṭān* (Satan). He is possessed of a specific personality and is not just an abstract force.

Iḥsān literally denotes doing something in a goodly manner. When used in the Islamic religious context, it signifies excellence of behaviour arising out of a strong love for God and a profound sense of close relationship with Him. According to a tradition, the Prophet (peace be on him) defined *iḥsān* as worshipping God as though one sees Him.

Īmān literally means faith and belief.

Jihād means "to strive, to exert to the utmost". The words *jihād* and *mujāhid* imply the existence of forces of resistance against whom it is necessary to wage a struggle. Moreover, the usual stipulation in the Qur'ān that *jihād* should be *fī sabīl Allāh* (in the way of God), it is clear that there are forces of resistance which obstruct people from serving God and pursuing His good pleasure, and that it is necessary to engage in strife and struggle to overcome those forces. The term, however, embraces all kinds of striving aimed at making the Word of God supreme in human life and is not confined only to fighting and warfare. The Prophet (peace be on him) even declared the striving to subdue one's self to the will of God is one of the forms of "greater *jihād*".

Jinn are an independent species of creation about which little is known except that unlike men, who were created out of earth, the *jinn* were created out of fire. But like men, a Divine Message has also been addressed to the *jinn* and they too have been endowed with the capacity, again like men, to choose between good and evil, between obedience and disobedience to God.

Ka'bah, literally a cube. It is a large cubic stone structure covered with a black cloth which stands in the centre of al-Masjid al-Ḥarām. It is also known as *al-bayt al-ḥarām* and *al-bayt al-'atīq*. It marks the direction to which the Muslims should face in their Prayers.

Kaffārah means atonement, expiation.

Khalīfah or vicegerent is the one who exercises the authority delegated to him by his principal.

Khayr does not mean goodness only; rather, it connotes wealth as well.

Kitāb, literally a thing on which something is written; a book or inscription; also a writ or command. The Qur'ān also called *Kitāb*.

Kufr, its original meaning is "to conceal". This word has been variously used in the Qur'ān to denote: (1) state of absolute lack of faith; (2) rejection or denial of any of the essentials of Islam; (3) attitude of ingratitude and thanklessness to God; and (4) non-fulfillment of certain basic requirements of faith. In the accepted technical sense, *kufr* consists in the rejection of the Divine Guidance communicated through the Prophets and Messengers of God. More specifically, ever since the advent of the last of the Prophets and Messengers, Muḥammad (peace be upon him), rejection of his teachings constitutes *Kufr.*

Maghfirah comes from the root word *ghfr*, meaning to hide or cover. *Maghfirah*, then, means to ask God to hide or cover one's evil deeds by forgiving them.

Malak means "message-bearer" and is used in the Islamic texts for angels.

Miskīn (pl. *masākīn*) denotes helplessness, destitution. Thus *masākīn* are those who are in greater distress than the ordinary poor people. Explaining this word the Prophet (peace be upon him) declared that *masākīn* are those who cannot make both ends meet, who face acute hardship and yet whose sense of self-respect prevents them from asking for aid from others and whose outward demeanour fails to create the impression that they are deserving of help.

Muhājirūn: Emigrants; those who migrated from Makkah to Madīnah in the way of God when it had become extremely difficult for them to live in their home town according to the requirements of their faith.

Munāfiq (pl. *munāfiqūn*), means a hypocrite.

Muslim (Literally means "one who has submitted to God"). Taken in its widest sense, it implies that everything in the whole universe is a Muslim, as it has submitted to the will of God, whether willingly or otherwise. In its narrowest sense it implies those who commit themselves to follow the teachings of the Prophet Muḥammad (peace be upon him) after reciting the *Shahādah* (q.v.). The Qur'ān also refers to the followers of all the Prophets before the Prophet Muḥammad (peace be upon him) as Muslims.

Nabī, a word for which we have used the word Prophet as an equivalent, refers to a person chosen by God to whom He entrusts the task to warn people against that which would lead to their perdition and to direct them to the way that would lead to their felicity. Prophets are enabled to perform this task because of the special knowledge that is providentially made available only to them, because of the special power that is bestowed upon them by God (which is evident from the miracles they are enabled to perform), and because of the special ability to live a life of absolute probity. The function of a *nabī* is close to, but note necessarily identical with that of a *rasūl* (q.v. *rasūl*).

Nadhr denotes the firm promise that a person makes to God to perform certain supererogatory acts of goodness over and above those he is obliged to perform.

Nuṣub signifies the place consecrated for offerings to others than the One True God.

Qiblah signifies the direction to which all Muslims are required to turn when offering their prescribed Prayers, namely towards the Ka'bah.

Qitāl, war, fighting.

Rasūl (pl. *rusul*), literally meaning "message-bearer", has been used in the Qur'ān with reference both to the angels who bear God's Message to the Prophets, and with reference to the Prophets who are entrusted with communicating God's Message to His creatures. In its technical sense, the word *rasūl* is used in Islamic parlance in the latter sense. There is some disagreement among Muslim scholars as to whether the terms *nabī* (Prophet) and *rasūl* (Messenger) are equivalents, and which of the two – *nabī* or *rasūl* – has a higher status. The majority of scholars are of the opinion that while every *rasūl* (Messenger) is a *nabī* (Prophet), every *nabī* is not a *rasūl*; and that the Messengers (*rasūl*), therefore, have a higher status and are entrusted with a greater mission than the Prophets.

Rukū' means to bend the body, to bow. This bowing is one of the acts required in Islamic Prayer. Additionally, the same word denotes a certain unit in the Qur'ān. The whole Book, for the sake of the convenience of the reader, is divided into thirty parts (*ajzā'*, sing. *juz'*), and each *juz'* consists usually of sixteen *rukū'*.

Ṣadaqah signifies whatever is given in charity with sincerity and the intent to please God. It is required that those who give charity should do so without flaunting it, without impressing upon its recipients that it was given to them as a favour, and without causing them any hurt.

Sajdah means prostration. It is one of the prescribed rites of prayer requiring one to put one's forehead down on the floor in humility and out of worshipful reverence for God.

Ṣalāh literally means prayer. In Islamic parlance *ṣalāh* refers to the ritual which is so called because it includes praying. *Ṣalāh* is an obligatory act of devotion which all adult Muslims are required to perform five times a day and consists of certain specific acts such as *takbīr,* which signals the commencement of *ṣalāh,* and includes such other acts as *qiyām* (standing), *rukū'* (bowing), and *sujūd* (prostration). Apart from obligatory *ṣalāh,* there are other categories of *ṣalāh* as well. (For one such *ṣalāh* q.v. *Tahajjud.*)

Shahādah, literally the act of witnessing, is the declaration of belief in the unity of God and the Prophethood of the Prophet Muḥammad (peace be upon him). Its pronouncement is considered one of the five pillars of Islam. When one proclaims it aloud, one is considered to have officially declared oneself to be a Muslim.

Sharī'ah signifies the entire Islamic way of life, especially the Law of Islam.

Shirk consists in associating anyone or anything with the Creator either in His being, or attributes, or in the exclusive rights (such as worship) that He has over His creatures.

Shukr means thankfulness. In Islam, it is a basic religious value. Man owes thanks to God for almost an infinite number of things. He owes thanks to God for all that he possesses – his life as well as all that marks his life pleasant, enjoyable and wholesome. And above all, man owes thanks to God for making available the guidance which can enable him to find his way to his salvation and felicity.

Sunnah, means a way, course, rule, mode or manner of acting or conduct of life. In Islamic terminology it denotes the way of the Prophet Muḥammad (peace be upon him) as evidenced by his authentic precepts and practices.

Sūrah, literally a row or fence, refers to any of the 114 chapters of the Qur'ān.

Tahajjud is the Prayer offered in the last quarter of the night, at any time before the commencement of the time of *Fajr* Prayer. It is a recommended rather than an obligatory Prayer, but one which has been emphasised in the Qur'ān and in the *Ḥadīth* as meriting great reward from God.

Taqwā, is one of the many words in the Islamic terminology whose exact equivalent is hard to find in English. It has been translated as 'fear of

Allah', 'God fearing', 'piety', righteousness', 'dutifulness', and 'God-consciousness'.

Tasbīḥ, has two meanings: (1) to proclaim God's glory, and (2) to exert oneself earnestly and energetically to do God's will.

Tashahhud, literally 'testimony', is a declaration of the Muslim faith towards the end of the Prayers, immediately after the recitation of *Taḥīyah,* while sitting with the first finger of the right hand extended as a witness to the unity of God.

Tawbah basically means 'to come back; to turn towards someone'. *Tawbah* on the part of man signifies that he has given up his disobedience and has returned to submission and obedience to God. The same word used in respect of God means that He has mercifully turned to His repentant servant and that the latter has once again become an object of His compassionate attention.

Tawḥīd, which is the quintessence of Islam, besides being the doctrinal affirmation of God's Oneness and Unity, it also represents man's commitment to render God worship, service and absolute obedience, and to consecrate them for Him alone.

***Waḥy* [*Waḥī*]** signifies the revelation which consists of communicating God's Messages to a Prophet or Messenger of God. The highest form of revelation is the Qur'ān, which, in every sense of the expression, is the 'speech or word' of God.

Wuḍū' refers to the ablution performed for acquiring the state of ritual purity which is pre-requisite to perform Prayers. It requires washing (1) the face from the top of the forehead to the chin and as far as each ear; (2) the hands and arms up to the elbows; (3) wiping with wet hands part of the head; and (4) washing the feet up to the ankles.

Zakāh literally means purification, whence it is used to express a portion of property bestowed in alms, as a means of purifying the person concerned and the remainder of his property. It is among the five pillars of Islam and refers to the mandatory amount that a Muslim must pay out of his property. The detailed rules of *zakāh* have been laid down in books of *Fiqh.*

Zinā means illegal sexual intercourse and embraces both fornication and adultery.

Biographical Notes

'Abdullāh ibn 'Abbās, see Biographical Notes, *Towards Understanding the Qur'ān*. Leicester, Islamic Foundation, 1988). All subsequent references, unless otherwise stated, are to the same edition. Vol. I

'Abdullāh ibn 'Amr ibn al-'Āṣ, see Biographical Notes, Vol. I

'Abdullāh ibn Mas'ūd, see Biographical Notes, Vol. I

'Abdullāh ibn 'Umar, see Biographical Notes, *Towards Understanding the Qur'ān*, Abridged Version. Leicester, Islamic Foundation, 2006.

Abraham (Ibrāhīm), see Biographical Notes, Vol. VIII

Abū Bakr, 'Abdullāh ibn 'Uthmān, see Biographical Notes, Vol. I

Abū Dā'ūd Sulaymān ibn al-Ash'ath, see Biographical Notes, Vol. I

Abū Ḥanīfah, al-Nu'mān ibn Thābit, see Biographical Notes, Vol. VIII

Abū al-Haytham Sulaymān ibn 'Umar, a Successor and a disciple of the Companion, Abū Sa'īd al-Khudrī. Narrated many *Aḥādīth* from al-Khudrī and Abū Hurayrah. Rated as reliable narrator of *Ḥadīth.*

Abū Hurayrah, see Biographical Notes, Vol. I

Abū Jahl, 'Amr ibn Hishām ibn al-Mughīrah, see Biographical Notes, Vol. I

Abū Lubābah ibn 'Abd al-Mundhir (d. during 'Alī's Caliphate). During the battle of Badr the Prophet (peace and blessings be upon him) had appointed him his deputy in Madīnah. There is an allusion to him in *Sūrah al-Tawbah.*

Abū Thawr, Ibrāhīm ibn Khālid ibn abī al-Yamān al-Kalbī (d. *circa* 240 AH/854 CE), was a leading *Ḥadīth* scholar and jurist.

Abū Ya'lā (d. 307 AH/919 CE): He was born in Mosul, Iraq. His *Musnad* is a major work on *Ḥadīth*.

Aḥmad ibn Ḥanbal, see Biographical Notes, Vol. I

'Ā'ishah, see Biographical Notes, Vol. I

'Alī ibn Abī Ṭālib, see Biographical Notes, Vol. I

Al-Ālūsī, Maḥmūd ibn 'Abdullāh al-Ḥusaynī, see Biographical Notes, Vol. I

Anas ibn Mālik, see Biographical Notes, Vol. I

'Aṭā' ibn Abī Rabāḥ, see Biographical Notes, Vol. I

'Aynī, Badr al-Dīn (763–855 AH/1361–1451CE): A *Ḥadīth* scholar, historian and Ḥanafī jurist. He hailed from Ḥalab, Syria. Among his notable works are *'Umdatul Qārī*, his commentary on al-Bukhārī's *Ṣaḥīḥ*, and his other commentary on *al-Hidāyah*.

Al-Bajlī, Jarīr ibn 'Abdullāh (d. 51 AH), a Companion. The Prophet (peace and blessings be upon him) had directed him to demolish the Dhū al-Khalsa temple. Took an active part in the Qadisiya and other expeditions.

Al-Bayhaqī, Abū Bakr Aḥmad ibn al-Ḥusayn ibn 'Alī, see Biographical Notes, Vol. V

Al-Bukhārī, Muḥammad ibn Ismā'īl, see Biographical Notes, Vol. I

Buraydah ibn al-Ḥusayb ibn 'Abdullāh ibn al-Ḥārith al-Aslamī, see Biographical Notes, Vol. V

Ḍāḥḥāk, Abū 'Āṣim al-Nabīl ibn Makhlad ibn Ḍaḥḥāk ibn Muslim al-Shaybānī, see Biographical Notes, Vol. VI

Al-Dārānī, Abū Sulaymān (d. 204 AH). A disciple of Successors, especially of Sufyān al-Thawrī. A native of Damascus.

Dāraquṭnī (306–385 AH/919–995 CE): He hailed from Baghdad. He is a leading Shāfi'ī *Ḥadīth* scholar and jurist. Amid his works on *Ḥadīth* the following two deserve special mention: *al-Sunan* and *al-'Alal*.

Al-Dārimī, 'Abdullāh ibn 'Abd al-Raḥmān, see Biographical Notes, Vol. I

Darrāj ibn Sam'ān (d. 126 AH). A *Ḥadīth* narrator rated variously by *Ḥadīth* scholars.

Fāṭimah bint Muḥammad, see Biographical Notes, *Towards Understanding the Qur'ān* Abridged Version.

Fiḍḍah, Fāṭimah's slave girl.

Fuḍail ibn 'Abbās (d. 187 AH) Teacher of Sufyān al-Thawrī. A Sufi master and pious, reliable narrator of *Ḥadīth*.

Ḥafṣah, see Biographical Notes, Vol. I

Al-Ḥākim al-Nīshāpūrī, Muḥammad ibn 'Abdullāh Ḥamdawayh, see Biographical Notes, Vol. V

Al-Ḥasan al-Baṣrī, see Biographical Notes, *Towards Understanding the Qur'ān* Abridged Version.

Ḥasan ibn 'Alī, see Biographical Notes, Vol. VII

Ḥassān ibn Thābit (d. 54 AH/674 CE): Belonged to the Khazraj tribe of Madīnah. He was acclaimed as a poet both before and after accepting Islam. He composed verses in defence of the Prophet Muḥammad (peace be upon him).

Ḥāṭib ibn Abī Balta'ah, see Biographical Notes, *Towards Understanding the Qur'ān* Abridged Version.

Ḥudhayfah ibn al-Yamān, see Biographical Notes, Vol. II

Al-Ḥusayn ibn 'Alī ibn Abī Ṭālib (d. 61 AH/680 CE), was Fāṭimah's son. He enjoyed great respect because of his many qualities, including piety, besides his distinguished lineage as the Prophet's grandson. Soon after Yazīd assumed power, Ḥusayn went to Kūfah at the invitation of his supporters who promised to install him as the caliph. Accompanied by members of his family and a band of staunch supporters, he was intercepted by Umayyad soldiers and brutally martyred along with his family members and followers.

Ibn Abī Ḥātim, 'Abd al-Raḥmān, see Biographical Notes, Vol. VI

Ibn Abī Shaybah, 'Abdullāh ibn Muḥammad, see Biographical Notes, Vol. VIII

Ibn al-Mundhir, Muḥammad ibn Ibrāhīm, see Biographical Notes, Vol. VII

Ibn Hishām, 'Abd al-Malik, see Biographical Notes, Vol. I

Ibn Isḥāq, Muḥammad, see Biographical Notes, Vol. IV

Ibn Kathīr, Ismā'īl ibn 'Umar, see Biographical Notes, Vol. I

Ibn Mājah, Muḥammad ibn Yazīd, see Biographical Notes, Vol. I

Ibn Marduwayh (323–410 AH/935–1019 CE): A renowned Qur'ān and *Ḥadīth* scholar and historian.

Ibn Sa'd, Muḥammad, see Biographical Notes, *Towards Understanding the Qur'ān* Abridged Version.

Ibn Taymīyah, Taqī al-Dīn Aḥmad ibn 'Abd al-Ḥalīm see Biographical Notes, Vol. I

Ibrāhīm al-Nakha'ī, see Biographical Notes, Vol. I

Ibrāhīm ibn Muḥammad (peace be upon him): Mary the Copt gave birth to him in 8 AH. He, however, died in 10 AH.

'Ikrimah ibn 'Abdullāh al-Barbarī al-Madanī, see Biographical Notes, Vol. VIII

'Imrān ibn Ḥuṣayn ibn 'Ubayd, see Biographical Notes, Vol. VIII

Isaac (Isḥāq), see Biographical Notes, Vol. VIII

'Īsā, see Jesus.

Isḥāq, see Isaac.

Ishāq ibn Rāhwayh ibn Ibrāhīm ibn Makhlad al-Marwazī, see Biographical Notes, Vol. V

Jābir ibn 'Abdullāh, see Biographical Notes, Vol. I

Al-Jaṣṣāṣ, Aḥmad ibn 'Alī, see Biographical Notes, Vol. I

Jesus ('Īsā), see Biographical Notes, Vol. VIII

Ka'b ibn Mālik al-Anṣārī, see Biographical Notes, *Towards Understanding the Qur'ān* Abridged Version.

Kalbī (d. 204 AH/819 CE): His full name is Hishām ibn Muḥammad al-Kalbī. He was a historian, hailing from Kufah. Amid his many works, *Kitāb al-Aṣnām* is highly acclaimed.

Khadījah bint Khuwaylid, see Biographical Notes, *Towards Understanding the Qur'ān* Abridged Version.

Khālid ibn al-Walīd, see Biographical Notes, Vol. I

Al-Khudrī, Abū Sa'īd Sa'd ibn Mālik ibn Sinān al-Anṣārī, see Biographical Notes, *Towards Understanding the Qur'ān* Abridged Version.

Lot (Lūṭ), see Biographical Notes, Vol. VIII

Lūṭ, see Lot.

Mālik ibn Anas, see Biographical Notes, Vol. I

Mary the Copt (d. 16 AH/ 637 CE): An Egyptian slave girl sent as a gift by the ruler of Alexandria in 7H to the Prophet Muḥammad (peace be upon him). She gave birth to the Prophet's son, Ibrāhīm. She passed away during the Caliph 'Umar's reign.

Moses (Mūsā), see Biographical Notes, Vol. VIII

Mūsā, see Moses.

Muḥammad al-Bāqir ibn 'Alī Zayn al-'Ābidīn ibn al-Ḥusayn, see Biographical Notes, *Towards Understanding the Qur'ān* Abridged Version.

Mujāhid ibn Jabr, see Biographical Notes, *Towards Understanding the Qur'ān* Abridged Version.

Muslim ibn al-Ḥajjāj al-Nīsābūrī, see Biographical Notes, Vol. I

Naḍr ibn al-Ḥārith, see Biographical Notes, Vol. II

Al-Nawawī, Yaḥyā ibn Sharaf, see Biographical Notes, Vol. II

Nīsābūrī, Niẓām al-Dīn al-Ḥasan ibn Muḥammad, see Biographical Notes, Vol. VII

Noah (Nūḥ), see Biographical Notes, Vol. VIII

Nūḥ, see Noah.

Qatādah ibn Di'āmah, see Biographical Notes, *Towards Understanding the Qur'ān* Abridged Version.

Al-Qurṭubī, Muḥammad ibn Aḥmad, see Biographical Notes, Vol. I

Rabī' ibn Anas see Biographical Notes, *Towards Understanding the Qur'ān* Abridged Version.

Al-Rāzī, Muḥammad ibn 'Umar Fakhr al-Dīn, see Biographical Notes, Vol. III

S'ad ibn Abī Waqqāṣ, see Biographical Notes, Vol. III

S'ad ibn Mu'ādh, see Biographical Notes, Vol. III

Sa'd ibn Ubādah al-Khazrajī al-Anṣārī, see Biographical Notes, Vol. VI

Sa'īd Ibn Jubayr (45–95 AH/665–714 CE): A Successor. He was a disciple of Ibn 'Abbās and Ibn 'Umar.

Ṣafīyah, see Biographical Notes, Vol. I

Sa'īd ibn Jubayr, see Biographical Notes, Vol. II

Ṣāliḥ, see Biographical Notes, *Towards Understanding the Qur'ān* Abridged Version.

Sawdah bint Zam'ah ibn Qays, see Biographical Notes, *Towards Understanding the Qur'ān* Abridged Version.

Al-Shāfi'ī, Muḥammad ibn Idrīs, see Biographical Notes, Vol. I

Shāh Walī Allāh, see Biographical Notes, *Towards Understanding the Qur'ān* Abridged Version.

Al-Suddī, Ismā'īl ibn 'Abd al-Raḥmān, see Biographical Notes, Vol. VIII

Ṣuhayb ibn Sinān, see Biographical Notes, Vol. VIII

Sulaymān ibn Yasār (34–107 AH/654–725 CE): A Successor. He was the freed slave of the Prophet's wife, Maymūnah. He ranks among the seven leading jurisprudents of Madīnah.

Al-Suyūṭī, Jalāl al-Dīn, see Biographical Notes, Vol. VII

Al-Ṭabarānī, Sulaymān ibn Aḥmad ibn Ayyūb, see Biographical Notes, Vol. VI

Al-Ṭabarī, Muḥammad ibn Jarīr, see Biographical Notes, Vol. I

Ṭaḥāwī (239–321 AH/853–933 CE): His full name is Abū Ja'far Aḥmad ibn Muḥammad a renowned Ḥanafī *Ḥadīth* and *Fiqh* scholar. Originally from Egypt, his *Sharḥ Ma'ānī al-Āthār* is a substantial work on *Ḥadīth*.

Ṭā'ūs ib Kaysān, see Biographical Notes, Vol. I

Thābit ibn Ḍaḥḥāk (d. 45 AH/665 CE): A Madinan Companion of the Prophet (peace be upon him), who belonged to the Aws tribe. He was among those who had pledged his oath of fealty to the Prophet (peace be upon him) at the time of the Ḥudaibīyah treaty.

Al-Thawrī, Sufyān ibn Sa'īd, see Biographical Notes, Vol. II

Al-Tirmidhī, Muḥammad ibn 'Īsā, see Biographical Notes, Vol. I

Ubayy ibn Ka'b, see Biographical Notes, Vol. I

'Umar ibn al-Khaṭṭāb, see Biographical Notes, Vol. I

Umm Salamah, Hind bint Abī Umayyah, see Biographical Notes, Vol. I

'Uqbah ibn 'Āmir, see Biographical Notes, Vol. VIII

'Uthmān ibn 'Affān, see Biographical Notes, Vol. I

Al-Wāḥidī, 'Alī ibn Aḥmad, see Biographical Notes, Vol. VIII

Walīd ibn al-Mughīrah, see Biographical Notes, Vol. VIII

Ẓāhirīs, see Biographical Notes, Vol. I

Al-Zamakhsharī, Maḥmūd ibn Muḥammad ibn Aḥmad, see Biographical Notes, Vol. IV

Zarkashī (745–794 AH/1344–1392 CE): His full name is Badr al-Dīn Muḥammad. His works are on *Tafsīr*, Qur'ānic studies, *Ḥadīth*, Principles of *Ḥadīth*, Jurisprudence, Principles of Jurisprudence and Literature. His major work is *al-Burhān fī 'Ulūm al-Qur'ān.*

Zayd ibn Ḥārithah ibn Sharāḥīl (or Shuraḥbīl) al-Kalbī, see Biographical Notes, *Towards Understanding the Qur'ān* Abridged Version.

Zayd ibn Thābit, see Biographical Notes, Vol. I

Zaynab bint Jaḥsh al-Asadīyah, see Biographical Notes, *Towards Understanding the Qur'ān* Abridged Version.

Zufar ibn al-Ḥudhayl, see Biographical Notes, Vol. II

Al-Zuhrī, Muḥammad ibn Muslim ibn Shihāb, see Biographical Notes, Vol. I

Bibliography

Abū Dāwūd, Sulaymān Ibn al-Ash'ath al-Sijistānī, *al-Sunan.*

Abū al-Ḥanafī al-'Izz, *Sharḥ al-Ṭaḥāwīyah fī al-'Aqīdah al-Salafīyah*, Riyadh, Wakālat al-Ṭibā'ah wa al-Tarjamah, 1413 AH.

Abū Ḥayyān, *al-Baḥr al-Muḥīṭ.*

Akmal al-Dīn Muḥammad ibn Maḥmūd, *al-'Ināyah Sharḥ al-Hidāyah*, 9 vols., Quetta, al-Maktabah al-Rashīdīyah, 1985 on the margin of Kamāl al-Dīn 'Abd al-Wāḥid, Quetta, *Fatḥ al-Qadīr*, 9 vols., al-Maktabah al-Rashīdīyah, 1985.

Al-Ālūsī, Maḥmūd ibn 'Abdullāh al-Ḥusaynī, *Rūḥ al-Ma'ānī*, 30 vols., Cairo, Idārat al-Ṭibā'ah al-Munīrīyah, n.d.

Al-'Asqalānī, Ibn Ḥajar, *Fatḥ al-Bārī*, 13 vols., Cairo, al-Maṭba'ah al-Khayrīyah, 1325 AH.

__________, *al-Iṣābah.* Beirut, Dār al-Kutub al-'Ilmīyah, 1415/1995.

Al-'Aynī, Badar al-Dīn, *'Umdat al-Qārī*, 12 vols., Dār al-Ṭibā'ah al-'Āhmirah, n.d.

Āzād, Abū al-Kalām, *Tarjumān al-Qur'ān*, New Delhi, 1970.

Al-Azharī, *Tahdhīb al-Lughah*, Cairo, 1967.

Al-Baghawī, Al-Husain ibn Mas'ūd Abī al-Qāsim, *Ma'ālim al-Tanzīl*, eds. Khālid al-'Ak and Marwān Sawār, 4 vols., second edition, Beirut, Dār al-Ma'rifah, 1987.

Al-Baghawī, 'Abdullāh ibn Muḥammad Abī al-Qāsim, *Sharḥ al-Sunnah*, ed. Zuhayr al-Shāwish and Shu'ayb al-Arnā'ūṭ, 16 vols., second edition, Beirut, al-Maktab al-Islāmī, 1983.

Al-Baghdādī, 'Alā' al-Dīn, *Tafsīr al-Khāzin*, eds. 'Abd al-Salām Muḥammad 'Alī Shāhīn, 4 vols., Beirut, Dār al-Kutub al-'Ilmīyah, 1995.

Al-Bayḍāwī, 'Abdullāh ibn 'Umar, *Anwār al-Tanzīl*, 5 vols., Beirut, Dār al-Fikr, n.d.

Al-Bayahqī, Abū Bakr Aḥmad ibn al-Ḥusayn ibn 'Alī, *al-Sunan.*

Al-Bukhārī, Muḥammad ibn Ismā'īl, *al-Jāmi' al-Ṣaḥīḥ*.

Al-Dāraquṭnī, 'Alī ibn 'Umar, *al-Sunan*, 4 vols., Beirut, 'Ālam al-Kutub, n.d.

Al-Dārimī, Abū Muḥammad 'Abdullāh ibn 'Abd al-Raḥmān, *al-Sunan*, 2 vols., Cairo, Dār al-Fikr, 1975.

Doughty, Charles Montague, *Travels in Arabia Deserta*, London, 1888.

Encyclopaedia of the Qur'ān, 5 vols., ed. Jane D. McAuliffe, Leiden and Boston, Brill, 2001–2006.

The Encyclopaedia of Religion and Ethics, 12 vols., ed. James Hastings, Edinburgh, 1959.

Al-Fīrūzābādī, *al-Qāmūs al-Muḥīṭ*, second edition, Cairo, al-Ḥalabī, 1952.

Al-Ghazālī, Abū Ḥāmid Muḥammad ibn Muḥammad, *al-Iqtiṣād fī al-I'tiqād,* Beirut, Dār al-Kutub al-'Ilmīya, 1403/1983.

Gibbon, Edward, *Decline and Fall of the Roman Empire*, fifth edition, London, Methuen, 1924.

Goitein, S.D., *Studies in Islamic History and Institutions,* Leiden, E.J. Brill, 1966.

Al-Ḥākim al-Naysābūrī, Muḥammad ibn 'Abdullāh Ḥamdawayh, *al-Mustadrak 'alā al-Ṣaḥīḥayn fī al-Ḥadīth*, 4 vols. Riyadh, Maktabat al-Ma'ārif, n.d.

Al-Ḥamawī, Yāqūt, *Mu'jam al-Buldān*, 5 vols., Beirut, Dār Ṣādir, 1977.

Hershon, Paul Issac, *Talmudic Miscellany*, London, 1880.

Al-Hindī, 'Alā' al-Dīn, *Kanz al-'Ummāl fī Sunan al-Aqwāl wa al-Af'āl*, Beirut, Mu'assasat al-Risālah, 1985.

The Holy Bible, Revised Standard Edition, New York, 1952.

Howley, G.C.D., *A Bible Commentary for Today*, London, Pickering & Inglis Ltd., 1979.

Ibn 'Abd al-Barr al-Qurṭubī, *al-Istī'āb*, Beirut, Dār al-Kutub al-'Ilmīyah, 1415/1995.

Ibn Abī Ḥātim, *Tafsīr*, Makkah, Maktabah Muṣṭafā, 1417/1997.

Ibn Abī Shaybah, *al-Muṣannaf*, 15 vols., Karachi, Idārat al-Qur'ān wa al-'Ulūm al-Islāmiyah, 1986.

Ibn Aḥmad al-Makkī, *Manāqib al-Imām al-A'ẓam Abī Ḥanīfah*, Hyderabad, India, 1321 AH.

Ibn al-'Arabī, Abū Bakr, *Aḥkām al-Qur'ān*, Beirut, Dār al-Kutub al-'Ilmīyah, n.d.

Ibn Baṭṭūṭah, *Muhdhdhab Riḥlat Ibn Baṭṭūṭah*, ed. Aḥmad al-'Awāmir Muḥammad Jād al-Mawlā, Cairo, al-Amīrīyah, 1934.

Ibn Ḥanbal, Aḥmad, *Musnad*, 6 vols., Cairo, al-Maktabah al-Maymanīyah, 1313 AH.

Ibn Ḥazm, 'Alī ibn Aḥmad, *Jawāmi' al-Sīrah.*

————, *Al-Muḥallā*, ed. Muḥammad Munīr al-Damishqī, 11 vols., Cairo, Idārat al-Ṭibā'ah al-Munīrīyah, 1352 AH.

Ibn Hishām, 'Abd al-Malik, *Sīrah*, eds. Muṣṭafā al-Saqqā et al., second edition, Cario, 1955.

Ibn Isḥāq, *The Life of Muḥammad*, tr. and notes by A. Guillaume, Karachi, Oxford University Press, 1955.

Ibn al-Jawzī, *Zād al-Masīr.*

Ibn Kathīr, Ismā'īl ibn 'Umar, *al-Bidāyah wa al-Nihāyah*, Cairo, Dār Iḥyā' al-Turāth al-'Arabī, 1988.

————, *Tafsīr al-Qur'ān al-'Aẓīm*, Riyadh, Dār Tayyabah, 1420/1998

Ibn Mājah, Muḥammad ibn Yazīd, *al-Sunan.*

Ibn Manẓūr, *Lisān al-'Arab*, Beirut, Dār Ṣādir, n.d.

Ibn Rushd, *Bidāyat al-Mujtahid*, 2 vols., Cairo, n.d.

Ibn Sa'd, Muḥammad, *Al-Ṭabaqāt Al-Kubrā*, 8 vols., Beirut, 1957–60.

Ibn al-Sinnī, Abū Bakr Aḥmad ibn Muḥammad, *'Amal al-Yawm wa al-Laylah*, Hyderabad (Deccan), second edition, Maṭba'at Dā'irat al-Ma'ārif al-'Uthmānīyah, 1359.

Ibn Taymīyah, Taqī al-Dīn, *Majmū' Fatāwā Ibn Taymīyah*, ed. Muḥammad ibn 'Abd al-Raḥmān ibn Qāsim, 37 vols., Riyadh, 1398.

Al-'Imādī, Abū Sa'ūd, *Irshād al-'Aql al-Salīm ilā Mazāyā al-Kitāb al-Karīm*, 9 vols., Beirut, Dār Iḥyā' al-Turāth al-'Arabī, n.d.

Al-'Irāqī, Abū al-Ḥasan, *Tanzīh al-Sharī"ah al-Marfū'ah 'an al-Aḥadīth al-Mawḍū'ah*, 2 vols., first edition, Cairo, Maktabat al-Qāhirah, n.d.

Al-Jaṣṣāṣ, Aḥmad ibn 'Alī, *Aḥkām al-Qur'ān*, 3 vols., Cairo, 1347 AH.

Al-Jazīrī, 'Abd al-Raḥmān, *al-Fiqh 'alā al-Madhāhib al-Arba'ah*, 5 vols., Beirut, Dār Iḥyā' al-Turāth, 1980.

The Jewish Encyclopaedia, 12 vols., ed. Isidore Singer, New York, KTAV Publishing House, n.d.

Kamāl al-Dīn Muḥammad ibn 'Abd al-Wāḥid, *Fatḥ al-Qadīr*, 9 vols., Quetta, al-Maktabah al-Rashīdīyah, 1985.

Al-Kardarī, Muḥammad ibn Muḥammad ibn al-Bazzāz, *Manāqib al-Imām al-A'ẓam Abī Ḥanīfah*, Quetta, Maktabah Islāmiyah, 1407AH.

Khān, Sir Sayyid Aḥmad, *Tafsīr al-Qur'ān wa Huwa al-Hudā wa al-Furqān*, Patna, Khuda Bakhsh Oriental Public Library, 1995.

Mālik ibn Anas, *al-Muwaṭṭa'*, ed. Muḥammad Fu'ād 'Abd al-Bāqī, 2 vols., Cairo, 1951.

Mawdūdī, Sayyid Abūl A'lā, *Rasā'il wa Masā'il* (Urdu), Lahore, 1957.

Muslim ibn al-Ḥajjāj al-Nīsābūrī, *al-Ṣaḥīḥ.*

Al-Nasā'ī, Aḥmad ibn 'Alī, *al-Sunan.*

Al-Nawawī, Yaḥyā ibn Sharf, *Sharḥ Ṣaḥīḥ Muslim*, Beirut, Dār al-Kutub al-'Ilmīyah, 1415/1995

al-Nīsābūrī, Niẓām al-Dīn al-Ḥasan ibn Muḥammad, *Gharā'ib al-Qur'ān wa Raghā'ib al-Furqān*, 30 vols., Beirut, Dār al-Kutub al-'Ilmīyah, 1996.

Polano, H., *The Talmud Selections*, London, Frederick Warne & Co.

Al-Qāḍī 'Iyāḍ ibn Mūsā, *Al-Shifā bi Ta'rīf Ḥuqūq Muṣṭafā*, ed. 'Alī Muḥammad al-Bajāwī, 2 vols., Beirut, Dār al-Kutub al-'Arabī, 1984.

Al-Qārī, Mullā 'Alī, *Sharḥ al-Fiqh al-Akbar*, Karachi, Muḥammad Sa'īd and Sons, n.d.

Al-Qurṭubī, *al-Jāmi' li Aḥkām al- Qur'ān*, 8 vols., Cairo, Dār al-Sha'b, n.d.

Al-Rāzī, Muḥammad ibn 'Umar Fakhr al-Dīn, *Mafātīḥ al-Ghayb*, 8 vols., Cairo, al-Maṭba'ah al-Khayrīyah, 1306 AH.

Al-Sa'ātī, Aḥmad 'Abd al-Raḥmān, *al-Fatḥ al-Rabbānī*, Beirut, Dār Iḥyā' al-Turāth al-'Arabī.

Al-Ṣābūnī, Muḥammad 'Alī, *Ṣafwat al-Tafāsīr*, 3 vols., fourth edition, Beirut, 1402/1981.

Sahāranpūrī, Khalīl Aḥamd, *Badhl al-Majhūd*, Beirut, Dār al-Kutub al-'Ilmīyah.

Al-Ṣālīh, Ṣubḥī, *Mabāḥith fī 'Ulūm al- Qur'ān*, Beirut, 1977.

Al-Sarakshī, Shams al-Dīn, *al-Mabsūṭ*, 30 vols., Cairo, Maṭba'at al-Sa'ādah, 1324 AH.

Al-Shahrastānī, Tāj al-Dīn Abū al-Fatḥ Muḥammad ibn 'Abd al-Karīm, *al-Milal wa al-Niḥal.*

Al-Suyūṭī, Jalāl al-Dīn, *al-Jalālayn*, Qatar, Mu'assasat al-Risālah, 1995.

————, *al-Durr al-Manthūr fī al-Tafsīr bi al-Ma'thūr.* 6 vols., Tehran, al-Maktabah al-Islāmīyah wa al-Maktabah al-Ja'farīyah, n.d.

————, *Lubāb al-Nuqūl fī Asbāb al-Nuzūl*, second edition, Cairo, Muṣṭafā al-Ḥalabī, n.d.

————, *al-Itqān fi 'Ulūm al-Qur'ān*, Riyadh, Maktabah al-Ma'arīf, 1416/1996.

Sykes, Percy, *A History of Persia*, London, Macmillan, 1958.

Al-Ṭabarānī, Sulaymān ibn Aḥmad ibn Ayyūb, *al-Mu'jam al-Kabīr*, ed. Ḥamdī 'Abd al-Mājid, 23 vols., second edition, Baghdad, Wazārat al-Awqāf, n.d.

_________, *al-Mu'jam al-Wasīṭ*, Cairo: Dār al-Ḥaramayn, 1405 AH.

Al-Ṭabarī, Muḥammad ibn Jarīr, *Ta'rīkh*, 8 vols., Beirut, Mu'sassat al-A'lamī, n.d.

_________, *Jāmi' al-Bayān 'an Ta'wīl Āyi al-Qur'ān*, ed. Ṣadqī Jamīl, 15 vols., Beirut, Dār al-Fikr, 1995.

Al-Tabrayzī, Muḥammad ibn 'Abdullāh, *Mishkāt al-Maṣābīḥ*, ed. Nāṣir al-Dīn Albānī, third edition, Beirut, al-Maktab al-Islāmī, 1985.

Ṭaḥāwī, Abū Ja'far, *Sharḥ Ma'ānī al-Āthār*, Beirut, 'Ālam al-Kutub. 1414/1994.

Thānawī, Ashraf 'Alī, *Bayān al-Qur'ān*, 2 vols., Lahore, Shaykh Ghulām 'Alī and Sons, n.d.

Al-Tirmidhī, Muḥammad ibn 'Īsā, *al-Sunan.*

'Uthmanī, Shabbīr Aḥmad and Maḥmūd al-Ḥasan, *Qur'ān Majīd: Mutarjam wa Muḥashshā* [popularly known as *Tafsīr 'Uthmānī*], Karachi.

al-Wāḥidī, Abū al-Ḥasan ibn Aḥmad, *al-Wasīṭ fī Tafsīr al- Qur'ān*, Beirut, Dār al-Kutub al-'Ilmīyah, 1415/1995.

Al-Wāqidī, Muḥammad ibn 'Umar, *al-Maghāzī*, ed. M. Jones, 3 vols., Cairo, 1966.

Wensinck, A.J., *Concordance et indices de la tradition musulmane*, 7 vols., Leiden, 1939-69.

Winston, William, *The Life and Works of Flavius Josephus*, Philadelphia, John C. Winston Company, n.d.

Al-Zamakhsharī, Maḥmūd ibn Muḥammad ibn Aḥmad, *al-Kashshāf 'an Ḥaqā'iq Ghawāmiḍ al-Tanzīl*, 4 vols., Beirut, Dār al-Kitāb al-'Arabī, 1366 AH.

Subject Index

Adhān, 142

Afterlife, 64, 80, 157, 206

Allāh Akbar, 142

Allāh's:
- appointed term, 96
- bounty, 4, 134
- chastisement, 125
- complete protection, 19
- displeasure, 18, 21
- forgiveness, 24, 25, 98, 99,136
- guidance, 3
- intervention, 20
- pardon, 25, 117
- pleasure, 189, 191
- promise, 132
- servant, 14, 118, 189
- way, 51, 110, 135, 144, 145, 153, 190, 192, 203, 232, 233
- will, 3
- wisdom, 207
- worst enemy, 6
- wrath, 17, 18

Angels, 3, 19, 20, 23, 69, 81, 82, 101, 106, 120, 121, 149, 150, 152, 173, 197, 200, 209, 233, 234

aqwamu qīlā, 129

Aṣīl, 202

'Aṣr, 10, 202

Atheism, 221, 222

Atheist(s), 165, 185, 187, 222, 226

awlā laka, 174

Bariqa al-baṣar, 164

Beggar, 86

Believer(s), 3, 4, 6, 19, 20, 22, 24, 26, 27, 31, 39, 41, 46, 57, 68, 84, 85, 88, 94, 103, 106, 116, 146, 151, 155, 168, 170, 171, 182, 198, 202, 203, 207, 213, 216, 222

Book of God, 58, 65

Bukrah, 202

Children, 23, 54, 60, 75, 80, 84, 98, 100, 101, 112, 132, 140, 147, 181, 190

Cleanliness, 88, 118, 143, 144

Command(s), 3, 11, 14, 15, 21, 22, 23, 57, 72, 95, 98, 99, 124, 125, 126, 127, 128, 133, 134, 139, 142, 167, 168, 181, 188, 201, 202, 217, 226, 227, 229, 230, 231, 232

Companion(s), 3, 4, 5, 6, 9, 22, 31, 45, 59, 105, 106, 134, 180, 181, 230, 237, 238, 243

Conscience, 22, 30, 46, 141, 148, 160, 161, 162, 163, 165, 170, 187, 226, 227

Contention, 201

Covenant(s), 58, 88, 229

Creation, 33, 39, 83, 99, 100, 108, 115, 176, 185, 187, 206, 212, 226, 232

Creatures, 30, 33, 39, 42, 69, 72, 107, 108, 121, 153, 182, 213, 229, 231, 234, 235

Culprit(s), 23, 33, 36, 45, 48, 57, 70, 71, 84, 102, 118, 131, 156, 165, 174, 197, 216, 237

Day:
- of Judgement, 48, 59, 64, 69, 70, 72, 80, 87, 91, 132, 141, 147, 155, 165, 171, 197, 205, 206, 210, 211, 213, 215
- of Resurrection, 31, 58, 68, 84, 98, 125, 161, 164, 208, 209

Deity, 101, 102

Deliverance, 30, 96

Devils, 34, 35, 115

Divine, 50, 62, 69, 80, 83, 94, 112, 146, 167, 182, 209, 225, 230
- blessings, 109, 141
- bounties, 117, 201
- chastisement, 80
- command, 21, 22, 57, 99, 139, 202
- decree, 61
- directives, 146
- dispensation, 36, 94, 108, 172
- displeasure, 193
- favour, 50
- guidance, 7, 36, 85, 94, 141, 232
- message, 96, 107, 109, 110, 112, 118, 127, 151, 232
- penalty, 66
- plans, 82, 83, 102
- punishment, 64, 80, 81, 87, 90, 95, 103, 120, 124, 125, 153
- recompense, 230
- reproach, 62
- revelation, 7, 20, 115, 139, 150, 152, 229
- reward, 182
- scheme, 83, 209
- scriptures, 112
- signs of His kingdom, 225
- statement, 167
- teachings, 21, 188
- throne, 69
- will, 2, 3

Divorce, 12, 13, 14, 18, 19, 20, 21, 22

Doing good, 33, 38

Enemy, 6, 16, 48, 82

Epileptic fits, 146

Error(s), 3, 4, 37, 43, 46, 112, 113, 138, 153, 154, 156, 158, 160, 163, 164, 197, 210, 222, 231

Evil(s), 30, 33, 38, 43, 52, 56, 57, 60, 70, 86, 89, 109, 114, 115, 143, 144, 157, 161, 162, 163, 170, 176, 186, 187, 188, 189, 195, 207, 211, 221, 222, 231, 232
– deeds, 24, 25, 28, 30, 80, 162, 165, 186, 206, 233
– doers, 6, 27, 72, 102, 165, 202, 217, 229
– doing, 53

Expiation, 11, 12, 13, 190, 193, 194, 195, 232

Fajr Prayer, 105, 235

False:
– gods, 95, 147, 187
– hood, 141, 157, 165, 169, 216, 217

Fasting, 22, 191, 194

Fate, 35, 36, 80, 118, 190, 206, 207, 211, 221

Feeding:
– the needy, 196
– the poor, 196

Feminine nature, 21

Fighting in the cause of God, 124, 135

Fiqh, 144, 231, 236, 243

Flood, 68, 101, 225, 230

Forgiveness, 24, 25, 33, 38, 94, 96, 97, 98, 99, 136

God's:
– behest, 100
– bounty, 135
– cause, 197
– chastisement, 23, 45, 82, 90, 94, 132
– commands, 98, 188, 229, 230
– control, 99
– court, 87, 132
– creative power, 154, 176
– creature, 231
– decree, 183
– decision, 187
– directives, 121
– displeasure, 61, 95
– divinity, 150
– earth, 117
– favourites, 57
– fear, 25, 57, 77, 98, 198, 216, 236,
– forgiveness, 96
– glory, 139, 236
– grace, 41, 42, 180
– grip, 90
– guidance, 153
– kingship and dominion, 70
– majesty, 98
– mercy, 42, 46, 61, 100, 171, 223
– message(s), 121, 130, 210, 234, 236
– Messenger, 60, 68, 95, 97, 121, 138, 143, 168, 188, 200, 223
– might, 143
– might and glory, 127, 143
– name, 118
– Oneness, 236
– partners, 109
– permanent law, 211
– pleasure, 23, 136, 190
– power, 121, 154, 170, 207, 214
– power and wisdom, 209, 213, 214
– promise, 198
– order, 231
– punishment, 39, 42, 48, 64, 95, 96, 109, 230
– reckoning, 82
– remembrance, 208, 224, 225

– revelation, 223
– scheme, 83
– servant, 118, 189
– severe chastisement, 76
– special favour, 200
– total control, 32
– treasures, 101
– vicegerent, 113
– way, 110, 145, 153, 190, 192
– will, 2, 158, 221, 222, 236
– wisdom, 15, 40, 183, 201, 207, 209, 213, 214, 222
– Word, 115, 149, 151, 152, 223
– working, 153

Godhead, 76, 118

Gospel, 98

Grand assembly, 26, 70, 71, 83, 84, 215, 216

Guidance, 3, 6, 7, 36, 37, 85, 94, 115, 117, 141, 145, 152, 153, 158, 186, 207, 217, 222, 232, 235

Ḥadīth, 6, 7, 9, 10, 19, 20, 23, 24, 40, 41, 52, 81, 88, 134, 144, 166, 169, 171, 190, 194, 230, 235, 237, 238, 240, 243
– scholars, 81, 166, 238, 239, 240

Ḥajj, 17, 138, 139, 146, 160, 192, 195, 231

al-Ḥāqqah, 63, 64, 66, 79, 85

Heaven(s), 33, 34, 35, 40, 41, 43, 81, 82, 97, 98, 99, 106, 107, 108, 114, 115, 120, 121, 132, 138, 142, 151

Hell, 6, 26, 27, 35, 36, 37, 79, 116, 119, 131, 141, 148, 149, 150, 152, 153, 154, 155, 171, 215, 229
– keepers, 36, 149, 150
– fire, 23, 36, 64, 79, 80, 116, 119, 141, 149, 155, 175, 216

Hereafter, 4, 5, 21, 24, 30, 38, 44, 48, 54, 57, 58, 64, 66, 68, 71, 75, 76, 79, 80, 85, 89, 98, 125, 136, 141, 146, 152, 155, 157, 160, 162, 163, 164, 165, 170,

171, 172, 175, 176, 182, 183, 185, 187, 188, 198, 203, 206, 207, 208, 211, 212, 213, 214, 216, 225, 226, 227, 229, 230

Hypocrites, 16, 26, 27, 150, 151, 165, 174, 223, 233

'Ibād al-Raḥmān, 189

Idols, 46, 58, 103, 142

Īlā', 12, 13, 20

Indecency, 27, 87, 221

Injustice, 36, 60, 116, 164

Intercession, 156

Intercessor, 156

'Ishā', 202

Islam, 6, 9, 16, 29, 38, 45, 48, 53, 63, 64, 101, 105, 106, 124, 133, 135, 138, 139, 141, 146, 148, 155, 160, 169, 182, 193, 202, 230, 231, 232, 235, 236, 239

Islamic:
- ethics, 38
- faith, 29, 160
- faith and concepts, 182
- law, 2, 169
- scheme of reform, 131

Jāhiliyyah, 109, 113, 144

Jinn(s), 35, 105, 106, 107, 108, 109, 111, 112, 113, 114, 115, 116, 117, 120, 150, 231, 232

Jinn listening to the Qur'ān, 105, 106, 112

Judgement, 38, 48, 57, 59, 61, 64, 69, 70, 72, 80, 87, 91, 132, 141, 147, 155, 165, 171, 197, 205, 206, 210, 211, 213, 215, 222, 231

Jurist(s), 11, 12, 189, 190, 192, 194, 195, 238

Ka'bah, 232, 234

Kayd, 60

al-Khayr, 53, 232

Last Day, 31, 44, 45, 66, 83, 160, 162, 164, 165

Lawful:
- or unlawful, 2, 3, 8, 9, 11, 12, 13, 14, 15, 135, 162, 165, 171, 190, 194, 197, 202, 221, 222
- sustenance, 135

Life after death, 57, 72, 89, 148, 161, 162, 163, 175, 176, 182, 184, 207, 212, 213

Maghrib, 202

Magician(s), 140, 141, 147

Mankind, 2, 3, 30, 32, 51, 59, 64, 68, 80, 91, 109, 118, 132, 139, 210, 225, 227, 231

Mahīn, 53

Man's:
- ability to acquire knowledge, 186
- birth, 185, 207
- capacity, 191
- creation, 100, 108, 212
- creator, 33
- faculties, 186
- freedom of choice, 221
- guardian, 14
- habitat, 41
- heart, 224
- knowledge, 83
- mind, 109
- moral, 163, 226
- nature, 41
- perception, 110

– refusal to be guided, 117, 158
– rejection to follow divine guidance, 117

Marriage, 13, 14, 87

Masājid, 117, 118, 171

Mercy, 4, 42, 45, 46, 62, 100, 127, 134, 158, 173, 183, 204, 209, 210, 221, 223, 224, 229

Messenger(s), 2, 5, 9, 19, 21, 30, 31, 36, 37, 41, 42, 60, 61, 64, 65, 67, 68, 73, 74, 76, 86, 95, 97, 101, 110, 112, 113, 114, 115, 118, 119, 120, 121, 124, 125, 126, 131, 132, 138, 142, 143, 145, 146, 151, 152, 155, 157, 168, 171, 174, 188, 192, 193, 200, 206, 210, 217, 223, 232, 233, 234, 236

Messengers':
– first and foremost duty, 142
– guidance, 3, 6, 7, 37
– teachings, 37, 223
– testimony, 206

Messengership, 11, 36, 49, 75, 114, 142, 145, 150

Meteor, 34, 35, 114, 115

Meteorites, 34, 35, 106, 108

Mi'rāj (the Night Journey), 81, 151

Monotheism, 42, 76, 119, 143, 221

Moral(s), 38, 48, 51, 52, 57, 66, 74, 75, 115, 143, 144, 145, 160, 162, 163, 175, 186, 202, 206, 221, 226:
– principles, 30, 188, 211
– values, 182
– and manners, 21, 48, 51, 128, 144, 146

Mursal, 9

Muslim:
– community, 169
– scholars, 5, 234
– wives, 21

Nadhr Lajāj, 190, 234

Nafl, 22, 133, 134
– fasts, 22
– Prayer, 133, 134

Nafs
– *al-ammārah*, 161
– *al-lawwāmah*, 161, 187
– *al-muṭma'innah*, 161

Next Life, 207

Nudity, 87

Nuṣub, 91, 234

Oath(s), 9, 11, 12, 13, 14, 50, 56, 74, 76, 90, 161, 162, 195, 208, 209, 225, 243

Obedience, 25, 98, 108, 191, 229, 231, 232, 236

Offering(s), 11, 12, 84, 86, 88, 125, 144, 155, 234

Orientalists, 169

Paradise, 6, 25, 26, 28, 57, 58, 64, 71, 79, 80, 88, 89, 90, 148, 152, 155, 171, 172, 197, 198, 199, 200, 216, 229, 230

Pardon, 4, 25, 26, 117, 141, 193

People of the Book, 98, 150, 151, 229

Perseverance, 47, 61, 83, 183, 197, 198, 202

Piety, 95, 98, 141, 186, 236, 239

Pilgrims, 139, 140, 146, 147

Poet, 63, 64, 65, 73, 74, 75, 140, 239

Poetry, 59, 75, 140

Polytheism, 41, 75, 109, 117, 119, 143, 221, 222

polytheists, 16, 46, 106, 108, 109, 112, 143, 187

Poor, 73, 80, 86, 155, 196, 233

Prayer(s), 10, 63, 80, 84, 86, 88, 89, 102, 105, 123, 124, 125, 126, 127, 128, 129, 133, 134, 135, 143, 155, 174, 183, 192, 194, 202, 203, 232, 234, 235, 236

Prisoner of war, 196

Prisoner(s), 180, 181, 196

Promised Messenger, 9

Prophet's:
- assignment, 198
- career, 106
- Companions, 3, 4
- core message, 43
- declaration, 75
- displeasure, 18
- domestic life, 20, 21
- emissary, 9
- excellent conduct, 48, 51
- excellent morals and manners, 52
- house, 9, 16
- illustrious life, 2
- letter, 9
- life and career, 52
- military plan, 5
- mission, 93, 106, 145, 147
- morals and manners, 51
- Night Journey, 203
- reward, 51
- role model, 3, 24
- sayings and actions, 169
- training, 3
- truthfulness, 151
- victory, 61
- wives, 1, 2, 5, 6, 7, 8, 10, 11, 14, 15, 16, 17, 18, 19, 20, 21, 22
- words and deeds, 132, 169

Prophethood, 50, 64, 76, 106, 123, 124, 152, 235

Prostrating, 59, 118

Punishment, 11, 23, 24, 30, 31, 33, 36, 38, 39, 42, 45, 48, 64, 76, 80, 81, 82, 87, 90, 94, 95, 96, 100, 102, 103, 110, 114, 115, 119, 120, 124, 125, 127, 132, 142, 147, 149, 150, 153, 157, 162, 173, 176, 209, 212, 215, 223, 226, 227

Purity, 2, 134, 143, 144, 236

Qur'ān:
- commentators, 54, 81, 84, 91, 105, 117, 128, 135, 144, 150, 151, 171, 173, 174, 179, 184, 196, 199, 200, 209
- recitation, 63, 105, 107, 109, 111, 115, 127, 134, 159, 160, 167, 236

Qur'ānic:
- allusion, 51, 54, 59, 68, 174, 237
- concepts, terms and commands, 167
- passages, 89, 107, 108, 109, 112, 139, 156, 186, 200
- statement, 59, 82, 107, 150
- teachings, 21, 29, 52, 55, 116, 157, 168, 223, 233

Raka'ah, 192, 203

Reason(s), 3, 8, 18, 36, 37, 40, 58, 59, 71, 90, 97, 101, 130, 151, 157, 161, 163, 165, 170, 181, 183, 186, 188, 196, 199, 203, 224, 227

Repentance, 16, 17, 22, 24, 25, 26, 98, 225

Resurrection, 31, 44, 58, 64, 66, 68, 69, 70, 76, 79, 80, 83, 84, 98, 103, 106, 114, 125, 146, 159, 160, 161, 162, 163, 164, 187, 205, 206, 208, 209, 211, 225, 226

Revelation, 1, 2, 7, 15, 20, 29, 47, 50, 54, 63, 76, 79, 82, 93, 105, 107, 111, 115, 120, 123, 128, 133, 137, 138, 139, 146, 150, 152, 159, 160, 166, 167, 179, 181, 205, 223, 227, 229, 236

Reward(s), 5, 21, 26, 30, 38, 39, 49, 51, 60, 64, 70, 71, 116, 125, 134, 136, 157, 162, 171, 176, 182, 188, 197, 216, 226, 229, 235

Rūḥ, 82

Rukū', 134, 177, 234, 235

Ṣā', 180

Safīhunā, 112

Ṣalāt, 52, 105, 111, 127, 166, 168, 171, 177

Salsabīl, 199

Sāq, 59, 173

Scriptures, 36, 40, 106, 112, 150, 186

Secular laws, 38

Sex outside of marriage, 87

Sexual relations, 12

Shahūd, 147

Sharī'ah, 8, 24, 168, 174

Sharī'ah duties, 174

Sinner(s), 25, 26, 36, 56, 71, 73, 80, 94, 103, 149, 150, 158, 162, 165, 172, 174, 187

Sins, 24, 25, 37, 87, 95, 102, 149, 155, 186, 224

Soothsayers, 35, 64, 65, 73, 74, 75, 140

Spirit, 28, 82

Steadfastness, 129, 183, 197, 198, 202

Straight way, 36, 85, 109, 115, 152, 197

Successors, 9, 22, 59, 181, 238

Sulṭān, 72

Sunnah, 169, 235

Supplication, 26, 28, 61, 94, 98, 127

Supreme Being, 82, 225

Tafsīr, 5, 9, 10, 11, 12, 19, 20, 22, 24, 26, 27, 52, 59, 84, 98, 105, 111, 113, 118, 125, 128, 133, 135, 137, 140, 152, 166, 171, 174, 177, 180, 243

Ṭāghiyah, 67

Tahajjud Prayer, 124, 125, 133, 134, 135, 202, 235

Ṭahārah, 144

Taẓāhur, 17

Temptation(s), 145, 197

Thankful(ness), 182, 186, 188, 201, 235

The people of the left hand, 154

Ties of kinship, 191

Towards Understanding the Qur'ān, 21, 27, 28, 32, 33, 35, 37, 40, 43, 44, 61, 69, 70, 75, 76, 77, 83, 85, 87, 88, 97, 98, 115, 129, 132, 135, 146, 151, 153, 154, 155, 162, 168, 177, 198, 198, 199, 201, 202, 210, 211, 212, 237, 239, 240, 241, 242, 244

True faith, 27, 38, 129, 149

Trumpet, 68, 69, 146, 231

Trust(s), 20, 31, 46, 50, 80, 88, 103, 130, 198, 230

Trustworthy, 73, 74

Unbelief, 16, 30

Unbeliever(s), 23, 27, 42, 45, 62, 77, 81, 89, 103, 146, 150, 151, 188

Unbelievers' rebellion, 60, 98

Unseen, 30, 35, 60, 61, 101, 107, 108, 120, 121, 209

Unthankful, 182, 186

'Utull, 53

Vices, 145, 182

Wakīl, 130

Wealth, 53, 54, 60, 80, 85, 86, 98, 100, 125, 135, 136, 147, 232

Weighty word, 127, 128

Wickedness, 113, 164, 221

Winds, 42, 206, 208, 209, 210, 224, 225, 226

Witness, 4, 31, 44, 68, 75, 84, 132, 147, 169, 235, 236

Women as role models, 28

Word of God, 64, 65, 74, 148, 168, 232, 236

Worldliness, 85, 203

Worship, 5, 14, 22, 46, 86, 95, 101, 109, 117, 118, 129, 183, 194, 207, 221, 229, 231, 234, 235, 236

Wrongdoing, 87, 187, 244

Za'īm, 58

Zakāh, 86, 124, 125, 133, 134, 135, 193, 236

Zanjabīl, 200

Ẓihār, 13, 14

Ẓuhr, 202

General Index

'Abd Yaghūth, 54, 102
'Abdullāh ibn 'Amr ibn al-'Āṣ, 191, 195, 237
Abū Bakr al-Ṣiddīq, 12, 20
Abū Dāwūd, 10, 40, 52, 127, 129, 133, 177, 190, 191, 192, 193, 194, 195, 245
Abū al-Haytham, 84, 237
Abū Hurayrah, 9, 20, 177, 190, 192, 195, 237
Abū Isrā'īl, 19
Abū Jahl, 14, 149, 174, 237
Abū Lubābah, 193, 237
Abū Sa'īd al-Khudrī, 84, 171, 237, 241
Abū Salamah, 11
Abū Thawr, 194, 238
Abū Yūsuf, 196
Ādam, 108, 149, 190
Aḥkām al- Qur'ān, 10, 12, 13, 14
Aḥmad ibn Ḥanbal, 14, 111, 238
'Ā'ishah, 4, 9, 10, 12, 17, 18, 19, 20, 22, 52, 128, 133, 191, 195, 238
Akhnas ibn Shurayq, 54
Alexandria, 9
'Alī, 24, 180, 181, 237, 238, 239
Ālūsī, 16, 179, 238
Anas, 10, 19, 20, 52, 59, 88, 127, 192, 238, 241
Anṣār, 18
Arab polytheists, 108, 109
Arabia, 9, 31, 75, 101, 102, 139, 140, 145, 147, 151
Arabic, 24, 53, 58, 59, 74, 75, 86, 111, 144, 156, 164, 168, 174, 175, 184
Arabs, 9, 35, 76, 98, 101, 113, 140, 143, 144, 148, 156, 199
Aṣbagh, 13
Aswad ibn 'Abd Yaghūth, 54
'Aṭā', 12, 144, 180, 238
al-'Aynī, Ḥāfiẓ Badr al-Dīn, 20, 238

Badā'i' al-Ṣanā'i', 13
Balkha', 102
Banī Jumah, 149
Banī Kalb ibn Wabrah, 101
al-Bayḍāwī, 179, 246
Bayhaqī, 88, 135, 166, 171, 177, 191, 195, 238
Bayt al-Maqdis, 192
Bayt-e Nasūr, 102
Bukhārī, 10, 11, 12, 17, 18, 19, 20, 23, 52, 105, 127, 128, 134, 136, 137, 138, 166, 171, 190, 191, 192, 193, 238
Buraydah, 194, 238
al-Burhān fī 'Ulūm al-Qur'ān, 181

Christian(s), 5, 112
Copts, 9

Ḍaḥḥāk, 16, 26, 166, 191, 238, 243
al-Dārānī, Abū Sulaimān, 196, 238
Dārimī, 52, 239, 246
Darrāj, 84, 239
Dāwūd Ẓāhirī, 195
Āl Dhu al-Kulā', 102
Dūmat al-Jandal, 101

Egypt, 1, 9

al-Fatḥ al-Rabbānī, 10, 18
Fatḥ al-Qadīr, 10, 13

Fāṭimah, 180, 181, 239
Fiḍḍah, 180
Fuḍa'il ibn 'Abbās, 239

Gabriel, 17, 19, 20, 73, 74, 82, 138, 142, 160, 166, 167, 180, 181
Ghassanids, 18

Ḥafṣah, 9, 10, 17, 18, 19, 20, 239
Ḥākim, 81, 128, 177, 239
Ḥamdān tribe, 102
Ḥanafīs, 12, 13, 190, 193, 194
Ḥasan al-Baṣrī, 12, 99
Ḥāshiyah al-Dusūqī, 14
Ḥassān ibn Thābit, 9, 239
Ḥāṭib ibn abī Balta'ah, 5, 9, 239
Hidāyah, 13
Hijaz, 102
Humayr tribe, 102
Ḥirā' cave, 138
Ḥudaybiyah treaty, 9
Ḥudhayfah ibn al-Yamān, 127, 239
Ḥudhayl tribe, 101
Ḥusain, 180

Iblīs, 107, 108, 112, 231
Ibn 'Abbās, 9, 10, 12, 16, 17, 20, 23, 24, 26, 27, 59, 81, 86, 105, 106, 111, 113, 129, 133, 144, 166, 180, 191, 192, 194, 195, 196, 237
Ibn 'Umar, 12, 23, 86, 171, 190, 237, 242
Ibn Abī Ḥātim, 10, 19, 24, 133, 177, 239
Ibn Abī Shaybah, 171, 240
Ibn al-'Arabī, Qāḍī Abū Bakr, 10, 12, 14
Ibn al-Mundhir, 10, 171, 177, 240
Ibn Ḥajar, 9
Ibn Hishām, 138, 140, 237, 240
Ibn Jubayr, 12, 53, 118, 125, 133, 144, 242
Ibn Mājah, 12, 52, 127, 172, 191, 192, 240
Ibn Marduwayah, 10, 135, 177, 180
Ibn Mas'ūd, 12, 16, 23, 24, 135, 136, 237
Ibn Sa'd, 9, 240
Ibn Taymiyyah, 181, 240
Ibn Zayd, 135, 166, 174
Ibrāhīm (the Prophet Muḥammad's son), 1, 9, 240, 241
Ibrāhīm (Abraham), 109, 146, 164, 237
'Ikrimah, 140, 240
'Imrān's family, 28
Isḥāq ibn Rāhawayah, 194, 240
al-Iṣ'ābah, 9
al-Istī'āb, 9
al-Itqān fī 'Ulūm al-Qur'ān, 181
'Iyāḍ, 10

Jābir ibn 'Abdullāh, 137, 138, 172, 192
Jaṣṣāṣ, Abū Bakr, 12
Jesus, 28, 240
Jews, 5, 28
Jonah (peace be upon him), 49, 61
Jurash, 101

Ka'b ibn Mālik, 193, 241
al-Kashshāf, 25, 99, 118, 135
Khālid ibn al-Walīd, 147, 241
Khawlah bint Tha'lbah, 41
Khaywān, 102
Khyber, 1
Kalbī, 101, 241
Kitāb al-Kharāj, 196
al-Kubrā, 9, 191

Lot (peace be upon him), 6, 27, 57, 67, 241
Lot's wife, 27

Madhjīh tribes, 101
Madīnah, 17, 106, 124, 133, 151, 152, 179, 180, 181, 233, 237, 239, 242
Makkah, 5, 45, 48, 54, 86, 89, 93, 106, 123, 124, 138, 139, 143, 146, 151, 152, 156, 159, 192, 233
Makkan; chiefs, 48, 156; disbelievers, 31, 41, 62, 65, 66, 73, 74, 76, 80, 81, 89, 93, 97, 103, 110, 124, 132, 139, 157, 163, 217
Mālikī(s), 12, 13, 14, 190, 193, 194; school, 12
Mary (Maryam), 6, 28, 156; the Copt, 240, 241; father, 28
Masrūq, 11
Michael, 20
Moses, 102, 106, 112, 200, 241

al-Mudawwanah, 13
Mughnī al-Muḥtāj, 12, 13
Muḥammad (peace be upon him), 2, 6, 29, 31, 64, 73, 76, 93, 101, 118, 120, 131, 140, 142, 148, 156, 168, 192, 229, 233, 235, 239, 240, 241; wives, 17, 18
Muḥammad al-Bāqir, 23, 241
Mujāhid, 23, 26, 50, 86, 128, 144, 166, 174, 196, 241
Muqawqis, 1, 9
Musnad of Imām Aḥmad, 6, 20, 52, 63, 84, 111, 127, 128, 166, 171, 177, 191
al-Mustadarak, 128
Muwaṭṭa', 41, 128, 193, 195

Naḍr ibn Ḥārith Kaladah, 81
Nakha'ī, 86, 144, 240
Nakhlah, 105, 106
Nasā'ī, 9, 10, 12, 17, 41, 52, 81, 127, 128, 136, 166, 191
Nasr, 101, 102
Naṣūr, 102
Nawāwī, 10, 194, 195, 241
Nīshāpurī, 179
Noah (Nūḥ), 6, 27, 68, 93, 94, 95, 96, 97, 100, 101, 102, 103, 142, 242; wife, 27

Pharaoh, 6, 28, 67, 102, 103, 124, 132, 200; wife, 6, 27

Qatādah, 12, 144, 166, 174, 242
Quḍā'a tribe, 101
Quraysh, 5, 17, 45, 63, 98, 101, 102, 119, 139, 140, 143, 146, 148, 149, 160, 203

Rabāḥ, 238
Rabī' ibn Anas, 59, 242
Rabī'ah, 11
Rafī' al-Dīn, Shāh, 16
Ramaḍān, 22
al-Rāzī, Imām, 16, 179, 180, 242

Sa'd ibn 'Ubādah, 194
Sa'īd ibn Jubayr, 12, 53, 118, 125, 133, 144, 242
Saba', 44, 70, 81, 102, 108, 109, 131, 156, 211
Ṣafīyah, 1, 10, 20, 242
Ṣaghw, 16
Ṣaḥīḥ Muslim, 10
Satan, 34, 107, 108, 109, 231, see also Iblīs
Sawdah, 10, 20
Sha'bī, 11, 53, 86, 166
Shāfi'ī school, 12, 13
Sharḥ Muwaṭṭa', 193
Sharḥ Muslim, 194, 195
Sīrīn, 9
al-Suddī, 23, 242
Sulaymān ibn Yasār, 12, 242
Sunan al-Kubrā, 191
Sunnat kī Āyinī Ḥaythiyat, 167, 168
Suwā', 101
al-Suyūṭī, 181, 243
Syria, 9, 238

al-Ṭabaqāt, 9
al-Ṭabarānī, 10, 166, 171, 243
Tabūk, 193; expedition, 193
Tafsīr (*al-*), 5, 9, 22, 26, 52, 128, 133, 152, 174, 243; *al-Basīṭ*, 180; *al-Kabīr*, 180; *Ibn Kathīr*, 20, 24, 59, 81, 98, 113, 118, 177; *Ibn Jarīr*, 24, 27, 84, 98, 213; *K. al-*, 10, 12, 19, 105, 111, 128, 137, 166, 171; *al-Ṭabarī*, 81, 111, 125, 128, 133, 135, 140, 166, 171, 177
Ṭaḥāwī, 191, 193, 243
Ṭā'if, 105, 106
Ṭāwūs, 12
Thābit ibn Ḍaḥḥāk, 191, 243
al-Thawrī, Sufyān, 16, 238, 239
Tirmidhī, 17, 111, 127, 128, 137, 166, 171, 177, 191, 243
Torah, 98

Ubayy ibn Ka'b, 24, 243
Uḥud, 4
'Ukāẓ, 105, 106
'Umar, 9, 12, 17, 18, 19, 20, 23, 24, 41, 63, 64, 86, 98, 135, 171, 190, 193, 194, 237, 240, 241, 242, 243, 246

'Umdatul Qārī, 193, 238
Umm Salamah, 18, 19, 20, 127, 243
'Uqbah ibn 'Āmir Juhanī, 192

Wadd, 101
al-Wāḥidī, 'Alī ibn Aḥmad, 180, 243
Walīd ibn al-Mughīrah, 54, 139, 141, 147, 149, 243
Walīullāh, Shāh, 16, 17, 193, 242

Ya'ūq, 101, 102
Yaghūth, 54, 101, 102
Yanbū', 101
Yemen, 101, 102

Ẓāhirīs, 11, 194, 243
al-Zamakhsharī, 25, 179, 180, 243
al-Zarkashī, Badr al-Dīn, 181, 243
Zayd ibn Ḥārithah, 106, 244
Zayd ibn Thābit, 12, 128, 244
Zaynab bint Jaḥash, 10, 20, 244
Zirr ibn Ḥubaysh, 24
Zufar, 193, 244
Zuhrī, 138, 193, 244